Dear Sammy

LETTERS FROM
GERTRUDE STEIN
AND
ALICE B. TOKLAS

Dear Sammy

LETTERS FROM

Gertrude Stein

AND

Alice B. Toklas

Edited with a Memoir by
Samuel M. Steward

Illustrated with photographs

HOUGHTON MIFFLIN COMPANY BOSTON

1977

Grateful acknowledgment is extended to the Estate of Gertrude Stein for permission to quote the unpublished letters of Gertrude Stein to Samuel M. Steward. These letters are separately copyrighted. Copyright © 1977 by Daniel Stein, Gertrude Stein Tyler, and Michael Stein. Notice is hereby given that these letters may not be used in any other work without the express permission of the Estate of Gertrude Stein.

Acknowledgment is made to the Estate of Alice B. Toklas for permission to print the hitherto unpublished letters of Alice B. Toklas to Samuel M. Steward on pages 155–245. Copyright © 1977 by Louise Taylor. Notice is hereby given that these letters may not be used in any other work without the express permission of the Estate of Alice B. Toklas and that of Louise Taylor.

Grateful acknowledgment is made for the kind permission of Random House, Inc., to reprint two excerpts from *Everybody's Autobiography* by Gertrude Stein, copyright 1937, renewed 1964, by Alice B. Toklas. Acknowledgment is extended to the Yale University Press for permission to quote a passage from *Alphabets and Birthdays* by Gertrude Stein, copyright © 1957 by Yale University Press and the Estate of Gertrude Stein. Acknowledgment is made to Liveright Publishing Company for permission to reprint the partial texts of letters from Alice B. Toklas to Samuel M. Steward that had previously appeared in *Staying on Alone: The Letters of Alice B. Toklas*, edited by Edward M. Burns, copyright © 1973 by Liveright Publishing Company.

Publication of the letters of Gertrude Stein to Samuel M. Steward has been courteously allowed by Donald C. Gallup, Curator of Yale University's Collection of American Literature in the Beinecke Rare Book and Manuscript Library; and by James D. Hart, Director of the Bancroft Library of the University of California at Berkeley. Grateful acknowledgment is also made to James D. Hart for permission to publish the complete correspondence of Alice B. Toklas to Samuel M. Steward as well as the unpublished photographs of Gertrude Stein and Alice B. Toklas, held in the Samuel M. Steward Collection by the Bancroft Library.

Thanks are due to Paul Padgette and Desmond Arthur of San Francisco for their helpful suggestions regarding the text, and to Drew Ponder-Greene for his kind permission to reproduce "To Sammy on His Birthday."

Library of Congress Cataloging in Publication Data
Stein, Gertrude, 1874–1946. Dear Sammy. Includes index.
1. Stein, Gertrude, 1874–1946—Correspondence. 2. Toklas, Alice B. 3. Steward, Samuel M.—Correspondence. 4. Authors, American—20th century—Correspondence. I. Toklas, Alice B., joint author. II. Steward, Samuel M. III. Title.
PS3537.T323Z547 818'.5'209 [B] 77–3519
ISBN 0–395–25340–3

Printed in the United States of America

W 10 9 8 7 6 5 4 3 2 1

FOR

PAUL PADGETTE

AND

DREW PONDER-GREENE

CONTENTS

ILLUSTRATIONS

following page 118

(All pictures, unless otherwise noted, are courtesy of the Bancroft Library, University of California, Berkeley, California.)

The Memoir

I

IN THE LATE 1920s there was a professor of English at Ohio State University named Clarence E. Andrews, who among other things wrote *The Innocents of Paris,* from which Maurice Chevalier's first American movie was made.

That alone made Andrews a glamorous figure to his students, but there were many other things. For one, he was a Francophile in the golden days when Paris was the magical Mecca for all of us young would-be "intellectuals," and for six months of every year, Andrews would disappear into the darkly romantic life of that city, returning regretfully to teach for the other six months. He was a true cosmopolite, one of a breed of professors seldom seen today. All of his students adored him — his elegance, his intellect, his wit, his polished lectures — and quoted his bons mots everywhere. The legend that surrounded him — aided by the air of mystery that developed from his living with a young painter named David Snodgrass — resulted in his classes being always filled to overflow.

It was Andrews who first introduced us to Gertrude Stein, of whom little was known in those days. He had visited her salon many times, listening and talking, and then returning to tell his classes about her. He was perhaps the first to point out her influence on Hemingway and Sherwood Anderson, and was our only link to the great world of which she was an important center. After his lectures on her and her influence there was the usual student race to the library to try to find out more. But we discovered very little, for Gertrude Stein had not yet made herself famous by writing *The Autobiography of Alice B. Toklas.*

Andrews had the wonderful faculty of being able to stimulate, and he was the great formative influence on many of us. The kind of life he made for himself could never have survived into the 1930s and '40s, and it was perhaps best that he should have died very suddenly in 1932 of pneumonia; his style and elegance were fast to disappear from the academic world.

There was no way for Gertrude Stein to learn of his death. It took courage, but I looked for her address and wrote to tell her about it. She replied, saying nice things to indicate she did remember Andrews, and then went on to invite me to write again because she wanted to hear more about me.

Flattered, I did as she asked; she answered, and our correspondence began. I was even brash enough to send her a copy of *Pan and the Firebird,* a collection of short Cabellian tales which I had done for one of Andrews' writing classes, and which had been published. She did not like them very much, except for "spots," explaining that she was bothered by the necessity of content without form, and creation without intention.

Then Gertrude Stein and Alice B. Toklas came to America in 1934–1935 on their whirlwind tour, attended by enormous publicity, to visit universities and lecture for modest fees. Fired with excitement, I tried to arrange for them to come to a small college in Montana where I was endeavoring to teach cowboys about semicolons. But the other universities in the northwest failed to show any enthusiasm, and they could not come. I followed their progress in the papers, to California and then gradually back to the east, and finally to Europe again. In her role as manager, Alice Toklas wrote me that Gertrude Stein very much regretted not coming to Helena, Montana, because she wanted to see a ghost town, a gold mine, and the Hangman's Tree; and Gertrude — before she left — sent me one of Carl Van Vechten's photographs of her, signed with a message on the large matting: "For Sam Steward and when we meet we do meet but we do meet as we have met and it always has been and will be a pleasure."

That sentence was puzzling until I saw that she was referring to our "meeting" by means of letters. It was one of Van Vechten's best photographs of her, profiled against an American flag, a strong sturdy craggy face with the beginning of a smile, her gray hair short, and a rolled lace scarf around her neck.

Meanwhile things were happening. I had moved from Montana to the State College of Washington, from which I had been summarily dismissed after a year's teaching for writing a novel called *Angels on the Bough.* The authoritarian college president, although he had not read it, had heard that it was "racy." It was, perhaps, for 1936 and Pullman, Washington (it had a lady of the evening in it), but today it reads like *Little Women.* Luckily at that time I was a member of the American Association of University Professors. After a lengthy investigation they published a report absolving me and condemning the administration, saying that the president's action restricted the creative output of a university and tended to make its faculty barren and sterile. The report increased the membership of the AAUP at the State College of Washington from thirty to over six hundred, and the president soon thereafter resigned. I told Gertrude Stein of my vindication, which delighted her so much that she referred to it twice in *Everybody's Autobiography,* which I read in manuscript the first summer we met in Bilignin.

But even more important to me was the letter she wrote me about *Angels on the Bough,* before making her comments in the second autobiography. By this time she was addressing me as "Dear Sam," and in the letter she told me that I had really created a piece of something, and that it did something to her, and that the book's effect had to do with the way I had met the problem of time. She promised to read the book again and to write me more, and asked my age.

I told her that I was twenty-seven, and that my Ph.D. in English was four years old; and then in 1937 I was able to go to France to meet them for the first time. I was extremely nervous about the visit, for despite my years I was callow and unsophisticated, with a narrow Ohio background. In those days people seemed to mature more slowly.

On August 26, 1937, she wrote to me in Paris, saying that she was pleased I was there and was going to be here, and giving me instructions about the train to Culoz and the meeting.

Neither of them was in sight when I pulled my luggage off the train in the early afternoon in the village of Culoz. The air was warm, I was sweating, and the sky seemed bluer than I had ever seen it before in Paris or America. But Gertrude and Alice were nowhere to be seen.

The next moments were bad. I waited, watching for them, and at last asked the stationmaster if he knew the two *mesdemoiselles américaines.*

"Oh, but certainly," he said.

"Have you seen them today?"

He shook his head. "Not for more than two weeks. Perhaps if Monsieur would like to telephone them at Bilignin . . ."

French telephones dismayed me. In my then halting French, I had to make the operator understand what I wanted, and when I finally reached the house at Bilignin, it was to talk with Madame Roux, the housekeeper, and she spoke a patois that was beyond me.

I did manage to understand that they were not there, and had gone to Culoz. I checked my suitcases, trembling a little and wondering if there had been an accident, and set out to scour the town for them street by street. An hour passed, and there was no sign of them at all. I could not know that as I was going up one narrow street, they were going down another (having decided to do some shopping before the train arrived), and gradually a good many of the townspeople of Culoz were out looking for us, trying to bring us together, for half the village had seen one or the other of us. And at that time I did not know of Gertrude's feelings about trains and meetings: "I hate meeting trains and saying goodbye to them and meeting people and seeing them go away."

It must have been a great annoyance for Gertrude and Alice; it was hell for me. At last, about four o'clock in the afternoon, I did what I should have done at the very beginning: I went to the station, unchecked my baggage, and sat down on it to wait.

It was not long. I looked up the street leading to the station, and there they were — Gertrude and Alice, large and small.

"Jesus," I said to myself, and started toward them.

"Damnation!" Gertrude shouted. "There he is, it's Sammy himself."

That was their name for me from then on. We spent the next half-hour alternately swearing and laughing and explaining, while they looked at me and I looked at them.

Gertrude was wearing one of her best pink silk brocaded vests with a pale yellow crêpe de Chine shirt, a kind of monk's cloth or burlap skirt, and flat-heeled walking shoes. Alice was almost all in black, save for the wild fruits and flowers on her yellow hat and purple beads that swung in a triple loop down to her waist. I found it difficult to take my eyes away from her faint mustache, which held me almost as intently as did Gertrude's gray hair, cut short and circling into a fascinating whorl at the back of her head. She looked like a Roman senator about to break into voluble Latin.

We climbed into their Matford and set off, with Gertrude driving and Alice sitting in the back seat, filing her nails.

"What with all this waiting and looking, it's the dogs I'm worried about," Gertrude said. "We'll have to stop at the butcher's and get some scraps. It's far beyond their feeding time."

"They can wait, Lovey," Alice said.

"Not on your life, Pussy," Gertrude said. "We can wait but dogs can't." And so we stopped at a butcher's shop in Culoz to get some meat for them, while the butcher's wife made us some raspberry syrup with a little wine mixed in.

The first evening was memorable. We got to Bilignin while it was still light, and they gave me a tour through the eighteenth-century chateau with its mansard roof which they rented each summer. "Tumbledown," Gertrude called it, but it seemed charming and in good repair. It was lovely and old with gleaming hardwood floors, a stone stairway to the second floor, and a formal garden behind the house with trimmed box hedges, where Gertrude took me to see the broad beautiful valley rising to the misty blue unforgettable hills of Ain and far in the distance the barely visible peak of Mont Blanc outlined and goldenly radiant in the setting sun. Then Gertrude took me upstairs to show me my room, and grabbing my hand led me into the bathroom at the end of the hall, where with a flourish she turned on the hot water in the washbowl. It came out with a gush of steam.

"There, what do you think of that," she said proudly. "We just had it put in. All that hot water as soon as a hotel and hotter too."

Alice had left us to go to the kitchen when we went upstairs. She had learned of my complicated allergies and was putting together a meal calculated to avoid the milk, wheat, egg, and potato products I could not have. Great cook that she was, it must have annoyed her to try to fit together a meal without such staples, but perhaps she considered it a challenge.

At any rate, when she called us to dinner, she had succeeded admirably: it was a simple but delicious meal of poached fish, *haricots verts*, rice with saffron, and white wine. I noticed that Alice drank sparingly of the wine, and Gertrude not at all, and governed myself accordingly. After dinner there was a mint infusion, taken in the sitting room with its great squeaking wicker chair for Gertrude, in which she rocked gently against the background of white woodwork and painted trompe l'oeil panels of corbeilles and hunting horns, and musical instruments in tones of gray, brown, soft yellow, and purple.

Gertrude was just a trifle hard of hearing, but she had a superb way of overcoming it. If one started to say something and she did not hear the first words, she never waited until the sentence was finished. Instead she shouted, "What" in a tone to make one jump. The device saved time and repetition. And as for question marks — you never heard them in her talk or saw them in her writing. "Everyone knows a question is a question, so why use a question mark," she was fond of saying. "They are all right as a brand on cattle but you never need them in writing."

That evening we talked of one of the young avant-garde men who had begun to be a publisher, James Laughlin, and Gertrude called him inarticulate.

"And so am I," I said.

"No, you're not at all," Gertrude said, and her deep hearty laugh followed the thin wisp of Alice's cigarette smoke out into the dark blue shadows. "You're just a bashful boy, that's all."

I turned red, bashfully, and was silent.

"That young Laughlin was a Scotch Presbyterian and his

family all war profiteers," Alice said, and Gertrude added, "Yes, and he was a snob to his inferiors and craven, absolutely craven, before his superiors."

"Even with all that money?" I asked.

"Money doesn't make you brave," Gertrude said. "It is everything and nothing."

"Speaking of being craven," I said, "I guess I was that in England. The British and I didn't get along too well."

"And why so?" Alice asked.

I explained that I found many of them considering me inferior, and that perhaps I had known the wrong crowd.

"Do you have any British blood in you," Gertrude asked.

"I'm part Scot," I said.

"Ah, there you have it," Gertrude said. "If you have a single drop of British blood in you, you're thought inferior. A mongrel. The higher classes consider you so and the lower classes think you're inferior to their upper. Now I, I am a Jew, orthodox background, and I never make any bones about it. So in England I had a wonderful time when I went for the Cambridge lectures because no one expected me to be anything but a Jew and I could say what I pleased, even before I was I." She rocked a few extra times in her rocker, which she did to emphasize her point, and laughed — her rich, hearty laugh flowing out into the night of Ain.

The two of them together could make a great racket. Often it was difficult to hear, for they were both shouting at once, or laughing — Gertrude rocking happily and noisily in her wicker chair, and Alice quieter but just as thoroughly amused. I was awestruck to think that I was actually there, hearing Gertrude's deep alto voice, listening to her opinions, and able to ask questions.

Everyone always retired early at Bilignin. Gertrude would look at the clock and say, "Humph, it's bedtime," usually about nine. I was ready, because I could hardly wait to get to my room to start making notes about the day's conversation. Teaching had developed an auditory memory in me, and I made the best use I could of it, since this was long before the easy availability of portable tape recorders. I took comprehensive notes of her talk, always trying to remember exactly the phrasing and delivery of her sentences.

But that first evening Gertrude had another surprise for

me. She gave me the longhand manuscript of the first completed part of *Everybody's Autobiography* to read. It was in the kind of notebook French schoolboys used — about eight by ten inches and three quarters of an inch thick, bound in heavy boards of mottled green and black.

"Read it," she said, "if you can. My handwriting is terrible."

"I'm used to it from your letters," I said, "and besides, the freshman themes gave me training."

I took the book to my bedroom, made notes of the day's talk, and then began to read it. It seemed equally as fascinating as the first autobiography, and had the additional reward of "joy of recognition" for me — the America I knew, people, universities, and towns, recorded with an eye made fresher by thirty years' absence.

For most of the nights of that two-week visit, I read steadily through the manuscript, and by the end of that time Gertrude's sprawling, difficult, abbreviated handwriting was almost as intelligible to me as my own. The script was drunken and wildly ill formed, but flowing and large. Many of the vowels were omitted from words: "existing" became "xisting" or sometimes just "xstng." "Appear" became "appr," and sometimes only the context could help one distinguish meanings.

Weather permitting, Gertrude took a walk at Bilignin every morning — either the upper route through the vineyards or the lower turn down nearly to the small river, often dry, that ran through the Ain valley. Sometimes if she felt good she would take both turns in one day. Although no great lover of walking, I always went with her, for these were opportunities to be alone with her and hear her mind at work. She strode ahead at a good clip as if there were a time limit set on her, and she always carried a strong thin stalk of a weed from which she had stripped the leaves, or else the dog leash if one of the dogs were along. She liked to swat at weed tops and behead them. I walked behind her on the narrow trails through the greenery.

On the first morning we took a turn, there was a gray sky and the rumble of faraway thunder.

"The farmers fear the *orage* — the storm," she said.

"I suppose."

"The hail would ruin the grapes," Gertrude said, "and yet the grapes need the rain."

I was not a talented Boswell, able to feed her good questions. But it did not matter. No leap was too great for her, no non sequitur too absurd for her to take up.

The King of England had just abdicated to marry Wallis Simpson. "What do you think of the Simpson case?" I asked.

Gertrude snorted. "Humph," she said. "She was divorced and that made her in most British eyes just a third-rate besmirched American. Put case. Suppose FDR married a Filipino girl, the American people wouldn't stand for it at all now would they."

"I doubt it."

"Of course not," she said.

After a pause I said something about the futility of lecturing — how most of what you said fell on skulls with no associational background, and the blank looks you got as a result.

"I agree with you absolutely," Gertrude said. "When I lectured in America I found the dull ones always wanted to talk and they had nothing to say. I even told a young man, a talker, once that after I had told him what I thought about a subject I was not interested in what he thought. The good ones always found their way to you anyway. Why discuss anything. You discuss literary problems only with dull people. Either you understand a thing or you don't so what's the use."

"Yes," I said, "all you ever really learn in the classroom is where to go to look things up."

Then the talk switched to religion. In those days I had been experimenting, and had finally decided on the Catholic church — for a year and a half. It hadn't worked.

"Why did you settle on that for Pete's sake," Gertrude said.

"Well," I said, "I had read all of Huysmans, and at the same time there was a history course in the Reformation under a professor at Ohio State, and he was so sly and nasty and full of innuendo about Catholicism that it called up the imp of the perverse in me, and I joined partly just to spite him."

"Did he ever find out."

"Oh, yes, a lot of people told him. He felt he had failed."

"Good," Gertrude said. "That's what he deserved for meddling." She whacked a thistle hard and cut it off clean.

"There are really only two directions to take today," she went on, switching wildly right and left. "Catholicism and Communism. Catholicism is the lesser of two evils. Now the French Catholic is intellectual, the average American Catholic not. And the French Protestants are as ignorant as the middle-class American Catholics because there is less tradition behind each of them. America will never be a Catholic country. Gide is a Protestant and that is why his work is so thin. Now I, I look at Catholicism from my background which is all Talmudic. And with an exclusively Jewish background two facts exist: a comprehensible world and an incomprehensible one. The Jew doesn't concern himself with the second one nor with the Christian attempts at a 'solution' of it. Therefore, any Christian religion attempting a solution is not really interesting to me."

I did not yet know how balefully meaningful that phrase of hers usually was: "I am not interested." It was her way of stating her rejection and thereafter putting a person or thing completely out of mind.

"I speak particularly of the Protestant attempts at a 'solution,' " she added. "The Catholic solution is made with much more delicacy. The Jews are the greatest enemies of the Christians because they are not interested in a solution of the unknowable. The Protestants' 'sure' solution, which is a personal one, makes them intolerably dull. Generally, Catholics have genuine humility and Protestants haven't.

"But I am nonetheless interested in all people," she went on, "and especially in their mind-play. The educated mind can play with all things, all sorts of topics, and it shines while doing it. It has no walls around it. Even the French say of Catholic education, one is educated in a box.

"Now Bravig Imbs did not have that mind-play. He was as dull as Gissing, thoroughly and perfectly. Too bad. He tried to buy a castle and he failed even in that.

"And now," she said, "that's enough talk about religion. I am really not all that concerned about it."

The two were as excited as schoolchildren when it came to showing off their adopted country. One day in the early afternoon we got into the Matford to take a drive.

"Why a Matford?" I said. "Isn't it just a Ford?"

"It's what they're called in France," Alice explained. "Some legal complication."

"But that's what it is just the same," Gertrude said, sitting heavily in the front seat and bouncing once or twice. "A jolly old Ford."

Gertrude always drove, and she handled the car like a drag racer. She got the cushions adjusted behind her back and beneath her, hunched over the steering wheel, and let fly. Everyone and everything got out of the way — chickens squawking and running with feathers coming loose, dogs barking, and the peasants keeping a respectful — and safe — distance away. Since there were no speed limits in France, you could go as fast or as slow as you wanted, and Gertrude usually went fast. Now and again Alice would murmur an admonition from the back seat about "not driving so fast, Lovey," but it never had much effect on Gertrude. Yet she was a very good safe driver.

"Shall we go to Aix-les-Bains, Pussy, shall we," Gertrude said.

"It's much too far for this late in the day, Lovey," Alice said. "We'll do it another day."

"Well how about Artemare then," Gertrude said, narrowly missing a chicken. "We can eat at the Hôtel Bérrard and give Sammy a taste of real French bourgeois cooking."

So it was Artemare. We drove down the macadam road. Poplars made sheltering leafy tunnels out of the road, and we looked out at the green fields.

"Do you know why there is no painting in America Sammy," Gertrude asked.

"No. Why?"

"Look at the sky over there," Gertrude said. "There's a helluva lot more of it than there is in America. You need sky to paint. What would any of the painters like Van Gogh have done if there were skyscrapers cluttering up everything now I ask you."

"Perhaps," Alice said, "a lack of talent in America might have something to do with it."

"Pshaw," Gertrude said. "It's the lack of sky. Look at that." The sky was deep blue, the clouds blindingly white and clumped down near the horizon in great cumulus masses.

We passed some religious shrines, holding weather-bleached statues of the Madonna and child, and then gradually began to see a few columns of stone and fragments of a low wall.

"Roman ruins," Gertrude said. "There's a lot of them. My favorite is a little farther on." Then she turned to me. "Did you bring your camera now did you."

"Ever hear of a tourist without one?" I said, holding up the first model that Argus ever made.

"Good," Gertrude said, "we'll stop and take a picture of it. It's just over the hill."

We crested a small ridge and there it was: a solid gray stone column about two feet in diameter, flat on top, placed on a small pediment and pitted with the erosion of centuries. It stood entirely alone, and behind it the hill sloped down to the greenery of a fertile valley.

"I'll stand beside it and you can take my picture," Gertrude said. We left the car, and she posed herself indomitably beside the stone. I snapped the picture, a little nervous because it was the first one I had taken of her.

"Now I'll take yours," Gertrude said. "You climb up on top."

I looked in dismay at the stone, and turned to her. "It's just too high for me to jump up," I said, "and too thick and awkward to get a purchase on it."

Gertrude handed the camera to Alice. "Do hold it Pussy," she said. Then she drew close to the column, spread her sturdy legs as far as her burlap skirt would allow, and clasped her hands, fingers interlaced and palms upward, bracing them against her knee. "Step here and I'll give you a boost," she said.

"It'll dirty your hands," I said reluctantly.

"Nonsense no matter," she said, waiting.

I put my foot in Gertrude's palm. She gave a mighty boost; my fingers scrabbled at the top edge, got hold, and then she pushed harder. I was on top, somewhat scuffed and scratched, but there nonetheless.

Gertrude took the camera from Alice and stepped back. "Now how do you work this thing tell me," she said.

I told her what to do. She snapped the shutter and then started to turn the film. "This is too fancy for me," she said. "It's all I can do to work my little Brownie box."

"I'll fix it," I said, looking around. "How do I get down off this thing?"

"Jump," said Gertrude briefly. I looked for a soft spot and jumped.

"Now wasn't that nice," she asked, grinning widely.

"It would have been better," I said somewhat ruefully, "if I could have taken one with you on top."

Alice burst out laughing. "A hard thing to do," she said.

Gertrude laughed too. "You're bats," she said, and grabbed me around the waist and hugged me. "Even if I got up there, maybe with a crane, I never would have got down and then what would you have done."

"Got you down with a skyhook," I said slyly.

"A skyhook, a skyhook, what's that," Gertrude said excitedly. "I like the idea of that, what is it."

I briefly explained the old American joke.

"It's a grand idea," Gertrude said. "Maybe I'll use it some day would you mind."

"We are a part of all that we have met," I said.

We got back into the car. The sun was near the horizon, but it was not far to Artemare.

The Hôtel Bérrard was a typical peasant hotel, painted white with gray green shutters and a cupola on top with a red weathervane. It had a front porch where two tables were set up. Both were empty.

"Let's eat on the porch, Lovey," Alice said.

"Won't there be mosquitoes," Gertrude asked.

"There never have been around here."

"Good then it's the porch."

Madame Bérrard came out to seat us at the small round table with its blue-and-white-checkered tablecloth. She was a ruddy-faced Frenchwoman, rather bosomy, and very polite to the "mesdemoiselles américaines" and "leur ami." After we had been seated and the meal ordered, one of those curious moments of silence descended on all three of us. Finally Alice sighed.

"We are just like a typical French family," she said, "waiting for 'the beast' to be brought to the table. Typically bourgeoise. We sit down empty-minded, *fatigués,* and sigh. Then we take one bite, and *scream* through the rest of the meal."

"Yes," said Gertrude, "and just to prove how typical, I have learned finally how they do their napkins." She unfolded hers on her ample lap, and then with one quick movement — one arm crossing the other, and each hand grasping a corner of the napkin — she put the corners under each arm at the ribs, quickly clapping her arms to her sides so that the napkin was in place. Alice shook her head.

"I can never learn to do that," she said.

I tried, but it slipped. "You'll have to practice Sammy," Gertrude said.

The meal was excellent. We started with a duck pâté, very rich and heavy. Then there were tiny red crayfish, seasoned well and cooked until the shells were soft, tomatoes like the American "beefhearts," a partridge for each of us, small new potatoes peeled and smothered in parsley and butter, vin blanc — and finally, tiny wild strawberries, picked by Madame Bérrard's son in the hills that afternoon. We ended with strong coffee, and my allergic reactions to the food began to make me itch.

All through the meal there was conversation about everything under the sun.

"I know why you got fired from the State College of Washington Sammy," Gertrude said. "You called your book *Angels on the Bough.* Now that, that being an agricultural college in the apple country, they probably thought it was some sort of blight. If you had called it *Apples on the Bough,* everything would have been quite all right."

She kept throwing scraps to Basket and Pépé, making Alice nervous. "You'll put them off their feed, Lovey," she said.

The demi of white wine went almost untouched, save by me. "Am I the only drunkard?" I asked.

Gertrude put her elbows on the table and spread her fingers under her chin. "We don't drink much, Alice doesn't really care for it and it's no good for me. It's funny, very funny, about this problem of liquor and writers. Now take Hart Crane when he came to Paris. He was too drunk all the time to call on us except twice when he was half drunk. You can't write of the 'furious quest' and be drunk all the time, your quest is not furious then. Take Sherwood, he wrote with genuine melancholy because of it. It is a paradox. Hemingway, Crane, Sherwood, they all believed life turns on passion but they were without passion themselves because physiologically liquor kills all passion. But they all had a sense of power, it is very curious the sense of power that alcohol gives, but it is a false sense."

I felt that she was talking directly to me, and took no more wine.

"Now sometimes they can't help it of course," Gertrude went on. "Take poor Fitzgerald, he was a congenital dipsomaniac."

Alice wrinkled her nose. "And not for me," she said.

"And then there was Jo Davidson the sculptor," Gertrude continued. "He had a couple of pals he drank with and one night when they were drunk Jo fell down the stairs and broke his leg. So he was in a wheelchair for about eight weeks and his wife kept all alcohol away from him, and one night his two buddies both came to see him and they were as drunk as hoot owls and they stayed a long time and his wife never left them alone because she was afraid they'd give Jo some. And when they left Jo turned to her and said wonderingly, 'Chérie . . . was I ever like that,' and she very gently said, 'Yes, Jo, but you were worse much worse,' and do you know that from that day to this, about five years, Jo hasn't touched a single drop."

"And I doubt if he ever will again," Alice said. I lighted her cigarette and then my own.

Gertrude did not smoke. We were of the generation for whom alcohol and nicotine were problems but not drugs. Neither Gertrude nor Alice ever touched a pill or drug except when a doctor prescribed it, and then they were reluctant. Even the famous recipe for "haschisch fudge" in Alice's cookbook was not one that she had actually devised, nor did she even realize until later what the mysterious ingredient was. The recipe had been sent to her by Brion Gysin from Tangier — but more of that later.

With her usual sympathy and concern for young people who had experimented with writing, Gertrude talked a lot about my problems. "You need money to live on yes," she said, "but the worst way to get it, the worst thing to do if you want to write, is to teach, and here is why. You teach all day and then that word-finding part of your brain is worn out and when you do go to write, say in the evening or nights, you can't find any words to put down because that part of you is exhausted. It would be better yes much to be a butcher."

"I might try for a Guggenheim Fellowship if you'd help," I said.

"Maybe we could do that but they don't like me much because of something I wrote in the past and Henry McBride published it, we ought to try a *petite conspiracie* of some kind. The time of the patron is past. I, I resent the pull you have to have to get a Guggenheim but if you want me to help I will. But you ought to do something anything else but teach. However all the people like the Guggenheims have to be treated with delicacy O my yes."

"A shame," Alice said.

"You're right it is it is a crying shame," Gertrude said emphatically.

It was by then about five o'clock and the shadows of the poplars were lengthening. Gertrude put her hands on the table edge and pushed back in her chair. "We'll have to go back, Pussy," she said. "The Rops are coming tonight to meet Sammy."

I looked blank.

"Henri Daniel-Rops and his wife, Madeleine," Alice explained. "He writes, mostly about Catholic things. He's a kind of popularizer."

The Daniel-Rops arrived about eight o'clock that evening. They were a curiously matched pair. He had a congenital defect that kept his eyelids at half-droop, so that he had to tilt his head backward to look at you to talk, and he was thin as a rail. Madeleine was radiant and lovely, a truly handsome woman with brown hair. Yet it was Madeleine who later contracted tuberculosis, while her broomstick husband made his way in perfect health to financial security — even wealth — as a writer.

The evening was a French one, since neither Henri nor his wife knew any English at the time. We talked of many things — his fifteen books, Huysmans, Gertrude's writing, Trollope's novels, and my own small efforts.

During that first visit in Bilignin, the Daniel-Rops were frequent visitors. The vitality and charm of Madeleine and the intellect and wry humor of Henri were continually interesting. He had introduced Gertrude and Alice to the monks at the Abbey of Hautecombe, which overlooked Lake Bourget.

After the first meeting with the Daniel-Rops, I went upstairs to make my usual notes, and then to continue reading *Everybody's Autobiography.* To my astonished surprise I discovered that in two places she had told the story of my dismissal from the State College of Washington for writing *Angels on the Bough,* saying that she had found it very interesting, that it had something in it that made literature — more than clarity — that it succeeded in saying something more than it actually said, and that its clear line "created something" which gave her pleasure. She ended with "We are expecting him this summer and I think that he is interesting."*

Gertrude wakened me the next morning by pounding on the door. "Get up Sammy," she hollered. "You sleep even later than I do. Get up, we are going to Aix-les-Bains and have lunch, do hurry now do."

And so we were off again, with Basket barking and Pépé yapping because they were left behind. There was a lot of light small talk on the way about the liveliness of the sky that morning and the green and tan of the French countryside, and the sudden appearance last night of mosquitoes, "when we have never had them before," Alice said with irritation.

Suddenly Gertrude said, "Are you superstitious Sammy."

"I avoid ladders and throw salt over my left shoulder."

"Me too," Gertrude chuckled. "But spiders are my new

* See Appendix, pages 249–50.

superstition. Did you ever hear the old French proverb about spiders." She quoted it in French. " 'Spiders in the morning, chagrin; at noon — care and worry; and in the evening — hope.' "

"Have you given up the cuckoos for spiders?" Alice asked.

"I have not," said Gertrude. "It's just that cuckoos are now second."

"I've never heard about the cuckoos," I said.

"If a cuckoo hollers at you and you have money in your pocket you'll double it before the week's out," Gertrude said. "It's true too. Only the last time I had a check in my pocket and it may not work, because is a check money or is only money money."

"The only thing to do is wait and see," Alice said calmly.

"I just hope it works on a check," Gertrude said.

When we got to Aix-les-Bains we went to a charming restaurant and since the weather was warm asked for a table under the tightly packed arbor of fragrant leaves that cast a cool and speckled shadow over all. The maître d'hôtel recognized them at once, and bowed. "We are honored," he said, "to have once again our good friends, the mesdemoiselles from America."

"*Que vous êtes tout à fait aimable*," Alice said.

He gave us the best table, and the waiters hovered over us as if we had just been hatched. The lunch started with a slice of Algerian melon, and with Gertrude having a spoonful, I snapped a picture.

"Oh, Lovey," said Alice. "You never ought to be photographed while you're eating."

"I didn't have the spoon in my mouth," Gertrude grumbled. But Alice frowned, and the large cyst on her forehead under her bangs was visible.

The luncheon went on, without any more pictures. We had the excellent fish of the region, *omble chevalier, a pâté de la maison* (very rich and delicious, of ham and chicken livers), a partridge for each of us, green beans, and wild *framboises* with cream.

On the way back to Bilignin Gertrude was a little sleepy from all the excellent food. We went by way of Chambéry in Savoie to look at the chateau, the elephant fountain, and the Roman ruins. In Chambéry Gertrude took a walk to waken herself, and Alice went with her while I got a haircut. From there we went on to stop at the Abbey of Hautecombe to meet the monks. The abbey was medieval and very Gothic, with tombs of long-dead bishops standing on the chapel floor, and thin effigies carved in gray stone lying atop each one. Our guide was their favorite young Père Bernardet, a special friend of Henri's, a tall courteous handsome priest who looked like an American football player.

In the car the talk never stopped. We discussed handwriting and how to analyze it, for Gertrude — besides being an amateur palmist — was also good at that. They passed me a letter from someone I did not know, and by good luck I hit the analysis right — probably, again, the result of long acquaintance with reading freshman themes. Alice spoke at length of the way she could always get American cigarettes, since they both had an admirer who worked at the American Embassy in Paris.

My visit to Bilignin was drawing to a close, and it made me unhappy. But on this first "literary pilgrimage" to Europe I had already planned to go to Zurich to visit Thomas Mann, who was then living in the suburb of Küsnacht. I had not mentioned the purpose of the Zurich trip to Gertrude and Alice, since I had sensed (knowing that one never mentioned James Joyce to them) that geniuses on the same level never speak of each other. It was quite a shock then to receive a postcard in English from the wife of Thomas Mann, confirming the arrangements for a meeting three days later. But neither Gertrude nor Alice said a word about the card, and perhaps neither of them was tempted to read it.

I was well into the last manuscript volume of the autobiography, sitting in a lounge chair in the rose garden, when Alice called from the house the next morning.

"We are going to Chambéry, Sammy," she said. "We must buy some milk and oil and things. Would you like to come along?"

It was just before noon. I put the manuscript on the low stone wall of the rose garden, and went to join the usual hubbub of departure — the dogs barking and everyone yelling. We raced down the roads to Chambéry, and on this occasion I sat in the front seat. The windows were all down; the air was clean and fresh. I decided to have a cigarette, and pushed in the lighter on the dashboard. Then with my mind on something Gertrude was saying, I very casually — as if I had been holding an extinguished match — tossed the lighter out the window.

I let out a howl of agony when I realized what I had done. Gertrude's foot went down heavily on the brake, nearly throwing us through the front windshield, and dislodging Alice from her Madame Récamier position in the back seat.

"What's the matter, my god, what's the matter Sammy," Gertrude asked.

I told her what I had done. Both of them laughed.

"Cheer up, Sammy," Alice said. "It's a natural mistake. You're white as a sheet."

". . . and feel like a complete fool," I muttered, starting to open the door to go back to look for it.

"No Sammy wait a minute and we'll back up," Gertrude said, and with a mighty jolt she reversed the car and drove it back about a hundred yards to the approximate spot.

Jesus. The postcard from Katia Mann . . . and now this!

"Calm down, Sammy," Alice said. "You're trembling and perspiring. We'll find it."

We all piled out of the car, which Gertrude had pulled to the side of the road, and started to look. Gertrude spotted it almost at once, on the red sandy soil by the roadside.

"Whoopee!" she hollered. "I found it, I'm pretty good."

"The b-best," I said, wiping the sweat from my face with my handkerchief. Gertrude gave me a bear hug around the shoulders.

"That's all right Sammy, relax, no harm done," she said.

"It makes a wonderful story," Alice said calmly. We all got back into the Matford and went on to Chambéry. But my knees were still trembling when we descended in front of the grocery.

Somehow with their sensitivity and concern they sensed my worry and embarrassment. I wandered around the small store and found some kitchen knives and hardware. One particular small knife with a serrated edge took my attention and I stood looking at it admiringly, unaware that Alice had come up behind me.

"It's beautiful, isn't it?" she said. "If you could only see the look in your eyes, and how you want it. It's what they call a tomato knife in France and I have one" — she looked closely at it — "just exactly like it, and I'm going to buy it for you."

"Oh, no, please."

She dug into her beaded bag, the one with long fringes on the bottom. "Indeed I am," she said. "A souvenir that will make you always remember the story of the cigarette lighter." And she purchased it for me, but I insisted that she accept one franc, so that the sharp edge of the knife would not cut our friendship.

"You *are* a superstitious one," she said, taking it.

We got back to the chateau at Bilignin about three o'clock in the afternoon. "Well Sammy," Gertrude said as we got out of the car, "it's time for our exercise, shall we take the lower turn, and do you want to ask me any literary questions because if you do now's the time to do it."

"Of course I do."

"Then let's go," she said. Outside the iron gates of the chateau she plucked a hard stiff weed and stripped the leaves from it in her usual way.

We passed a few peasants, the women greeting her respectfully and the men removing their hats to say "Bonjour." Soon we left the dirt road and went into the trees leading down to the Ain River. The scent of the loam was fresh and pleasant, and the leaves were moist and soft under foot.

"I know that everyone asks you the same thing," I said tentatively. "But I can't help it. Why do you not write as you talk . . . or vice versa?"

"Simple," she said, beheading a weed. "If you invited Keats to dinner and asked him a question, you wouldn't expect him to reply with the 'Ode to a Nightingale' now would you."

"Hardly," I said. Then recalling the stationery she had given me to write some letters back to the States, I said, "Everyone is fascinated with that little sign of yours — the tiny rose inside the circle of 'rose is a rose is a rose.' Why did you invent that?"

She laughed. "I was wondering when you'd ask that. Most everyone who comes here on a visit asks it the first day or the first hour. That's why I like you for one reason, you waited nearly two weeks."

I was glad to be walking behind her, for I must have turned scarlet. It was probably the first time I'd blushed in ten years.

She laughed again. "You are a silly bashful boy," she said without turning her head, "and I betcha you're blushing right here and now."

Having plunged, I decided to go ahead. "You're right, I am," I said, "so what did you mean by the rose poem?"

"Well, I'll tell you," she said. She took the end of the switch and stuck it down between the crevice of two fingers of her left hand, half turned and stopped. "Poetry is made up of the addressing, the caressing, the possessing, and the expressing of nouns. Now when the poet first used the word 'rose' it called up a beautiful picture to the reader. But gradually as the years went by it meant less and less" — and here she slowly slid her hands farther apart on the switch until she held it at both ends — "and there was no meaning at all and no reader could ever see a rose. Now when I wrote 'Rose is a rose is a rose' " — and with that she drew her hands toward each other slowly, moving along the length of the switch until one palm finally rested against the other — "I slowly brought the meaning back to the word by repetition, I put the picture back in the word and I am the first person in two hundred years to do that thing."

I had the feeling that standing here on the fragrant needle carpet of the forest floor was one of the few women in the twentieth century who was developing a metaphysical mind, and I said so, adding: "I think you are one of the few women today who can get a physical sensation from a syllogism."

She laughed and resumed walking. She was smiling, her broad face crinkled into lines of warmth and friendliness. "You're right," she said, "they make the hairs on my neck stand up. And perhaps you're right about the metaphysical too, anyway it's a nice compliment it really is and I thank you for it, and maybe just maybe it is really and truly true."

"You know," she went on, "the creative act is wonderful. Remembering is not the way of creative thinking and writing. Creating is not remembering but experiencing. It is to look and to hear and to write — without remembering. It is the immediate feelings arranged in words as they occur to me. But only a minority, a very small number, of artists reveals a sensitivity to materials and to the world in general. That is, I mean, acting according to their experiencing and to be really living and creating. I am always a part of the picture as a writer. Nowadays everyone pretends nobody wrote the book a reader is reading, that they are all written while an author is doing something else. All the other writers do this thing. But someone wrote it so why pretend. All writing is necessarily or partly autobiographical so why pretend. You just rearrange and you don't bother about remembering. The bottom natures, the really bottom natures of people are revealed not so much by the actual words said or the thoughts had but by their thoughts and words endlessly the same and endlessly different, always repeating. Society can only find the right ways and the new ways, or the new ways only, by creating, by finding rather than remembering, and the way of finding and creating is by talking and endlessly discussing. And anyone who writes a masterpiece is not concerned, not at all, with any attempt to influence people one way or another."

"Yet you have influenced them," I said. "And you will go on influencing."

"I'll be happy, damn happy," she said, "if people come back to my writing every twenty-five years because they will slowly begin to understand what I'm trying to say."

During all her long speech she had been smiling and chuckling. I felt the metaphysical mind at work, but metaphysics by an artist in a mood of gaiety is sometimes difficult to follow.

"They will, they will," I said, "for we agreed you are the grandmother of modern American literature. And maybe, just maybe, it will be twenty instead of twenty-five years, or even a continuing thing."

"Four times a century's enough for me," Gertrude said.

We walked a short distance in silence. There was still one distracting question on my mind that I was almost afraid to put into words.

"Some people say your writing is a . . . er . . . fraud," I began timidly.

Gertrude snorted. "Because of that automatic writing experiment before I left America," she said. "Nothing to it.

College experiments pure and simple, that's all they were. My teacher William James was interested in whether the unconscious mind could furnish messages, any sort of messages from what he called 'the summer-land,' and so Leon Solomons and I tried to test whether the un- or sub-conscious could produce writing under certain conditions of fatigue or reverie, or distraction. But I, I always knew what I was writing, it was not automatic."

"And punctuation?" I asked.

"It's nonsense mostly. I already told you that everyone knows a question is a question so why use a question mark. And commas, they help you put on your coat and button your shoes for you and anyone can do that. But I believe in periods because after all you have to stop sometime." She chuckled.

We had come to the bottom of the ravine and slowly started back up toward the old chateau.

"You really have two styles of writing," I said.

"Maybe more than that," Gertrude said. "The style in the autobiographies is what I call my moneymaking style. But the other one is the main one, the really creative one."

I ventured an analogy. "It reminds me of the improvisations of Eastern music," I said. "It sort of goes on and on, maybe like water running, a little different sometimes, mostly the same. And you wait for a crescendo or a climax and none comes, and just when you begin to feel thwarted, the music turns soothing and then there is a kind of twitch, and it becomes really and truly interesting."

"I like that Sammy, I really do," Gertrude said. "That is nice, you are *perspicace*."

We went on climbing. "You know," she said, "you're going to Zurich and I am going to give you a note to Thornton Wilder and you can say hello to him. He's writing a play just now and I think it may be a good one."

"Thank you," I said. "I would like that."

We reached the chateau, always more out of breath than when we started, and had a very light evening meal. After it was over we sat and rocked a while and talked in the living room, and then Gertrude gave a mighty yawn.

"I'm sleepy that's what I am and tired too and I'm going to bed."

We went our separate ways. After I had finished packing I was really exhausted, but not too tired to be able to stay awake until I was sure they were asleep. Then I stole quietly downstairs, tiptoed into the kitchen, and very softly opened the drawer where Alice kept her knives. With a small flashlight I looked at them and found the duplicate of the tomato knife she had bought for me. I extracted it from the drawer, careful to make no sound, and replaced it with the one she had given me. Then I closed the drawer carefully and crept back upstairs. After all, I would much rather have the knife that she had used than the brand-new one. I often wondered if her sharp eye ever saw the difference.

My alarm went off at nine the next morning. I lay dozing for a few minutes, when there came a small knock at the door.

It was Alice. "Are you awake and decent?" she said. My god, I thought — could she have discovered my small theft so soon?

"Yes, I am," I said, opening the door. Alice was standing there with what for her was a deep scowl. She came into the room and closed the door.

"I am going to have to scold you a little, Sammy," she said. "Do you know that you left the last volume of *Everybody's Autobiography* out on the garden wall all through the night?"

I sank into a chair. "Oh, my god," I said.

She came over and patted me on the shoulder. "There, there," she said as one would to a wounded animal. "Luckily there was no harm done, and I won't tell Gertrude. But it was lucky, really. Suppose it had rained — where would the manuscript be?"

"Oh, oh," I groaned.

"Never mind," Alice said. "I know you didn't mean to. And I really won't tell."

I kissed her hand. "That's very sweet of you."

And that was that. As far as I know, she never did tell Gertrude.

Gertrude hated departures. Nonetheless, they both drove me to Culoz and left me at the station. Gertrude kissed me on both cheeks in the French fashion, and so did Alice.

"And you will come again next year," Gertrude said.

"I hope so if I can afford it," I said, wondering if all the mishaps of the last few days would be held against me.

But they were evidently not, because when the time came — two years instead of one year later — along came another invitation. And I accepted.

II

MY FIRST THOUGHT on returning to Chicago from the visit to Bilignin was that I wanted to send Gertrude and Alice a token to thank them for their hospitality to me. But what? Something for Gertrude alone? Something for Alice alone? Something for both of them together?

I thought a long time about it and then finally headed for the largest department store in Chicago, to the floor of kitchen utensils. There I picked out all the unusual household and kitchen gadgets that I could find, things I did not remember seeing that Alice had, and sent them.

It seemed a long time before there came word from Gertrude that they had arrived, but in November 1937 she wrote that the gadgets had arrived at the rue de Fleurus and that Alice was delighted with them and kept them on a shelf of the best Italian furniture in the atelier with the best treasures, showing them with so much pride, finding them so useful and pale blue and beautiful that they were a joy to both of them. She wrote also that they were leaving the rue de Fleurus for the rue Christine, that they and the Rops had "talked endlessly" about me, and that she was writing a life of Picasso in French.

A score or more of letters came from Gertrude in the two-year interval before I left for France again, letters telling me that the Père Abbé had said that I was always welcome at Hautecombe, or saying that "Alice's joy in the gadgets is as great as ever, and now she is to have a refrigerator and there is a cover to that for things in your collection, it seems to be a regular Swiss Family Robinson collection . . . and everybody says how Sweet is Sammy and he is and perhaps he will be sweet enough to be happy that is our wish . . ."

Or again: "Whenever anybody says Sammy somebody says he is a darling or somebody says he is an angel, that is the way somebody always seems to feel about Sammy . . ."

Indeed I must have had them fooled . . .

Gertrude and Alice were long settled in the rue Christine, and when the summer of 1939 arrived they went once more to Bilignin. Back in Chicago I prepared to visit them again in the south of France. I saw the Daniel-Rops first in Paris, arriving there in early July and after a few days going on to Bilignin.

This time there were no complications about meeting Gertrude and Alice. They were at the station in Culoz when the train arrived.

It was a happy reunion. We embraced and kissed each other on the cheeks, and then started to talk — of the Rops, the Abbey of Hautecombe, literature (Gertrude said, as the French say, "We are having a bad quarter of an hour in it"), the failure of both Wendell Wilcox, another young writer, and myself to get Guggenheim Fellowships ("because of that thing I wrote about them," Gertrude said — and she had sponsored both of us), and a dozen other topics.

"The Rops think you are quite angelic in appearance," Gertrude said, and guffawed heartily. "And that seems funny to me but that is the way they feel about it. And did you leave a pair of shoes behind you all done up in nice little shoe bags."

"Yes, I did," I said. "Walking shoes. I guess it must have been Freudian — if you leave something behind it means you want to come back again."

"And now you have," Alice said, still at work on her fingernails.

I considered the Rops's statement and said to Gertrude, "But you don't think I look angelic."

"You damn betcha I don't," she said, hunching over the wheel of the Matford as we sped breakneck over the country roads. "It's more Machiavelli, it's that mustache."

I had remembered Gertrude and her superstitions, and I

took from my pocket a small rabbit's foot and passed it over to her.

"What's that," she asked.

"It's a rabbit's foot, Lovey," Alice said.

". . . to keep us on the road," I added.

Gertrude took it and put it into an ample pocket in her beige-colored blouse. "Thanks," she said, "it'll probably work better than a Saint Christopher. Speaking of superstitions I've got *Faust* finished and it's got spiders and vipers in it and Lord Berners is going to do it, at least that's the plan, and Alice made a carbon copy just for you, and I corrected all the mistakes in it with my new thirty-five-franc pen."

"I'm overwhelmed," I said. "Thank you in advance."

Alice humphed mildly. "There weren't *many* mistakes," she said.

"No not many at all," Gertrude said. "But the corrections were in my handwriting and that may mean something."

"Makes it a collector's item from the grandmother of American literature." I grinned at her.

She grinned back, and gave me a hard whack on the leg. "It's good to see you again Sammy," she said. "And we have a surprise for you too, Henry Luce and his wife Clare are here giving us the 'rush' and tomorrow they've invited us for lunch at the Hôtel Royale-Splendide in Aix-les-Bains and will you go or would you rather read the *Faust*."

"I'd rather read *Faust*," I said, "but let me go along because I'd never have a chance to meet them except through you two."

"Sweet," Alice said.

"Very," said Gertrude, "and very diplomatic. Our Sammy is the last gentleman. And no I don't mind not really, there's plenty of time to read the *Faust* and even some more things."

"Henry Luce and his wife are taking the cure at Aix-les-Bains," Alice volunteered. "It seems they've both been eating and drinking too much on this trip to Europe."

"Tell Sammy what they do during the cure, Pussy, do tell him," Gertrude said excitedly, chuckling.

"Well," said Alice, "at one point they have to be separated, male from female, while they get massaged; and each time before they do, they give each other a thought to think about.

And then when they come out from being broiled and whacked they exchange their conclusions about the thought."

I whooped with laughter. "Not a wasted moment — an executive's combination of business and benefits," I said.

"Or something like that," Gertrude said. "You'd think an ordinary person would just want to relax and be thumped."

"Oh, they're not ordinary people," I said.

"That was a bitchy play she wrote about women," Gertrude said. "But I liked it, at least I liked it a little. Now she's taken up knitting or crocheting or something like that."

"She's all tied up in little blue French knots," Alice said enigmatically.

I turned to look at her. "A mysterious statement," I said.

"You'll see tomorrow," Gertrude said."

Something seemed a bit different about Alice, and shortly I discovered what it was. Although she still wore her bangs low on her forehead, the huge cyst under them had been removed. The faint scar of it was visible when the wind blew through the open windows and disarranged her hair.

"Thornton said Clare was rather like granite," Alice said. "And Sammy, do you know he liked you? He was writing *Our Town* in Zurich and was stuck at the end of the second act, and you walked all night in the rain with him and he struck a match on you, he said, and wrote the whole third act the next day while you were sleeping."

"I might have guessed that," I said, "from the way he kept pumping me. It was drizzling, horrible weather, and I kept hollering about my feet being wet and wanting an umbrella, and now I see that act three opens with a crowd of people under umbrellas in the rain in a graveyard. Thornton's nice, even though he nearly gave me pneumonia waltzing me around in the wet to show me where Dadaism began with the reading of laundry lists into poetry. And we had to stay up all night until the bells began to ring because he wanted me to hear them in the morning the way Max Beerbohm described them. And of course we had to see the house where Nietzsche 'in great loneliness,' as he said, wrote *Zarathustra* . . ."

"I don't know why it is people can create things in Zurich," Alice said.

"Probably because there's nothing else to do except bank your money," I said cynically.

Gertrude laughed. "I think maybe that's it, it really could be that. Pussy, do you remember the story about Whistler's going there, do you now," she asked.

"Yes," said Alice.

"I'm not sure I ever heard it," I said.

"Well," said Alice, "Whistler was going to live in Switzerland for a year and they gave him a going-away party, he was going to paint and write, and a little old lady came up to him and said, 'Oh, Mr. Whistler, what an inspiration it will be for you to look at the Alps, think of the lovely things you will produce with all that inspiration,' and Whistler looked down at her and said, 'Madame, the Swiss have been looking at the Alps for hundreds of years and all they have ever produced is the carved wooden bear and the cuckoo clock.' "

Finally we arrived at the old chateau in Bilignin, and I opened the iron gates. The two dogs barked furiously at our arrival. Once again I savored the ancient pleasing odor of the old house with its oak paneling and the windows shuttered against the sun. There was the same rose garden, with its beds of flowers outlined by the clipped low lustrous green hedging and the sweet odors of ivy, box, and roses, the same valley of the Ain River with the land rising to the remembered circle of blue misty hills on the other side, and the peak of Mont Blanc far in the distance, catching the last rosy glints of the sun. It was like coming home again.

Gertrude went out into the garden and sat on the low wall, close to the pointed cupola in its center, and I joined her. "It's good to be here again," I said. "Nothing's changed. It's just the same, and I feel as if I belonged here."

"We like to have you here, you can bet on that or you wouldn't be here," Gertrude said, laughing. As she sat on the wall, her feet dangled about four inches from the ground and she swung her sturdy legs like a little girl, banging her heels against the wall.

The stillness was wonderful. In the Ain valley a late bird sang now and again, and a cowbell tinkled rhythmically far away. From the house drifted the voice of Alice, speaking in English on the telephone.

"Do you still have your allergies Sammy, now tell me," Gertrude said.

"Alas, yes," I said, "although I think that I may be losing one or two of them."

"Allergies are becoming very fashionable," — Gertrude grinned — "but trust our little Sammy, he was the first to have them and know about them, and it is always good to be first, even though it is sometimes a nuisance, isn't it."

I nodded.

"I've got a dirty book for you to read," Gertrude said. "It's got lots of dirty words in it, it's called *The Young and Evil,* but it's still good to be first, no matter whether with allergies or dirty words."

"Well, you were the first, too," I said, "not with allergies or dirty words but with exploding and renewing the language. More and more people are realizing your influence. In my classes back in Chicago I talk a lot about you every time I can bring your name up, and I tell them what changes you've made and are making in language, and how language and literature will never be the same again because of you."

Gertrude smiled radiantly and kicked her heels again. "Thank you Sammy," she said. "If anyone ever knows me well and understands my position it will be because of people like you endlessly talking and Wendell Wilcox and Carl Van Vechten and Thornton and Donald Sutherland and some others. Did you know," she then asked excitedly, "that the Picasso book is going wonderful well and that the first autobiography has been translated into Italian and we are very pleased to hear that."

Then she looked at the sky and the sunset. "It's too late for our walk," she said, "and anyway Alice will have dinner soon, but we can walk the upper turn tomorrow before the Luces come."

She climbed from the wall and I stood up. "I'll go tell Pussy about the allergies," she said, "and you, you can go up to the bathroom and make yourself fresh and then come down for dinner, and you can take your bags up and put them in the same room you had before."

We went into the chateau and I carried my suitcases up the worn stone steps. Coming down from the servants' quarters in the attic was a young Oriental man, who bowed from the waist and very politely said, *"Bon soir, Monsieur."*

Who the hell was that? I wondered. Later I learned that it was Chen, the new Annamite houseboy, come all the way from Indochina to study at the Sorbonne. Gertrude and Alice, having heard of his financial plight, had hired him for the summer to do odd jobs about the house.

By the time I had washed and refreshed myself, the last rays of the sun were almost gone. Alice had prepared a delicious sole with a lemon sauce and rice, and some leafy lettuce from their garden in a salad, together with *haricots verts*. There was a demi of white wine on the table.

We sat down and were served by Chen, under the directions shouted at him from the kitchen by the ever-faithful Madame Roux, who had been with Gertrude and Alice ever since they started to spend their summers at Bilignin.

It was a delightful and simple meal, and Gertrude reached for the decanter of wine. "How are you coming with your drinking Sammy, do you want some wine," she said, ready to pour it for me.

"Much better," I said. "I'll take just a half glass, please." I wondered if Thornton had told them of the quantity of Pernod and cognac I had consumed that wet night in Zurich.

"I'll have just a drop, Lovey," Alice said. "It's delicious with the sole and salad."

Gertrude poured her a little and then spoke to me, returning to the matter of drinking. "I'm glad," she said. "As we told you the last time Sammy, if there's anything neither of us can stand, just really not stand at all, it's drunks."

"Have no fear," I said, but my hand trembled as I took a swallow of the sauterne — and then no more. After all, there was still a large bottle of cognac in my suitcase . . . for emergencies.

We finished the meal, catching up on much of the gossip, and then Gertrude pushed back from the table, sliding it over the gleaming dark yellow hardwood floor. "Let's all go sit in the living room and have our *infusion*. What would you like Sammy, tea or coffee or *verveine* or mint or what, now tell us. There are lots of different herbs in the kitchen to make infusions and we are having a spell with *verveine,* it's very good and it makes you sleep well."

"I'll try the *verveine,"* I said, "for the very first time."

"Who knows," Gertrude chuckled, "you may abandon the grape entirely as we almost have, both Pussy and me."

It was only about nine o'clock but we were all tired, so after the infusions we said our good nights and went to our beds, Gertrude and Alice in theirs next to the bathroom and myself in the guest room with its secret cupboards camouflaged behind the wallpaper. I sat up for an hour to make my usual notes about the day's conversation.

Bright and early (for Gertrude) the next morning she hammered on my door. "Do get up Sammy it's nine, and we'll go for a walk at ten and the Luces are coming for us at eleven with their real chauffeured limousine now isn't that nice."

I had to scramble to be ready at ten, but it was managed, and Gertrude stood at the gate, switch in hand. "Let's take the upper turn," she said. "It's a little shorter and I've gotta be at my best for the Luces."

Despite the prominence that Gertrude had achieved by then, and despite the fact that the Luces had come courting her, she still seemed somewhat nervous about them because of their own eminence in America.

We set off on the upper turn, following a footpath that wound through the vineyards to the hilltop. The odor of the ripening grapes was heady and sweet and strong, and they were already a dark purple with a silvered pearl gray frosty sheen on them. I liked the fragrance and said so.

"Yes and I do too, I like things of the senses especially sights and odors," Gertrude said. "My nose is pretty good."

The whole world that year was nervous about Hitler, and the rumblings from the high world of diplomacy to the low one of the ordinary man were everywhere. It was only natural for me to ask Gertrude: "What do you think of that madman in Germany?"

Gertrude used her switch violently on some weeds. "I think that's one reason the Luces went to Poland, for one thing, and why they are here for another, because he's convinced there'll be a war and there won't be any more Poland. But as for what you call that madman himself, well, somehow though I am worried I am not too worried, but I am still glad the future is hidden. Hitler is an Austrian and the Austrians hate the Germans as much as the Danes hate the Swedes and vice versa. So what I think is, Hitler really hates Germany so much that he has set out to ruin it systematically, and at present, mind you only at present, I am rather calm in the head. It is not very interesting to me right now, it may get more so when fall comes."

"What would you do if there's a war?" I asked. "Would you stay here or go to Paris or come to America again?"

"Who knows," she said. "We might stay here, we might go again to America and lecture, or we might go to Hollywood and make a movie about the first autobiography. That, I think that would be really and truly exciting. But let's talk about something else, maybe literature, did you like Thornton, really now."

"Yes, I really liked him a lot, if only he hadn't made me get so wet."

Gertrude chuckled. "Poor Thornie, he wants to take care of the whole world. I remember Sylvia Beach once said about him, he reminded her of a man taking everyone in the whole world on a Sunday school picnic and trying to get them all on the train at the same time. He's a funny mixture, his background and bringing up, I suppose. He likes the gypsy world of the theater, that's his green go-ahead light, but then that New England part of him turns the light red just when he is about to kick over the traces and have a really good time."

I agreed with her silently.

"Trouble is," Gertrude said, "Thornton lacks that quality of *lascivetė* which Whitman introduced. Really no Americans have it or if they do they bury it deep but it is bound to come out sometime, maybe in the works of some dramatist who follows Thornie, or in novels. Hemingway didn't have it and Sherwood Anderson didn't either. An American would say 'cock' before a woman only if he expected to take her to bed, the French might use the same word in their own language, '*bitte*' I guess it is, but it would be accompanied with the 'eye.' Whitman was really the first to live the life of the senses and he got into a mess, really he did. Americans say keep away from the bottle and you've got a great life ahead, but the

French say keep away from women and you've got a great life ahead. I once wrote a book with some of that *lascivetè* in it or maybe only a little, Carl Van Vechten has the manuscript, maybe some day it will be published but it's not for anyone to read unless they already know about such things, or are themselves."

"What did you call it?"

"*Q.E.D.*," Gertrude said briefly. Then: "What time is it Sammy, we've got to be back to the house by eleven."

"Twenty minutes of."

"Ohmygod, let's go," she muttered and took off at a very rapid pace down the hill through the vineyards. Gertrude was like an athlete and almost as sure-footed, and I followed as best I could. We arrived at the chateau with ten minutes to spare, time enough to change shoes and allow Gertrude to put on her best pink brocaded vest with a yellow blouse and clean monk's cloth skirt.

Then there was a horn in the road, and Chen ran out to open the huge old iron gates. In drove a black limousine that seemed about a half block long. The chauffeur sprang out to open the door, beating Chen by a split second, and Clare Boothe Luce stepped out—tall, willowy, blond, and beautiful. From the other side descended Henry Luce, tall, craggy, Ciceronian, a man with a face that seemed to hold a great deal of power. Preceded by Chen, who seemed to be doing more than his usual bowing and gesturing, the Luces walked into the house — to be met by Alice (I was listening from the hall above) and escorted to the rose garden. And then Gertrude came out from the living room, and finally I summoned my courage and went down the steps.

The introductions were pleasant enough, but I realized I was the zero in the crowd. To make up for it, when I was introduced to Mrs. Luce, I bent to brush her hand with my lips and murmured, "What an extraordinarily beautiful woman you are!"

I think all of them were startled except Clare, who thanked me prettily.

"Trust Sammy," Gertrude said. "He lives in the States but he was really born spiritually here in France."

We all laughed, and then there was a moment's silence.

Clare was holding a small square of crocheted blue wool, or linen, on which a design was beginning to appear, and she said to Alice, "I wonder if on the way to Aix you'd show me how to make a French knot on the underside. I simply cannot seem to master it."

"Delighted," Alice murmured, but I could see that she was madder than hell underneath about something. Perhaps Clare had done it too quickly, making Alice think that such a remark relegated her to the status of a domestic, or an instructor in needlepoint.

"Will there be room for all of us in your car or do you want us to go in the Matford and you follow us," Gertrude asked.

"Oh, there's more than enough room," Clare said. "The men can sit on the jump seats."

"We'd better get going," Henry Luce said. "I made a reservation at the Royale-Splendide for twelve-thirty." He looked at his watch and at the sky, which had clouded over. "And it looks like rain."

We climbed into the car, Henry Luce on one jump seat and myself on the other, facing three of the most dynamic women of the decade. Gertrude was in the middle, flanked by Clare and Alice. As we started off, Clare leaned across Gertrude and said to Alice, "Please — will you show me?" and handed her the needlework.

Like lightning Alice took the needle and made a stitch at the bottom. "Like this," she said. "It's really quite simple. You haven't been pulling it through far enough."

"Oh, thank you," Clare said, taking the square. It had been done so fast that no one could have seen.

Henry Luce made himself as comfortable as he could on the jump seat, but his legs were long and his feet tangled with his wife's. He folded his arms and spoke to Gertrude. "Well, what do you think of Hitler?"

Gertrude leaned forward a little, put one large hand on each of her kneecaps, and said, "Just as I was telling Sammy this morning . . ." And she went on to detail her theory about Hitler. The day darkened, the rains came, and then the sky lightened again, as did the curious and unaccountable tension in the car. By the time we reached Aix-les-Bains,

Gertrude and Henry Luce were joking over a proposed collaboration between themselves about a play on the generations and he had asked Gertrude to do some articles for *Life* magazine.

"You're a brave man," Gertrude said.

The arbor was dripping when we got to Aix. "We'll have to eat inside," Luce said.

"Unless we want to get damn good and wet," Gertrude said. "I don't mind, a lot of people think I'm all wet anyway, but Clare's dress . . ."

"Ah, we'll eat inside," he said. "And you ladies will probably want to freshen yourselves a little, and young Steward and I will do the same."

We made a rather odd-looking group, but the word had got around, and there was a good deal of attention bestowed upon the five of us. Henry Luce led the way to his room and while I washed my hands he started for the telephone. "I have to call the Paris office," he said.

"You'll never get it in time."

"Why?"

Laughing, I explained my theory as to why the French hated telephones: being used to gestures while talking, they resented an instrument that denied their seeing each other's movements. But I had not reckoned with Henry Luce. Before I had finished my explanation, almost, he was talking with the Paris bureau of *Time* magazine, giving instructions. When he hung up the phone, he grinned. "There, you see," he said.

"It just shows what the magic name of Luce can accomplish, even in Aix-les-Bains," I said.

We went down to join the ladies, and the maître d'hôtel showed us into the faded gold and white splendor of the dining room, pulling out the fragile and spidery chair for Gertrude, who looked at it dubiously and even more carefully let her weight down on it.

It was a delicious luncheon, marred only by the fact that Gertrude could not eat two or three things because they disagreed with her — asparagus being one. But the conversation was full of laughter and wit and, though concerned with modern topics, had a kind of nineteenth-century quality to it.

There were also, however, some small bubbles of nervous quiet now and again. Henry Luce came more and more to the front as the meal progressed, but something told me that the meal ought not to last too long. The silences of Alice were very unusual. I made my only profound remark of the meal when I said, over a Benedictine: "Look! The sun is shining again."

"So it is," Gertrude said. "I tell you what, let's stop at Hautecombe on the way back, maybe the Rops are there, and then we can all meet each other."

"Such a crowd of us will worry the Père Abbé to death," Alice said.

We had gone out of the dining room, and Alice and I were behind the others. "At the Abbé's age," I whispered, "it will be hard to change from a shepherd to a zookeeper."

Alice laughed. "That's my Sammy," she said, clutching my elbow momentarily. "He's got thorns." None of the others had heard our exchange, or so we thought.

The sun had cleared the skies magically, and it was not a long drive to Hautecombe. Both the Rops were there, in an earnest and rather loud discussion with the handsome young Père Bernardet about the powers and merits of the Holy Ghost; they broke it off as introductions were made. The young priest seemed momentarily discomfited by the descent of such a troop on him, but he recovered quickly, told us the Père Abbé was at his devotions, and begged us to stay long enough to meet him.

Meanwhile, Clare was as busy as any midwestern tourist, snapping pictures of everyone, especially Gertrude, and then Henri Daniel-Rops when she found out who he was. She even took one of me, and then approached while the others were talking.

"What did you say your name was?" she asked.

I told her, politely enough.

"And you wrote a novel, *Angels on the Bow?* To whom were they bowing?"

"No," I explained. "It's b-o-u-g-h. The title comes from William Blake." And I added, "He was a late eighteenth-century poet," but I smiled as I said it.

Clare's head came up quickly and her eyes went wide.

Then she smiled and said, "You *do* have thorns." Then she extended her hand in her pretty way.

"Truce?" she said. This time I shook it.

"To the end," I said.

The Père Abbé came out just as we were preparing to leave, and the introductions had to be made all over again. He was an ancient and venerable man with a crown of white hair, visibly impressed with the presence of so many notables. But he shook a finger at Henry Luce, saying something about his magazines; I caught the words "sex" and "violence."

"But that's what news is made of," said Luce, laughing a little.

"Alas, too true," said the Abbé. "The world cannot live in its own Hautecombe."

Alice was standing close. I leaned down to whisper: "Do you think we should ask him if we may all come to a retreat here?"

She drew in her breath sharply in a muffled "Oh!" and dug her elbow into my ribs. We both laughed. "Sometimes I think you need a good spanking, Sammy," she said, but then she slipped her arm through mine and looked at Clare flattering the Abbé.

Gertrude broke off chatting with the others, saw Alice and me standing apart, and said heartily in English, "Well, let's all go now, we can go by way of the d'Aiguy's chateau and they can meet Clare and Henry and Sammy."

Alice squeezed my arm and whispered. "I don't know about this. May d'Aiguy has got one of the sharpest tongues in France and we'll have to keep Clare as far away from her as we can." She looked up and gave me a slow solemn wink. "Just in the interest of good international relations," she said slyly.

"As far as I'm concerned —" I began.

"Sh-h-h, Sammy," Alice said. "Even non-Christians have crosses to bear."

With many farewells, we arranged ourselves in the limousine again, leaving the Rops behind, and drove to the Château d'Aiguy. The conversation grew wild, even hilarious, with arguments both for and against Franklin Roosevelt and American politics and the Americanization of Europe. And when we got to the chateau, the charming old Baronne Pierlot was there, and the comtes d'Aiguy, her sons. Madame la Baronne had a broadbrimmed hat trimmed with shining black feathers that glistened blue in the sunlight, and she wore an old-fashioned net collar to conceal her ancient neck. A rope of pearls and a long black silk dress made her a gracious figure from the past century.

Somehow Clare and May d'Aiguy got their heads together. "Go break it up, Sammy." Alice nudged me.

I wandered toward them, just in time to hear Clare describing her seasickness on the way over, how oxygen had to be used, and sleeping tablets at night. "It's a great price to pay to come to France," she said.

May clucked her tongue. "We are sorry that our country has unwittingly put you to so great trouble. Perhaps it would be wiser to stay at home next time." May turned and walked away.

I felt that I had walked into a theater at the final curtain.

Clare was speechless. She was still holding the square of linen on which she had been working, and I said, "Have you conquered the problem of the French knots yet?" as if I had heard nothing at all.

It took her a moment to answer. "The knots, yes," she finally said. "But the French are beyond me." I tried to look puzzled.

With that she walked toward her husband, linked her arm in his, and said, "I have a frightful headache, darling — shall we go soon?"

Henry was extremely gallant. "Of course, my dear," he said with solicitation. "It has been a long day." He turned to Gertrude. "Do you mind if we deposit you, and I take Clare back to Aix? She hasn't been well recently."

"A minor indisposition," Clare smiled, her lovely face a mask. Alice, standing beside me, clucked sympathetically.

And so the day came to an end, but not without one last event. When Gertrude and Alice and I got out of the car at Bilignin, Clare opened her blue eyes to their widest and said, "Dear Gertrude — would ten be too early for you tomorrow? I'll come with the limousine to see those ruins, and we can have a good talk. I know I'll be feeling all right by then."

With that, the limousine drove off. How it had been arranged, and when, neither Alice nor I knew. For the only time

I ever saw her so, Gertrude looked somewhat shamefaced. She said, "Well, I told you she was giving us the rush and I guess she wants to talk, that's all. You don't mind do you now, Pussy. And Sammy," she asked.

"Of course not," I said. Alice said nothing. "I guess she's building her salon, too."

Then Alice said, "They're a pretty smart couple. *They're* not fooled by anything. They know who's who and what's what."

Thus Alice and I were left alone the next morning. I got up about ten, after Gertrude had gone, and about eleven went down to Alice's domain — the huge old kitchen with the wood-burning stove and the earthen floor. I hung at the doorway, not daring to enter without an invitation.

"Good morning," I said in a tentative way. Alice looked tinier than ever, diminutive in the huge old kitchen. She was whipping something in a bowl. "Good morning, Sammy," she said, her face unruffled. "Tell me — can you eat corn-meal mush? Fried with syrup on it?"

"It's one of my favorites," I said.

"I left the carbon of *Faust* on the dining room table. It's for you to keep and cherish. I'll have breakfast ready in a moment."

"Not too much, please. When will they be back?"

"About two o'clock, I suppose," Alice said. "Well, what did you think? That any William Dean Howells heroine could be so modernized?"

"Oh, I thought just what you did," I said evasively.

"Ah," said Alice, tasting a spoonful of something. "And that you'll never know."

I grinned. "Are you sure? I might trade you. I know something you don't."

Alice paused with the spoon in the air. "What is that?"

"I heard what Clare and May were talking about yesterday."

Into her eyes came a glint, and she smiled. "Do I have to bribe you?"

"Not at all," I said, and with that told her the whole story. When I finished she was shaking with laughter.

"Oh, are you sure, are you sure that's what May said?"

I repeated it, this time in French. "It sounds even worse in

French — *rester chez vous la prochaine fois,*" she said. "Oh, Sammy," she chortled, eyes shining, "you have really made this a beautiful day. This is the sort of thing I eat with a spoon."

"I'm glad you're happy."

"And now," she said, "you go read *Faust* while I toast the mush. It'll be about ten minutes."

But it was more like an hour, and I could hear her humming happily in the kitchen. Alice might have hurried to meet the King of England, but not if she still had something to fix in the kitchen.

I finished the excellent breakfast to which she had added a slice of thick country bacon; as the taste of the madeleine in his tea took Proust back in time, so the bacon returned me to my Ohio childhood.

Then I wandered out in the garden to go on with my reading of *Doctor Faustus Lights the Lights.* I dawdled for another hour over about ten pages of it, wondering why it was easier for me to read her writing in longhand than in typed form. And then there was a honking at the gate. I picked up the *Faust* (no more of putting anything on the garden wall) and went around to the front entrance. I opened the gate and helped Gertrude out of the limousine, said "Good day" to Clare — and then the car drove off.

"How's things," Gertrude said. "You're reading *Faust.*"

"Quiet," I said, "and yes I am and I like it a lot. Did you really get bitten by a viper?"

"O my yes and it was quite an experience. How's Alice."

"Unruffled, calm, beatific."

"Boy have I got some things to tell her and you," Gertrude said excitedly.

"May I come along?"

"Sure thing," she said, and strode into the house.

Alice looked up from a pot. "Well, Lovey, I see you're back. What happened?"

"The usual," Gertrude said. "We saw the Roman ruins and then we stopped near Artemare and just looked out over the valley, and it really is a lovely thing you know."

"Yes," murmured Alice. "I know."

"And we talked a lot and then I read her palm and she tried to read mine but she was all wrong. And do you know what,

Pussy, she has a whore's hand." She stopped suddenly, and looked at me like a child caught stealing jam.

I grinned at both of them and made a small gesture with my thumb over my lips. "Sealed," I said. "Under the rose tree for a very long time."

They both smiled and Gertrude went on. "And then I'll tell you something else she doesn't want known. Do you know Henry is thinking of wanting to be President, not this election but maybe the next one, did you know that."

"Oh, my God," said Alice, really stunned this time. So was I.

"Well," Gertrude said, "there's the power of the press and all that, but really honest and truly I was bowled over."

And with that she said one of her truly memorable things. She clapped her hand to the whorl at the back of her close-cropped head, and said, "Her maybe yes, but him no my god, not him, not ever!"

Both of us laughed. The meal that night was superb, and all calm restored.

"I tell you what," Gertrude said during dinner. "We'll have to do it sometime so why not now when Sammy's here and can enjoy, we've planned all along to drive to Switzerland, to Geneva, and see the Prado paintings they sent over for safekeeping during the Spanish Civil War, so why don't we have a picnic lunch on the way, we've just got to see the paintings so why not now."

Alice's dark and somber eyes gleamed with real delight. "I'll steam a chicken in white wine," she said, "and we'll make a real day of it. But do you think you can stand the Swiss that long, Lovey?"

"You know I don't like them," Gertrude grumbled. "They're stupid and I can stand anything, yes anything but that. Now you take a French *paysan*, when he sees you coming in a car down the road he moves to the side out of his instinct for self-preservation I suppose. But what do the Swiss do. Nothing. They stand there really stupid right in the middle of the road and you have to go around them. And all those little old Swiss ladies in the towns especially Zurich clutching their handbags on the way to the bank, they've got tight lips and all they can think about is three things, how to hold on to their money, how to get more of it, and how to get more interest on what they have."

"Well, we're not going to Zurich," Alice said, "and in Geneva it's a lot more cosmopolitan, and they don't do that so much."

"Well, maybe you're right, maybe they just don't hang on to their handbags so tight, but I still don't like 'em but we've got to go anyway so shall we."

"I'd enjoy it," I said.

"It's settled then," Gertrude said, giving the meal-end sign by pushing her chair away from the table.

It was drizzling a little the next morning about nine o'clock. Gertrude looked at the sky. "It'll clear off soon," she said, "but we have to drive into Belley to the garage before we start, there's something the matter with the axle and I hope to God it's not the transmission."

"Speak English," I murmured.

Gertrude turned to me. "Do you mean to say you don't know anything about cars, you really are unusual, you are the first American male I ever met who didn't know anything about cars."

"If I ever bought a car," I said, "it'd be just to get around in, and not a status symbol to impress people, not a thing like that big black limousine."

Gertrude and I got into the front seat of the car. Even to my inexperienced ear there seemed to be a great sickness in the motor. But we made it into the garage in Belley, three kilometers away, and jolted into the work area as best we could. Gertrude and the mechanic knew each other very well. She spoke to him in her peasant French until she came to the word "axle."

"What's the word for that now Sammy," she demanded.

"Might as well ask me for the word for the stuff you fill a tooth with," I said. "I'm sorry; I just don't know."

Gertrude solved the problem by getting down on her hands and knees and pointing. It jolted me to see her thus on the greasy floor, but she didn't seem to mind, save that when she rose she had two black spots on the knees of her thick lisle stockings.

"Good news," she said, rubbing her black hands on an old

rag. "It can be fixed in a few minutes, just a loose bolt or something. I don't know the French for it any more than you do. But axle is '*essieu*' and now we've both learned a new word."

We stood looking at the gray day outside and the thin lines of rain that were now coming straight down. Gertrude said, "I think it is sad the way rain comes down outside a garage, it is sadder than outside a house and why it is I don't know."

"Nor I," I said.

"Well anyway," she said, "I just know I wish he'd get the damn thing fixed, he said ten minutes and already it's twenty and we've got to get started if we're going, today that is."

It was about thirty minutes when the mechanic climbed from under the car, slapped the hood, and told her the car was "in good health" again; and we went back to Bilignin to get Alice. The rain stopped just as we started, the sun was shining wetly through the poplars that lined the roads, and the countryside was green and fresh.

Around twelve o'clock, Alice said, "Where should we eat, Lovey?"

"There's a nice flat spot with a stone in about two kilometers," she said, "and some bushes growing around, a pretty spot."

"Let's eat there then," said Alice — and soon we came to it. The ground was flat and close to the roadside. The slope behind it was dotted with bushes and dropped down to a green valley with many poplars. We pulled the old Matford off the road and parked it.

"Excuse me," Gertrude said, climbing out and heading for the bushes. Meanwhile, Alice was busily unpacking the picnic hamper, a huge rattan thing with several rattan separators fitted inside it.

Gertrude returned, and we all sat on the ground, which was completely dry, splashing ourselves with the juice of red tomatoes from the Bilignin garden (hoed by Gertrude herself) and eating the flavorful chicken, the rice (for my diet), and ripe pears to finish our meal.

I helped Alice repack the basket and pick up the litter, and then we drove on. Somehow the countryside seemed to change; it had a more southern look — and yet we were headed northeast. I said as much to Gertrude.

"So you noticed it too now did you Sammy," she said.

"Noticed what?" I asked.

"The southern part of a country is more southern than the northern part of the country just south of it," she said. "Have you ever been in the Midi before Sammy."

"No, never."

"You'll love it," Alice said. "You stay your two weeks there and then come back for some more time with us. But you be mighty careful when you get to Marseille. It's a bad town. And stay out of the Old Town section or you'll get your throat cut. And you be even more careful in Algiers."

"Good grief," I said.

"The *transbordeur's* still up, isn't it, Lovey?" Alice asked.

"I think so," Gertrude said, "there was some talk of taking it down but yes I think it's still up."

"What's the *transbordeur?*"

"A kind of bridge across the square port," Alice said. "It's got hooks and it hauls freight and things from one side to the other on high rails. It looks ghastly and spoils the view."

"Why not just walk or drive around the water?"

"Trust the French," Alice murmured. "The *transbordeur* saves a kilometer."

Just then there appeared a shepherd in the middle of the road, holding a shepherd's crook. He made no move to get to the side and Gertrude had to swerve around him.

"There you see," she said. "I guess we're pretty near the Swiss border, some of the stupidity slips across, it doesn't have to be declared at customs." She laughed. "We'll have to be careful from now on."

Then we saw the *douane* ahead with a striped barrier lowered across the road. "All passports ready?" Alice asked.

The Swiss customs guard was as healthy and tall and handsome a young man as I'd ever seen, dressed in a decorated dark blue uniform. And he was very polite.

He looked at the passports that we all three stuck out the side window and addressed us in perfect English: "May I ask where you are going and your purpose?"

Alice spoke. "To Geneva, to the Musée du Prado, to see the pictures sent over from Spain," she said, "and then back home again to France this evening."

"Does Madame have anything to declare?" said the guard politely.

"A total of four packages of cigarettes," said Alice, evidently counting mine along with hers.

The guard signaled the sentry box and the bar lifted. *"Au revoir, mes amis,"* he called. "Enjoy yourselves."

"Wel-l-l," I said slowly. "That particular young Swiss gentleman didn't seem too stupid."

"They pick the best ones for such jobs, it gives the country a good face," Gertrude said. "It's from now on we have to be careful."

She was right. Between the border and Geneva we must have passed a dozen peasants tending sheep — and not a single one of them moved out of the way. At the rate Gertrude was driving she had a lot of swerving to do, at one time getting so far off the road that she hit the shoulder and raised a great cloud of dust. I looked out the rear window and thumbed my nose at the cause of our near-accident. He did not move, but merely stuck out his tongue at me.

"You're right, they are stupid," I said.

"What do you think you accomplished by cocking your snoot like that," Gertrude said.

"Not a thing," I said, "except it made me happy."

The Swiss in that region, even though they might have been as stupid as Gertrude said, were all nonetheless extremely handsome — the young workers in the fields heavily tanned and slim of figure.

We had no trouble finding the museum that had been reserved for the Prado paintings, paid the modest admission fee, and went in. Even before the El Grecos, I had to see Rogier van der Weyden's *Deposition from the Cross,* and Grünewald's *Crucifixion,* since Huysmans' descriptions of them were still so fresh in my mind. Gertrude and Alice headed for the El Greco rooms, and I joined them ten minutes later.

It is difficult to analyze and describe an exhibition of such magnitude as the Prado paintings unless you are an art critic and have plans for several volumes. The comments of both Gertrude and Alice were sensitive and astute, and in their company I spent the next two hours in almost orgiastic pleasure before the paintings. I slowly developed all the symptoms of being drunk, or high on some powerful drug. Trembling, sometimes staggering, I endured it for two hours and then excused myself, saying that I would meet them at the door. The truth was that I felt in need of a drink, since this was long before tranquilizers, but the only "bar" in the museum was a "milk bar." Then I remembered the trouble the Swiss had had with their drinking problems and what Thornton had told me about the massive government propaganda to get the young people to drink milk instead of alcohol. So I slipped out of the building to get a demiliter of cognac, against the tumult which those paintings had caused in me. Gertrude and Alice caught me as I was coming back, about to pay another admission fare.

"Too much for you Sammy," Gertrude asked. "Almost too much for us too."

"I'm sorry," I said, still trembling. "I just had to have a drink to calm myself. All those El Grecos at once . . ."

"I'll join you," Gertrude said, and she poured a jigger into the bottle's metal cap. It was the only strong drink I ever saw her take.

"And I'll have one too," said Alice. "There really ought to be some kind of law passed, I think. It really is too much to see them all at once, Lovey."

"Even in Spain we didn't see that much so close together," Gertrude said. "It's an awful blow but a wonderful one."

After a few moments we felt somewhat better and got into the Matford again.

"Do you want to see the rest of Geneva Sammy, the old League of Nations or anything," Gertrude asked.

"No, please," I said. "If I ever want to see Lac Léman and the Château de Chillon I'll come again, but I can't stand any more today."

"I feel the same way," Gertrude said, and Alice nodded. We headed back toward France.

That night in Bilignin it rained, but scarcely enough to spoil our turn the next morning, the upper one, because the mud on the lower turn was heavy and unpleasant despite the loam and leaves.

Gertrude began things by saying, "Down here in the country we pay four thousand francs a month for seven rooms, all this view and a garden too, and six hundred to Madame Roux and four hundred to Chen, and in Paris we pay seven thousand a month for what we've got, which is nice enough but not as nice as this."

"Have you ever thought of moving down here and staying all year?"

"We have, but said no at once. All our friends are there not here, the art galleries and all the rest. People wouldn't make the long trip to Culoz and who would blame them, and we'd probably end up staying more in Paris than Bilignin anyway."

"And the paintings, all the Picassos and Picabias and Juan Gris, belong in Paris more than Belley. And Matisse," I said.

"Yes, and Sammy did you ever hear the way Alice says '*le cher maître*' when she speaks of Matisse, you ought to get her to say it. Well, all those paintings are worth a helluva lot Sammy, let me tell you. But when we first got them they were worth nothing, that is we paid next to nothing for them. I paid about" — and here she did some figuring in her head — "oh about twenty-nine or thirty bucks for that Rose Period thing, *Jeune Fille aux Fleurs,* and now it's worth thousands. And do you know why it's worth thousands Sammy, because I wrote about Picasso, I talked about him, I said he was the best there is, that's what, and that's why. But we were all starving together, and Pablo would do a picture and I would say I just had to have it and then we'd haggle over it and sometimes some food changed hands too, and now look at him he's good, he's famous and certainly partly because of me, and would you like to have a note to him when you go to the Midi because if you're a friend of mine you're a friend of his but don't expect him to fall all over you, he's not that way."

"I'd love to have a note," I said. "I'd go out of the way to meet him."

"Well but he wouldn't to see you so it's all on your own."

We walked farther along, rounding the crest of the hill, and then she abruptly made a great jump in topics. "Jo Davidson," she said, "he said a ghetto is a Jew surrounded by Christians. Neither he nor I liked each other the least little bit at first, and then one day we met each other when there was nobody else around and we liked each other a lot."

". . ." I said.

"Generally speaking," Gertrude said, flicking at a post, "I don't like the intelligentsia. Now you, you have intelligence but you're not one of the avant-garde crowd and that's good, that's very good, because they all have to use too many words to explain their work especially their painting and tell you what their paintings mean, and that's bad, it cannot stand alone the way mine can.

"Jesus was an intellectual," she went on. "And Hitler is madder than hell because he can't become the Messiah for the Jews the way Jesus was, because naturally the Jews wouldn't hail a non-Jew as the Messiah, of course not."

A little farther on, she suddenly said, "Are you a good teacher Sammy."

"I really don't know," I said. "My classes are always full but maybe that means I put a lot of sex in my lectures. I try to liberate the students, or increase their backgrounds, or train them to teach themselves. They say I have a sharp tongue and am a disciplinarian. Once I overheard one say, when he got back a paper with a low mark: 'Oh, that Doctor Steward — I never know whether to kiss him or kill him.' "

Gertrude's laugh boomed out. "That's perfect," she said, and started down the path to the chateau.

When we opened the iron gates and went in, Madame Roux came out talking excitedly. Chen had developed an infection on both arms. We hurriedly took him to Doctor Chaboux in Belley, where it was diagnosed as poison oak — of which Gertrude was deathly afraid — so for the next few days it fell to me to dress his arms and apply bandages. They teased me about being Florence Nightingale, and laughed when I said I had been worried that the surrounding skin was so yellow until I remembered that Chen was Annamite.

A day later, Alice sent us into Belley to get some milk and oil. "You can take Sammy along," she said to Gertrude.

"And give him a chance to practice his French," said Gertrude, looking a little crafty.

"More like keeping you from having to get in and out of the car," Alice said, grinning.

"Humph," Gertrude said, and away we went, the Bilignin chickens squawking again as the car roared past.

"Now that *Hero and Leander* thing you gave me, that thing

you're writing, it has some fresh charm to it but that's about all," Gertrude said. "It's like James Branch Cabell out of Hemingway if you can imagine such a thing. You've got to do something about it, such a thing wouldn't sell at all. Take out all those horrible dull conversations between men, or maybe just throw the whole thing away. Now I think a better idea is the story of those eleven women you escaped from, the ones who wanted to marry you or mother you, now why is that do you suppose."

I squirmed, remembering the fat one in the English department from whom I had escaped only by coming to France that summer. "I don't know — maybe they really do want to mother me for some reason."

"Yes that could be it," Gertrude said. "You're a motherable person. I think you really ought to do a book about the Eleven. You can begin it in Algiers and go on for your gentle success because I think you ought to be a writer Sammy, honest to God I do."

If the bottle doesn't get me first, I thought silently — and miserably. "Yes," I said, "well, maybe I will, although Algiers from what I've heard isn't the quietest place in the world to begin anything."

"Where are you going to stay there."

"The Rops recommended the Hôtel de Cornouailles," I said.

"That's a good one, it's about halfway up the hill and it's cheaper than all git-out," Gertrude said. "You get a room with a double bed and balcony looking out over the bay of Alger and three meals a day, all for about six bucks, to say nothing of the spiders and centipedes in your shoes, they're free."

"Ugh," I said. "It sounds great."

"But you listen now, you stay out of the Casbah alone, it's more dangerous than hell, when you start down the Casbah the women on the rooftops call across and say there's a foreigner on the way, so you got to get a guide, get a Cook's man, they're reliable and they speak Arabic, most of them."

"Don't you suppose I could find Hedy Lamarr and Charles Boyer there to protect me?" I said slyly.

"Of course, you could find all the Boyers in the world there but they're tough. They would do anything *but* protect you, so you promise me you'll get a Cook's man," she said.

"Promise," I said.

"Cross your heart," she asked.

I did, and we both laughed.

"Have your little Algerian time and its adventures and then come back to us the end of August, Francis Rose and Cecil Beaton will still be here probably but they won't worry you at all, and there's plenty of room but you may have to take another bedroom. You have to meet Francis, he's my present artist, but I'm not sure yet that he's really good and I'm not sure he'll be good for you."

Cecil Beaton had just been fired from *Vogue* and blacklisted, because in one of his layouts for an advertisement he had put a background of very fine print that contained some violent anti-Semitic statements, and the Jews called for his dismissal. I thought it odd that he should come to visit a Jewess but I suppose that Francis Rose had invited him, or that Gertrude was above caring.

Suddenly she grabbed my knee. "Sammy," she said, "do you think that Alice and I are lesbians?"

I had a genuine hot curl of fire up my spine. "I don't see that it's anybody's business one way or another," I said.

"Do you care whether we are," she asked.

"Not in the least." I said. I was suddenly dripping wet.

"Are *you* queer or gay or different or 'of it' as the French say or whatever they are calling it nowadays," she said, looking narrowly at me.

I waggled my hand sidewise. "Both ways," I said. "I don't see why I should go through life limping on just one leg to satisfy a so-called norm."

"It bothers a lot of people," Gertrude said. "But like you said, it's nobody's business, it came from the Judeo-Christian ethos, especially Saint Paul the bastard, but he was complaining about youngsters who were not really that way, they did it for money, everybody suspects us or knows but nobody says anything about it. Did Thornie tell you."

"Only when I asked him a direct question and then he didn't want to answer, he didn't want to at all. He said yes he supposed in the beginning but that it was all over now."

Gertrude laughed. "How could he know. He doesn't know what love is. And that's just like Thornie. We are surrounded by homosexuals, they do all the good things in all the arts, and when I ran down the male ones to Hemingway it was because I thought he was a secret one. If Shakespeare had had a psychiatrist then we would never have had the plays or sonnets. I like all people who produce and Alice does too and what they do in bed is their own business, and what we do is not theirs. We saw a part of all this in you but there was a dark corner and we were puzzled and now we have the right answer, haven't we."

"Yes, you do," I said, "and I'll never say a word —"

"Pshaw," she interrupted, "most of our really good friends don't care and they know all about everything. But perhaps considering Saint Paul it would be better not to talk about it, say for twenty years after I die, unless it's found out sooner or times change. But if you are alive and writing then you can go ahead and tell it, I would rather it came from a friend than an enemy or a stranger."

"Well, I can keep my mouth shut," I said.

"But your pen sometimes runs away with you," she said. "Now you take that novel you let me read, that one about the homosexual scene in Chicago, well, you used all the dirty words there were and then some, some I'd never even heard and I've heard a lot, but it didn't work, it was too sad, and then the ending was horrible, everything cut off that poor fellow. You tried to do Henry Miller but without the gusto."

My ears burned. Gertrude plowed on.

"Now that one I did, the one I mentioned to you the other day, the *Q.E.D.* one, I wrote that about, oh, thirty-five years ago, it was about the same matters but it was all done with restraint, restraint of course was part of the times then. But naturally I was ashamed of it —"

"Why?" I interjected.

"Well for one thing it was too early to write about such things in our civilization, it was early in the century and everything was puritanical and so it was too soon, maybe not if we were Greek but Greek we weren't, and of course it was a kind of therapy for me just like writing yours was for you, you had to get it off your chest. But once it was written I was ashamed, it was not done the way it should have been done, it was too outspoken for the times even though it was restrained."

"Are you going to let it be published?"

She shook her head. "No," she said, "maybe later, maybe after I'm dead and gone. Anyway, I took it and changed it around and made a man out of one of the women and it became *Melanctha*. But it would not have been a graceful thing to publish it then."

"Well," I said laughing, "I will control *both* my mouth and my pen and this will all be secret."

"Yes, for now," Gertrude said. We talked no more about it, but the exchange seemed to make her even more affectionate toward me.

We drove in silence for a while.

"When you sent me that first book, that little book of Cabell short stories you did for Clarence Andrews, I wasn't at all sure about you and your writing either, it was too derivative, it wasn't fresh. The novel, the *Angels* novel that got you fired, that was better. You see I am bothered, much bothered, by the necessity of content without form, and I do not like creation without intention. You have to have something in mind, some intention, or your creation is just words, just playing with words. That is the trouble with most of the writing being done today. If you had included the content in the form and the creation in the intention then you would have made something. But when the intention is only the intention then it is no good.

"And that," she said, "is really what's wrong with that new thing you're doing, those few pages you gave me about *Hero and Leander*. You are stepping backwards from what you did in *Angels on the Bough,* which I really and truly did like. And above all, you must not have a literary short breath, and the new thing looks like it would be short. You have to learn to *hold* the reader, now I do it in my short pieces with my style, but if you use the ordinary style like your Leander, then you have to hold him another way. Vignettes and short things ought to be out, because when you use the ordinary style it's really only by length, by piling things up that you can affect the reader."

I sighed. "Well, I see the advantage in being first, because if anyone ever writes like you again everyone will say he's imitating you."

"Yes," she said, "you shouldn't imitate directly, then no one will read you. But you can be influenced, your style can, by a thing and it will show the effect without being a copy. Both Hem and Sherwood read and studied what I had written and my rhythms show in their styles although they are as different from each other and from me as they can be."

"I see," I said, and then thought it my turn to shift the topic. "I hope you'll read my palm, everybody says you're a whiz at it, and I brought along a palmistry book with some specially treated paper in the back of it, so maybe you would give me your palm-print."

"Yes, of course," she said, "that is very exciting. Tell me Sammy, are you going to stay in the States."

"Even though you and Alice say I may actually belong in France," I said forlornly, "I don't see how I can manage to come over here to live right now, really I don't."

"Well," Gertrude said, "anyone can manage anything any time if he really wants to, look what Alice and I did."

I said timidly, "But don't you think things have changed by now?"

"Of course they've changed, thank god, suppose it was still the year I came over, but up to a certain point it's fun to starve."

"If you have someone to do it with you," I said. "But in the days when you first came over, everyone was starving, you and Picasso and all the rest."

"We all leaned on each other and we got along, as the French say we did not 'let go of the banister.' Now all you have to do is find the right person, man or woman, and come over and starve together."

"I think I did find the right woman once," I said, "but unfortunately she didn't think I was the right man so that was that. Besides," I said craftily, "I'm not sure there's room for a woman's things in my drawers anymore."

Gertrude laughed. "Then you'd have to keep separate places."

"But what about all that good advice Thornie gave me?"

"Like what," she asked.

"Well, first he said I must think how to run my classes most easily and not let them take too much of my time; and then he said I must consider my childhood thoroughly, calling up all the sexual or disgusting things and why they were disgusting; and third — for which I see no connection at all — write some essays; and fourth, consider the great artists from Michelangelo through Leonardo to Shakespeare and Whitman and beyond — and then my psyche would readjust itself and all my allergies would disappear. I tried all that for a year but it was unfortunate that none of my allergies knew anything about psychology, nor could they read, because they went on just as merrily as ever before."

"That sounds just like the two-bit psychology that Thornie is always passing out," Gertrude said. "I'd forget most of it if I were you." And then with another of those surprising shifts she was always making, she said — with tongue in cheek — "I think Sammy we ought to write something together and I have just the idea. *I'll* apply for a Guggenheim Fellowship and *you'll* recommend me, and when they ask me what the topic is, I'll very seriously say 'an abstract novel about the Duchess of Windsor illustrating the importance of publicity in America.' "

With that she laughed so loud you could have heard her two streets away, and she enlarged on the theme with much gaiety until by the time we had run our errands ("Get out and get it, that's a good boy, it's hard for me") and got back to Bilignin, it was almost lunchtime.

"And after lunch, don't forget, we are going to read palms," Gertrude said.

But we did not get to read palms that day, for after we finished eating one of the Bilignin neighbors came to borrow some tools; his outdoor bread oven had developed a crack, so we all went over to help him fix it, and Gertrude and I came home with soot all over our faces and hands.

That night after making the day's notes I finished reading what she had completed of *Paris France*, and was pleased to see that I had become one of her anonymities, for she was quoting what we had talked about a few days before, when she wrote that "an American who had read as far as this as far as it had been written said to me . . ." that she had not mentioned the relation of French men to French men, of French men to French women, and on down the line.

The following morning Gertrude did not take the usual daily turn, and did not come downstairs until noon. It was odd how lonely I felt without her and the morning walk (and Alice was usually occupied in the kitchen during those hours), but I passed the time having a sunbath in the good hot light of southern France. When she finally did appear she had two hoes in hand, and we went to work weeding the tomato patch. Someone once said that she never did any physical work of any kind, but she did — at least in the garden. And then unaccountably — or perhaps on hearing that lunch would be delayed — she changed her mind and decided to take a turn, the lower one. I hastily pulled trousers over my bathing trunks, grabbed my shirt, and we set off once more.

Pépé, the chihuahua, went with us this time, chasing the neighbor's chickens on the way. "Once in a while one of them turns on him," Gertrude said, "and he runs yapping to hide behind my skirt. Poor Pépé I think he's getting old and we may have to replace him the way we did Basket."

"What number Basket is it?" I asked.

"This is number two," she said, switching a weed.

"Doesn't it bother you, having to replace them?"

"For a month," she said. "And then everything is fine and I am I again because my little dog knows me. That's the whole problem of identity, who are you.

"That problem is really a hard one," she went on. "If you call a Paul by the name of George he gets mad because you have taken away his identity. Identity is a hard thing to understand."

"There was an old Doctor Goddard, a psychologist, at Ohio State University," I said, "and he once told a young man suffering from inferiority that when he went to his next party he should call all the males George and all the females Mary. It overcame his feelings of inferiority all right, but he lost all his friends after that."

We were both silent for a while as we clumped downhill.

"There have been a lot of changes in France," she said

suddenly. "It is becoming more and more a 'classified' society like that in America."

"Oh," I said sardonically, "but we have no classes in America. It's a democracy. Why, even the dirtiest old wino in rags could go right up to the finest apartment on the Gold Coast in Chicago and ask for Mrs. J. Witherington Harris and go in and sit down and talk with her for a half-hour."

"Sammy," said Gertrude severely, "stop teasing now, stop pulling my leg."

"All right." I grinned. "But anyway, America is going to be ruined sooner or later, classes or not."

"How come," Gertrude asked.

"Because of installment buying and buying on credit. Everyone in debt up to his ears. Luckily it hasn't come to France yet."

"Not yet," Gertrude said, "here you pay cash unless you've got a tab at your local bistro. But you forgot one thing. Unions. They are the last refuge of the incompetent. Everyone will grow more hoggish and strike for more money, and finally everything will crash again."

The idea of classes was still bothering her. "Now you take the Académie," she said. "Everyone wants to get in. But the great writers, the only really truly great ones in France wrote under the Seigneurs. When they wrote under the Republic they were no good at all. I think it takes a monarchy, needs a monarchy, to produce really good writers, really I do, at least in France. But just why I don't know unless it has something to do with pleasing your patron or else they all just had more time and didn't have to worry about where the next meal was coming from. Rops wants in the Académie but they don't want him, well maybe some day. What we call 'taste' under the Republic belongs almost entirely to the monarchists. Well, that's that. Do you really like Chicago Sammy."

"I had a hard time getting used to it," I said. "All those dirty backyards when you rode the Elevated, but finally I didn't see them anymore. The façade, the front face of Chicago is wonderful. I like the gray color; it's a lot like Paris."

"I liked it too," she said, "and some of the best audiences I had were there as well as some of the worst, and it was there that we rode in a police car and that was exciting, and Bobsy

Goodspeed was a perfect hostess and so was Thornton except in a sense you were a prisoner of love if you know what I mean."

"Perfectly," I said.

"Yes, well Alice protected me all she could, and I'm sorry we never did get to that funny little college where you were in Helena Montana, is that the way you pronounce it."

"No," I said, "it's HELL-uh-nuh, not Hell-EE-nuh."

"It sounds better the other way," Gertrude said, "and I especially did want to see the Hangman's Tree and the gold mine and the ghost town."

Ahead of us a peasant was digging with a spade. *"Bonjour, Monsieur le Grand,"* Gertrude said, and introduced me. We chatted about the weather, and then moved on.

"That's his favorite spot to dig for bait," she said. "Worms and things."

"You speak a nice French," I said.

"It's a peasant French," Gertrude said. "I really never learned to speak it until Alice and I were thrown with the French soldiers in the World War and we drove the Red Cross truck. And then you picked it up from them and of course they were mostly all peasants so it was peasant French I learned. Henri Rops says it sounds as if I were living in a stable and just came out for air, he wrinkles his nose every time I speak French." She laughed heartily.

"Now Alice," she continued, "she learned it in the States under very good French instructors and she speaks the pure French of Lyon or of Paris and when there's any telephone talking to do in French, well she always does it and I don't mind, not I, not in the least."

After we got back and had lunch, Gertrude pushed away from the table and said, "Now and really now this time, Sammy and I are going out into the garden and read palms, we didn't get to the other day, and he's going to take a palm print, so why don't you go up and get your things Sammy, and I'll meet you in the garden."

She was sitting on the low stone wall when I got there with my book and camera. I sat down beside her and she seized my right palm. "Are you righthanded Sammy, yes I seem to remember that you are," and with that she launched into a long and interesting reading, complaining about my "girdle of

Venus" and the promiscuity it indicated: "That's the Eleven again I suppose," she said, "but they should really show up here on the side and they don't there's nothing there. I thought you said you'd just missed getting married by eleven women," she said severely.

"But I never had affairs with them," I said.

"No," Gertrude said, "there's really just one and a half." And then she complained about my crooked little finger. "It's the sign of a con man," she said.

"Maybe it's just that I broke it once," I said.

"Then you broke it being a con man," she laughed.

After she finished reading my hand, I looked at hers — at her insistence and against my will. I saw what was almost a man's hand, with "physical" fingers and one large affair mark — and a life line that cut off dreadfully and sharply at a year or two past seventy — perhaps seventy right on the head. Between the ages of twenty and thirty-five there were many small cut-up lines, stars, and crosses, of struggle and confusion, and after that her "destiny line" went straight and sure — again to a point about seventy.

"You're holding things back now Sammy aren't you," Gertrude said in a stern tone. "You might as well tell me about the seventy thing, I can see it myself and that gives me six or seven more good years, but a lot, oh a very lot to be done, and the question is can I do it."

"Of course you can do it," I said. "You are just turning things out a mile a minute, and like any good apple tree, everything you turn out is good once you have learned to grow apples."

"That's sweet," she said.

"And now let's take a hand print, shall we?"

"Of course, of course," she said excitedly, "how is it done."

"I need some soda and soapy water for the solution," I said, and hurried to the kitchen, where Alice gave me the ingredients. Then with a wad of cotton and a thick towel I went back to Gertrude and swabbed her palm with the solution. I folded the towel, tore out one of the prepared pink sheets of paper from the book, and she pressed her hand down firmly on the paper and towel beneath — and there was her palm print with the lines showing distinctly.

"Dandy," she said, "except now I've got soda and soap all

over me." I handed her the towel. Then I took the pink sheet into the shaded living room to let it dry in the dark.

When I got back again to Gertrude in the garden she said, "We've got a coupla busy days ahead of us. First, tomorrow, that's Saturday, we are going to the agricultural fair at Virieu-le-Grand, *le ministre* of agriculture will be there and all the farmers in their Sunday best, it's really a kind of small carnival, and the Rops are coming too."

"Sounds exciting," I said, although country fairs were not very appealing.

Gertrude laughed. "Hardly. And then Sunday the whole commune at Chamonix is coming, they live there under André Breton, he founded surrealism you know, and there will be lots of his disciples including Yves Tanguy and Matta from Chile and there will be a party in the rose garden."

"That sounds better," I said, "and Sunday the twenty-third is also my birthday."

"No now is it really," Gertrude said. "Then Alice will have to bake you a torte or something."

"I'd like to see her do that out of cornmeal," I said. "Please, I'm old enough without being reminded of it."

She laughed. "You're just like Thornton. There's nothing worse than a young man hollering about being old, it makes him seem younger and that's what Thornie always wants. Well, we'll think of something if not a torte."

"It's not that I don't want one," I said, "but I've always thought birthdays should be days of mourning unless you managed to hit a hundred."

"Do you think you'll ever get over those allergies now do you," she asked.

"My father outgrew his hay fever when he was forty, so there's hope."

"You've got a ways to go," Gertrude said. "But you'll make it, your hand says you will, so maybe things will be all right then."

I did not know until many years later what was taking place in the deep well of her imagination, but I found the amusing use she made of my allergies under the letter 'S' in her *Alphabets and Birthdays.**

* See Appendix, pages 251–52.

Gertrude looked around the garden. Then she said, "I've just got a copy of my new child's book, *The World Is Round.* Do you want me to read it to you do you."

I had a small chill. Suppose Coleridge had asked one of his disciples at Highgate if he wanted to hear him recite the fragment of "Kubla Khan"!

"I'd be delighted," I said, gulping a little.

We went into the living room, and Gertrude seated herself in the big wicker rocker, picked up the book, and began.

It was before the days of tape recorders and cassettes, but the record of the intonations of that great contralto voice, the resonance and golden timbre of it and her inflections stay in my mind. Her deep warm tones tolled and echoed through the room, sometimes breathlessly tumbling, sometimes slow and measured, full of assurance and life. There were no interruptions, save for a moment when Alice appeared in the doorway, a bowl in hand, reminding me of the Man Ray photograph taken when the two of them lived in the rue de Fleurus — but when she saw what was happening she vanished as silently on sandaled feet as she had come.

Gertrude read on. It took her about forty minutes and then she put the book down. "Did you like it," she said.

"Wonderful. You have really found your way into the mind of a child."

"Children always seem to understand my books better than grownups," she said.

"Oh, the adults are gradually learning," I said.

"Do you really think so," she said, somewhat anxiously.

"Of course," I said. "You are the mother of Hemingway and Sherwood Anderson and many others not yet here. They will all owe something to you."

"The grandmother," she corrected, smiling. "But I can't stand Hem anymore. He's always putting on the big man act. And he's about this size." She put her thumbnail halfway down her little finger.

"Compensation," I said, and she nodded.

"I think he resents your influence on him," I went on. "When you get a reputation of your own you think that you alone are responsible for your greatness."

"Of course he resents it," Gertrude said sharply. "And one of these days when he sees fit he'll really attack all those he thinks had anything to do with his 'greatness,' Fitzgerald and Zelda and Alice and me and all the rest, just the way he attacked Sherwood."

"Well," I said, "he makes me tired. I read him with boredom. He repeats the word 'black' twenty times in one short paragraph describing grasshoppers. That's not my idea of a good style."

Dinner that evening was as usual a gourmet one — beef niblets with Alice's own *sauce béarnaise* on it, a salad with tarragon dressing, small balls of saffron rice fried in oil and cornmeal, and a dessert of fresh fruits in kirsch. I skipped the wine completely.

The next day we set off for Virieu-le-Grand about ten in the morning, but first Gertrude and Alice had a discussion about whether the dogs should go along. It was finally decided to leave them behind with Madame Roux and Chen; Chen loved the dogs and played with them endlessly.

Virieu-le-Grand was a small French village — thatched roofs and whitewashed houses — and it probably had more people in it that day than ever before. We wandered around and found the Rops almost immediately. Trust Henri — he was talking to Georges Monnet, *le ministre* himself, and we were all introduced. The minister had already heard in Paris of the "*mesdemoiselles américaines*" and was properly impressed. He was a funny little man, balding and dressed in the shiniest of suits with a bow tie, pleasant and charming, bowing to brush the hands of Gertrude and Alice, and giving me a short snappy bonecrusher handshake.

Later we listened to his speech, a very political one: he slipped in a few sly barbs about the Americanization of France and its agriculture. Everyone applauded when he finished, and then we went looking at the exhibits, Alice fascinated with a mushroom nine inches in diameter and Gertrude much taken with butter in small molds that looked like sheep. There were many little old ladies who had arrived on bicycles, and Gertrude commented on their bicycling at such advanced ages: "Those French — they have good hearts and good legs, very stout."

"But bad livers," Alice added.

Gertrude found something that absorbed her completely: a shooting gallery with whirling grouse and moving ducks as targets. She picked up a rifle and let fly at them, doing it again and again. I snapped her picture, and Alice tugged at her between loadings.

"Lovey," she whispered, "others may want to have a go at it."

Gertrude turned. "You know how I love things that go round . . . the world, whirling grouse, gramophone records and all the rest, anything that goes in a circle." And at that moment I knew what to send her and Alice as a house present when I got back to the States.

We stayed until the dust from the shuffling feet made the air so thick it was difficult to breathe. Alice began to cough, and so did I — and the crowds moved in a dust cloud made visible by the afternoon sun, moved like golden shadows, almost obscured. Finally Gertrude said, "This is long enough, don't you think, our clothes and shoes are all dusty, so what do you say, let's go."

So we departed, having made our appropriate farewells to the Rops, the mayor, and the minister of agriculture.

"I'm glad to get away from there," Alice said. "I'm filthy."

"We all are," Gertrude said. "We all need baths."

Dinner that evening was very quiet, for we were all tired from our excursion. We went into the living room for our infusions and very little was said. I spoke rather desultorily about love affairs among my students and how they grew and died, but somehow the conversation never left the ground at all.

The next morning at ten o'clock there came a great hammering at my door. "It's me," Gertrude said loudly. "Are you decent."

I grabbed my dressing gown and said, "Yes!"

She came in the door with a heavy gray woolen bathrobe wrapped around her. It nearly touched the floor. She was grinning widely and had not yet combed her hair, which stood up at several angles. Her mood was euphoric.

"Happy birthday Sammy," she said and threw one arm around my shoulder, giving me a big wet kiss right on the forehead. She had a sheet of her large blue writing paper in her hand, which she waved at me.

"I have written you a birthday poem," she said, "and here it is and many happy returns and many more of them."

She thrust the paper into my hand, not waiting for me to read it, and sailed out of the room. I looked at the poem. At the top of the blue sheet she had written "Bilignin 1939" and beneath it was scrawled the poem:

To Sammy
On his birthday

For which is what it is
That which is that Sammy is
With us with our love
On his birthday

Bless little Sammy
Which he is
All little Sammy
What he is
Which is what he is
With us which he is
With our love
On his birthday

And she had signed it with her characteristic "Gtde."

The sentiment was flattering, and to have a poem addressed to me on my birthday was better than any torte that Alice could have baked.

I was overcome with emotion, but I managed to dress and go downstairs. Gertrude was sitting in the rose garden, sprawled comfortably in a chaise longue.

"Dear Gertrude," I said. "You have done the sweetest thing that has ever been done for me," and I reached out and grabbed her big hand.

"You know we are glad to have you here Sammy," she said, "or it would not have been written at all. I have not written many birthday poems, you can betcha, but I could not resist writing one for you because we are very fond of you and hope you are of us."

"You are two great kind women," I said. "Only one thing could ever make me want to stay young forever and that would be always to be able to sit beside you here looking out over the valley, with Alice rattling pans in the kitchen. This is the only birthday present I'll always remember."

"Well, I'm glad you liked it, now stop it, you silly bashful boy you, and let's talk about the Chamonix crowd, there's some pointers I have to give you, they're a rather strange bunch. Separately they are fine but together they make a, what do you call it, phalanx."

"I'm listening."

"Well," she said, "the first thing is André Breton, he's about as big as I am, and he's the leader and everybody has to kowtow to him, and certainly you must because he founded surrealism, but don't genuflect. As for me, I won't kowtow, we meet as equals. And then there's Yves Tanguy, he's all tangled up but he's a nice person. And Matta who comes from Chile and really can paint and he's the handsomest of the lot. Then there will be Madame Breton or at least I guess that's what she is and they have a little girl — well, they'll all be coming and who knows who else — and it'll be quite a crowd and the Rops will be here too. Oh my god, I hate parties like this I really do, and people will be taking pictures and spilling punch all over everything the drunker they get."

"It sounds like quite an afternoon in the making," I said. "I think the best thing for me to do would be go to bed right now and stay there."

Gertrude laughed. "Well, I certainly wish I could do that very thing or else sit up there and write."

"When do you write, by the way?" I asked. "You always seem to be really free of such a chore."

"Well," she said, "I used to write at night and then there got to be too many visitors so I changed it to mornings, and I don't come down for breakfast until about ten as you know and very little of that but I wake up about seven or sometimes six and then I just sit up in bed and write and it's very comfortable."

"How many words do you count as a good day?"

"Sometimes I do one thousand, sometimes two and if there's absolutely nobody around why I find I can even sometimes do three thousand, and if you could do that much every day you'd get a helluva lot done, now wouldn't you."

"Yes," I said. "You could write potboilers and detective stories all over the place if you did three thousand."

"Well believe me I can't do that much every day," Gertrude said, "it's more like a thousand. And you too as a beginning writer, you know very well that sometimes you squeeze and groan and pace and not a word, not one single word will come out. Speaking of writing, why don't we all send a round-robin postcard, I like round robins, to the Wendell Wilcoxes, they'd love it, and maybe also one to your sister and Emmy, she's your current flame, number eleven, isn't she."

"They'd all be tickled pink," I said.

"Have you got any postcards that aren't used up or any from the region here," she asked.

"Oh, I have plenty of postcards, but not of the scenery; they're all of paintings by Picasso or Van Gogh or Cezanne or Matisse."

"Well, they'll do fine," she said. "You just run up and get them and we'll do some round robins and leave space for Alice to write something too."

I had quite a few cards and Gertrude made the selection, using her own pen and writing very small at the top. Then I wrote my message on the lower third of the correspondence space, leaving the middle for Alice. "Now we'll have Alice fill them in, in the middle," Gertrude said, "and do you think they'll really like getting them."

"Yes, I do," I said. "They'll treasure them."

She laughed. "You know it's really nice to be famous," she said. There was no trace of immodesty in her statement; it was merely an observation. "And it all came about because of the smallness and intensity of my audience, at first that is, not the bigness. You and Claire Andrews and the Wilcoxes and Carl Van Vechten and Thornton and people like that."

"The Wilcoxes will be pleased when they hear that," I said. "And I am too."

We sat for a moment looking out over the valley, taking in the blues and greens and the massed white clouds near the horizon.

"I feel that we're waiting for the hurricane," I said. "The party."

"Me too," Gertrude said. "That's an awful bunch of people to be having."

"When are they arriving?"

"Oh, about two o'clock," Gertrude said. "If I had my way there'd never be more than two people here at a time and one would be better. Now you take Sir Francis Rose and Cecil Beaton, they'll be coming on the same train you leave on to go to Algeria, and Francis I can stand all right because you can put up with a lot from a genius and he may be one, he just may be one, but I am not sure in my head if he is, anyway I am buying his paintings the same way I did Picasso's and maybe Francis is good and maybe not, and if he is good maybe I'll make Francis famous too just the way I helped to make Picasso but I am not yet sure about Francis."

"And if he is good then you'll have a lot of paintings by Francis and they'll be worth something."

"You betcha," Gertrude said, "but I wouldn't say they were good if they weren't, and I am not at all sure yet they are."

"What's he like?" I asked.

"Oh, Francis looks as harmless as a titmouse," Gertrude said. "He's got a big droopy mustache and baby blue eyes, he's a kind of combination of Shelley and Byron but he's got something they didn't have, he's vicious. He fell in love with an American named Billy who was the *mignon* for that gangster Dutch Schultz, Billy was a collection man, and he really collected everything Francis had, he even sold a villa that belonged to Francis down in the Midi and the family silver and all. And it got so bad that I had to go to the British Embassy in Paris, the British Intelligence Service and say, 'See here, here's an Englishman who's made a bad choice, that's all, and you really ought to keep Billy, Maher I think his last name was, to keep Billy out of England,' and they were very polite and said, 'Thank you, Miss Stein, we will, we don't want people like this Billy in England,' and it was hard for me to talk to Francis for a long time after that, and I gave him hell the next time I saw him because I don't like going to the British Intelligence Service any more than anybody else and meddling that way, but it had to be done and I was the one who had to do it. And then I introduced him to Cecil and I know they have a lot of fun together and perhaps you're what he needs Sammy, Cecil is anti-Semitic and I know that but he doesn't know I do, so maybe when you come back from Algiers something may boil up and be delightful."

"Maybe," I said. "He may not like me and I may not like him, but we may have something in common."

"You said it, I didn't," Gertrude laughed. "And with Francis the commoner the better. He goes out to the gates of Paris and talks with the workingmen and gets drunk and has a good time."

I did not know until much later that Francis had for one summer as his houseboy a stranger who he discovered (sometime after) was his own illegitimate son from Spain — but that's another story.

"Well, I think if you have any preparing to do now's the time," Gertrude said, and I went upstairs to wash my face.

Car by car, I heard the arrivals at the gate. There seemed to be five or six automobiles. I looked out the front window and could see little but the tops of heads — one balding, another with thick wavy black hair, another with straight brown. The Breton child was easily identifiable — a little golden-haired girl whose clothes were an exact copy of her mother's.

I finally went downstairs. The thick wavy black hair was Matta, and he was very handsome, with cream-colored skin; the taller one was Tanguy, and there were several new ones Gertrude hadn't counted on. All of them were *surréalistes.* It was good to see a familiar face in the crowd and I made straight for Henri and Madeleine Rops.

Such gatherings are all the same, and all different; this one was hard on me because I knew few of the persons about whom the gossip swirled. And there was about the same amount of bitchiness that you would find in a cocktail party in America.

The punch was delicious, a wine and kirsch one, and very strong. Madame Breton took a good deal of it. She and her daughter wore pink gypsy dresses with yellow and orange flowers. And Madame wore a necklace of hollow glass balls, large ones, each partly filled with colored water.

The party went on a long time, for several hours, and then Madame Breton had to take her child upstairs to the bathroom. Madame, a little unsteady, stumbled and fell on her daughter on the stone stairs, causing the child to knock out a front tooth.

At once the Breton child naturally became the center of attention — there was a flurry of cloths to catch the blood, and toys to distract her wailing, while Alice applied some mysterious herbal concoction to stop the bleeding of the girl's cut lip. Madame seemed to be more worried about breaking one of the glass balls of her necklace, but the rest of us hovered around the child, probably frightening her more than the fall.

At any rate, it was the reason for ending the party — which I think both Alice and Gertrude were secretly wanting to do — and there were apologies, farewells, and invitations for everyone to visit in the house near Chamonix. The last of the crowd departed, and it was over.

"Whew," Gertrude said. "I am really glad that's ended and as for going to visit that menagerie, not on your life."

Alice was holding her ropes of beads together at her waist and bending over to look at the food left on the buffet table. "We'll have enough to last for a week," she said, "except I don't know what to do with the punch."

"Let's take it and give it to the neighbors here in Bilignin," Gertrude said. "You can fill however many jars there will be and then we, Sammy and I, we'll distribute it."

"We'll have to see how much there is," Alice said, "so that no one will be insulted."

By leaving about an inch empty at the top of each liter jar, we found that there was one apiece for each family in Bilignin, and so Gertrude and I set out like Saint Nicholas to distribute them. I carried the basket, which got very heavy indeed. But Bilignin had only eight or nine families; in each case Gertrude asked them to bring back the jar, according to Alice's last shouted instructions.

"Some party," I said. "It really ended just as it got going."

"And I don't mind," Gertrude said. "There's never any really good talk at parties like that even with people who know how to talk, no conversation, just gossip. I've heard enough gossip in my life to last me several lifetimes and most of it untrue and vicious."

"I imagine you have," I said, swinging the now nearly empty basket.

She chuckled, just as we entered the gates to the chateau. "Did you hear about the woman who came over from America to 'protect' me from all the world," she said. "She didn't know French and she thought the word *'château'* came from the French word for cat which is *'chat'* and she thought Alice and I lived in a cathouse."

I laughed. "I'm going to miss being here," I said, "and hearing things like that. There won't be anyone to talk to in Algiers."

"Oh yes there will," she said, "you can always talk to strangers there, strangers sometimes talk better than friends, and it will be fun and exciting, your first introduction to a non-Christian culture, the Arab one. Did you know that their fezzes, their *chéchias,* have a linen lining around the inside edge that touches their foreheads because they're afraid if it's leather it might be from a pig.

"And when you come back," she went on, "you can stay another week or two, Francis and Cecil and you will overlap but that's all right, there's plenty of room in the old cathouse." She laughed in high good humor.

"Are you all packed," she asked, with a sudden switch.

"Almost," I said, "I just have to get the toilet things together."

"Good," said Gertrude. "Alice and I will get you to the noon train at Culoz and maybe there will be time for a brief meeting with Francis and Cecil and maybe not, but you will see them eventually."

That night I went into the bathroom after they had gone to bed. I left the light on and the door open and was engaged in gathering up my razor and toothbrush and stuffing things into my kit. Their bedroom door was closed; it was set at a right angle to the bathroom door. I was being as quiet as I could, thinking that they had already gone to sleep.

Suddenly I heard their door open and looked up, startled. There at the bathroom entrance stood Gertrude completely naked. She covered her pubis quickly with both hands, said "Whoop!" in a loud voice, and vanished back into her bedroom, slamming the door until the bathroom mirror rattled. I had only the barest glimpse of her, and my shocked eyes noted the glistening hollow pink scar that remained from the excision of a part of her left breast. The tumult of her whirlwind vanishing left me confused, and as I stuttered something like "I was just packing —" she was at the same time saying, "I thought you'd left the light on in the bathroom —"

Upset and trembling, I made it back to my room, this time thoroughly convinced that I had really done it, that there would never be another invitation — for aside from the doctor who delivered Gertrude, I was convinced I was the only male who had ever seen her naked. With shaking hands I poured a large drink of my "emergency" cognac, and went to sleep with nightmares.

But nothing was said of it at all. The next morning I awoke at nine, had breakfast, and chatted with Alice, who in a way had become my personal barometer; she reflected for me the emotional state of Gertrude and the ambience. Gertrude came down about ten, her face as bland as Buddha's, with no signs of embarrassment, recrimination, or disapproval. It was as if nothing had happened.

The trip to Culoz was an excitement. Gertrude started singing "Frère Jacques" in her near-bass golden alto, Alice joined in contralto, and I came along in my turn, tunelessly.

The train that would take me to Marseille was on time, and Francis and Cecil got off. Francis embraced them warmly while Cecil stood aside, and then hasty introductions were made. I climbed on the train with my suitcases (no *porteurs* at Culoz) and went toward the southland, still quivering slightly when I remembered the scene of the night before. Then I began to smell the grapes and the melons in the heady and intoxicating air. It was tropical and tranquil and golden.

I spent three weeks in Algiers and its environs, going to the edge of the Sahara, going to a sheep market, buying a magic amulet from a sand reader, watching the camels and the Arabs in fez and burnoose, going through the Casbah (protected, as I had promised), and in general enjoying a thoroughly hedonistic and leisurely vacation.

Then it was time to return to France. On departure day came a card from Gertrude: "Hurry up and get back Sammy and stay a few days and then get the hell to Le Havre, we are all afraid of war and it may come, really it may."

On the way back, I did not pause at Marseille and could not even spare the time to deliver Gertrude's note of introduction to Picasso. At the train station I was lucky enough to catch a train to Culoz after only an hour's delay. From the station I called Bilignin and spoke with Madame Roux, who told me that Gertrude and Alice were shopping, but that she would deliver the message. Then I asked if the two British persons were still there.

"Oh yes," she said. "They seem not to be worried about the war at all." Then in her patois she muttered something about "that *merdeux* Chamberlain and his umbrella." I said, "Yes, yes," and hung up.

There was something new in the faces of the French men and women on the train; it was not fear, but a kind of resigned and fatalistic concern.

At Culoz, all four of them were there to meet me.

It was the twenty-eighth of August. "I won't be staying long," I said. "The *Normandie* leaves on the sixth of September and I must be in Le Havre." No one knew that the *Normandie* had never left New York for that trip, and instead of being in mid ocean was safely docked in a thus far neutral country, leaving six thousand stranded and badly frightened tourists to get home as best they could.

When we got to Bilignin I was installed in a new room; Francis and Cecil had my former one.

I liked Francis, although I did not find him "wicked and evil" (to use another of Gertrude's phrases about him); I think that she was afraid he would "corrupt" me. Cecil, more British than British, paid little attention to me, possibly because I was that "mongrel mixture" of Scot and American.

The twenty-eighth of August was Monday; Britain and France were to declare war on Germany the following Sunday, September third, after Hitler's invasion of Poland on September first. Francis had a small radio and we were clustered around it — until tiring of the same news bulletins endlessly repeated, I wandered out into the rose garden. Cecil was sitting there in a sun chair, completely relaxed, and sketching the Ain valley.

"Why aren't you listening to the war broadcasts?" I asked. He was wearing a thin jacket over a light summer sweater with broad red and white horizontal stripes, and on his head as a sun hat was one of Gertrude's high-crowned Korean straw creations with a very wide brim. He had on a pair of khaki knee-length shorts, and was fiddling with a rose in one hand, twirling the stem, while he sketched with the other.

"Ch-chamberlain . . . has ar . . . arranged things," he said. "There will be no war." His slurred speech indicated that he was completely drunk.

I went back into the living room and beckoned to Francis. When he came out I said, "You know Gertrude's rules about alcohol. Cecil is smashed."

The remark galvanized Sir Francis. "My God," he said. We went toward the chair, which was turned away from us. It was empty, save for the sketch pad and Gertrude's straw hat. Cecil had vanished.

"Oh my God," said Francis again. "I'll have to find him and take him for a ride or a walk and get some coffee in him."

"Coffee won't help," I said. "Instead of a sleepy drunk, all you'll have will be a wide-awake one. You'd better get him straightened out before dinner."

"I will, I will," Francis said. "But he'll have to be found first. Come along."

"Where are you going?"

"Belley, first," he said anxiously. "He can't really have got very far. He'll be on the road. I'll take over when we find him."

"All right," I said, "I can telephone Gertrude from there with some sort of excuse."

But Cecil was not to be found. We came back to Bilignin. By then the sky had clouded over and it had started to drizzle. "You'll have to tell Gertrude," I said.

"You do it," he said nervously. "I'm really afraid."

"Not I," I said. "You march right into the living room and tell her."

I stayed in the car. Soon Gertrude came out, wearing a kind of droopy Garbo rainhat. Francis was behind her. She got in the car. By then it was nearly dark. "Where do you suppose he is," she said anxiously, and a little angrily.

"I haven't the foggiest," Francis said.

"Well, let's go back to Belley and we'll leave you Sammy, you've got a raincoat and can wander around looking for him."

We returned to Belley and they deposited me. "Be sure to look in all the bistros," Francis shouted, as they left me in the dismal wet night of the square, lighted by only one feeble street lamp.

I looked and asked in all the bistros. No Cecil. After about two hours I called Gertrude.

"Go right to the *gendarmérie,*" she said. "Tell them I said to call out the troops from the *caserne* because Cecil is lost."

I went to the police station and was met with subdued laughter and raised shoulders.

"With all due respect to Mademoiselle Stein," an officer said, shrugging. "War is near, Monsieur, and after all it is only one man. When dawn comes he will be found."

I reported this to Gertrude over the telephone.

"Go see the mayor," she said.

"But he has no control over the troops," I said.

"Go see the mayor," she shouted excitedly.

I did not, because I knew what his answer would be, and I phoned Gertrude a third time and told her the mayor could do nothing. "He's a stupid man," she shouted, "and if you see him again tell him I am not interested in the war, I am interested in where is Cecil Beaton." She was very upset. "We are going out again to look for him ourselves," she hollered. "We'll pick you up in Belley in the square."

Another hour passed while I sat under an umbrella at the small table of a sidewalk café and had a Pernod. Meanwhile — although I did not know it until later — Gertrude and Francis went to the local *caserne,* which was a barracks for a detachment of Senegalese soldiers from Africa, very tall and very black. There Gertrude with her remarkable powers of persuasion had talked the commandant into filling a truck with Senegalese soldiers armed with flashlights and pressing them into the search. Yes, Cecil had been there earlier, and — as Francis told me later — the black soldiers seemed to be enjoying some huge joke among themselves, but since no one could understand the language they spoke, it remained a mystery.

Finally the Matford came around the corner from Bilignin, Gertrude at the wheel, Alice and Francis in the back, and between them a very wet and bedraggled Cecil.

"Where on earth did you find him?" I asked.

They told me that two huge six-feet-four Senegalese soldiers from the *caserne* had been walking him home between them, all of them fairly well snockered, and they were all singing "L'Alouette" at the top of their lungs as they walked down the road.

"Cecil was up there at the *caserne* all afternoon," Alice said, "drinking."

Francis murmured something I did not hear, and then said to me, "I told him to behave while he was here, but you know Cecil . . ." He looked straight ahead.

"Well, all is quiet now," I said. "We have found the lost sheep."

Cecil struggled upward from his collapsed position but Alice pushed him back. ". . . no sheep," he muttered.

"There, there," said Francis. "Everything will be all right tomorrow morning," and then he added, "except for your headache."

Gertrude caught the sentence. "Well, everything won't be all right," she said. "I think you'd all better leave tomorrow while you still can. You have to get to Le Havre Sammy, and god knows how the trains will be, maybe all taken by the military for troops, and Cecil and Francis, you'd better get to the embassy in Paris to be safe."

"But what about you two?" I asked.

"Never mind about us," Gertrude said, "we'll be all right. The peasants will hide us if necessary. We are just going to set it out, it may be dangerous but we have almost decided that's what we're going to do."

"But the pictures in Paris!" I said. "The Germans will take them all!"

Gertrude turned almost completely around and even in the dark I could see her wink. "We are going back there secretly if war comes and bundle some of them up and bring them here."

"Oh my god," I said. "If Paris falls and the Germans find you, they'll kill you for sure. You should just stay here and eat things from your garden."

"I had rather be killed for a Picasso than a tomato," Gertrude said. Later I learned that Gertrude and Alice did indeed make a hurried trip to Paris but could not bring the paintings back with them — except for Picasso's portrait of Gertrude and a Cézanne.

On that horrid night in August I packed quickly and early the next morning caught the eight o'clock train for Paris. It was full of standing people, packed together, and it was only with difficulty that I found a place to fit my feet. What happened to Cecil and Francis I never heard.

The last glimpse I had of Gertrude was her waving goodbye, still in the droopy rain hat from the night before, with Alice standing beside her like a small black bird . . .

Interlude

THE WAR acted as a kind of paralyzing agent, and I delayed for a few months in sending a gift to Gertrude and Alice, because there was no assurance that anything might reach them. I knew what I was going to send — a Mixmaster blender, for I remembered the village fair at Virieu-le-Grand, and how Gertrude had said she liked things that went around — gramophone records, whirling grouse, eggbeaters, and the world. The Mixmaster seemed like the perfect gift, and useful to Alice as well.

But troubles lay ahead. There had to be communications with the company that made the Mixmaster, and arrangements for a specially wound armature, and Continental round-pin plugs. They warned me that the machine would run faster in Billignin than in Paris, since the voltage was higher in the country; I could hear Alice murmur that such an arrangement was against all nature. Finally, the French Trade Commission (or what was left of it in Chicago) had to be consulted; they gave me a difficult time, as did the export authorities, claiming that the mixer had a "commercial value" and could not therefore be sent in wartime.

Then there was the mode of sending and the costs: $6.10 by parcel post, $11.00 by express, and $386.00 by Transatlantic Clipper, a service just then beginning (passenger fares one-way were just $350.00). The package could not be insured, and a waiver had to be signed because there was no certainty that the blender would arrive at all.

At last everything was ready, all papers signed and forms filled. One day before sending it, a letter arrived from Gertrude, saying, "No no no, no Mixer, $25 is not cheap it is a helluva lot of francs" and that there were better things to do with the money. Besides, she added, everybody has time enough now to mix by hand all the things that need mixing, and money is money, and not now to be spent on mixers . . .

I thought of all the trouble — the special wiring, the wire-strapped wooden shipping box — and sent it anyway, by parcel post.

That was in late November. About five months later, after Easter Sunday 1940, there arrived a euphoric letter from Gertrude, saying that the Mixmaster had come Easter Sunday and they had not had time to more than read the literature and put it together and gloat. It was oh so beautiful, she said, and Madame Roux said, *oui, il est si gentil*, and Easter morning, what a spring, lovely as she had never seen anything lovely, and Alice all smiles and murmuring in her dreams, Mixmaster . . .

The next few letters from Gertrude arrived together, having been delayed somewhere, and all of them asked how much they owed me for the blender. It was not until well into midsummer 1940 that it finally became clear to them that the Mixmaster was a house present.

Meanwhile, things had become so difficult for them that they wavered in their resolution to stay in France. Gertrude's letters were full of plans to come, and perhaps go to Hollywood. I knew a second-rate "agent" who had wanted to handle their lectures for tremendous fees during their first American tour. This man, Ford Hicks, saw in their second coming nothing but a lining of his pockets with greenery, and, using the remarks that I unconsciously made in front of him, held out for them the prospect of really going to Hollywood and making a film about the first autobiography. My naiveté did not allow me to discover until two years later that Hicks was a fraud and had no more connection with Hollywood than I had. This infuriated me and sadly disappointed Gertrude and Alice.

The letters between us during the war years were sporadic. Sometimes my letters stayed in occupied Paris a year before reaching them, and theirs to me were similarly delayed. The war psychosis had its effect on me, too; because so many months elapsed between letters, I often thought there was no point in trying to write. When word came in July 1940 that Alice had broken the green spinning bowl of the Mixmaster and could another be sent, I had neither the will nor the energy to go through the whole procedure again.

Bennett Cerf sent Gertrude *War and Peace* to read; she wrote me that she enjoyed that, but kept importuning me to send her some "*mystères*" — detective novels and whodunits — complaining that she had read everything in the house at least five times over; and all that she could find now were *The Cloister and the Hearth*, four Dickens novels, *Uncle Tom's Cabin*, and *The Vicar of Wakefield*, none of which suited her taste precisely. I wrapped up three separate packages of paperback *mystères* and sent them to her. Her gratitude was profound, almost pathetic. She thanked me for the packages and at the same time scolded me a little for "being so neglectful in your ways." She said that they were enjoying the experience of the war, that they would not have missed it for anything, and that the daily conversations they had with their neighbors were alone worth the price.

"We garden, we work," she wrote, "and we see a great many people, one might not think so but we do." She told me again that "not by name but just the same" I was mentioned in *Paris France*, and that her current plans included doing a similar piece on America, which she thought would be "rather fun," and that she might also go back to doing "portraits" once again. *Superstitions* had been done originally in French and then translated by herself into English. She said that she and Alice had so far not been homesick for Paris, "but I suppose that when fall comes we will be." And then with that extraordinary childlike naiveté that she sometimes had, she asked if I were coming over that summer (in the middle of the war!), since I must now be rich after being named an associate professor in Chicago.

In the next batch of letters she referred again to the agent in Chicago, saying that it didn't sound so bad, really — that they might come over in the fall and do their movie — but would anyone come to hear her lecture while the country was in the process of electing a president? I wrote that her lectures would be a welcome relief from any campaign, and that everyone would come to hear her speak. But I knew that I was wrong; the spirit of the country had changed so much that it seemed doubtful their second reception would be as enthusiastic as the first.

In another letter, dated May 1, 1940, and received in the late fall, she wrote that it did seem that if they were ever to be in Hollywood it would be the work of Sammy dear Sammy, and that it would be nice if they wanted them and gave them so much money they could buy a car and drive a car ("we and Sammy at the wheel"), and that "we never got to the Chartreuse but we might all get to Hollywood."

Ford Hicks was possibly frightened at the prospect of arranging things for such a notable person as Gertrude; he kept finding all sorts of excuses — the difficulty of getting them out of the country, the death of his Hollywood contact (whom I doubted ever existed), and other nonsense, until we finally stopped all communication with him.

Then several of my letters arrived together in France, and Gertrude answered them with a long one, asking me once more to send a bowl for the blender, saying that all of the substitutes — of stainless steel and ceramic — did not work properly, the contents rising and spilling over the side. This time I pulled myself together and did send a replacement.

She spoke of her continuing interest in predictions and said that Saint Odile was their present favorite, for Odile had said that the war would end in Italy and that the Germans would withdraw, having contracted a "strange illness."

She complained that the butchers had banded together and refused to deal in contraband any longer in Belley, and that one now had to stand in line; Madame Balthus, a neighbor, had announced the other day that she lived two days a week *honnêtement* and the rest of the time by contraband. She ended that particular letter by asking me to try to write to Sir Francis Rose; she said that she would like news of him if nothing more than fish and chips, that the British were covering themselves with glory on their tight little island and that she supposed fish and chips helped.

In another letter arriving in the same group, she spoke again of their food, saying that they ate lots of luxuries but that my specialties alas did not exist; there was word also of their new neighbors, a half-Scottish, half-Mexican wife and a French husband, and of the Rops in Aix-in-Provence at Christmas to say how do you do, and the d'Aiguys in Tunisia eating dates.

My brother-in-law had gone into the army with a commission. He stopped in Paris to see the Rops, Gertrude and Alice not yet being back from Bilignin, and then he got killed in Germany. At once, in 1945, came a letter of sympathy from Gertrude, saying she had telephoned the Rops and they were very upset. "Will you tell your sister how sorry we all are . . . Spring has come and never have I seen Paris so lovely, so abundantly warm, soft skies and lovely buildings and everybody and the American Army, it is sad not to be a soldier bold but there are lots of compensations, lots of love to you, always Gtde."

And a last one saying, "sure some day you will come back, there are lots of new ones, but you will be a welcome old one, you bet."

But I didn't make it before July 27, 1946, when she died.

III

THE LETTERS from Alice began in 1946, after Gertrude's death, and her strong and vital personality emerged from the shadow in which she had deliberately kept it during Gertrude's lifetime. They were often voluminous, done with the thinnest of Spencerian nibs in the delicate spiderwork that was her handwriting, which someone once said was done "with the eyelash of a fly." She wrote on both sides of translucent paper, so that one side confused the other; a lengthy letter would sometimes take an hour to read with a strong magnifying glass. They were filled with humor and tidbits of gossip, sharp and sometimes hilarious in observations, witty and often sentimental. But the number and length of her letters, the outpouring, seemed almost to result from the desolation that she felt because of Gertrude's absence, as if by maintaining a contact with those who had known them both she was drawing life from the past to help her continue in the present.

When I arrived in the summer of 1950 at the Hôtel Récamier on the Place St. Sulpice, there was a vase of flowers waiting for me with a note in her tiny script: "Welcome to Paris once again, dear Sammy, and come for tea tomorrow at four if you can."

The rue Christine was not far from the Récamier. The next afternoon I walked toward it, pausing at a stall to buy some of her favorite flowers. Then I went up through the market crowds on the rue de Buci to reach the quiet short street where she lived. Across the way from number 5 was a horsemeat shop with a classically carved horse's head above the open counter and a customer or two buying meat.

Alice had never thought of leaving number 5. The place looked shabby and dirty from the outside; there were a laundry and printing establishment in the gloomy courtyard. But like so many dingy fronts in Paris, one could never tell what kind of apartment might be within.

The concierge, an old harridan in house slippers, directed me to the second floor, up solid oaken steps. The knob and the letter-drop of Alice's door were brightest polished brass. I pushed the button and waited, and the door was opened by Madeleine, her maid, whom I had met before.

"*C'est vraiment le monsieur Steward, le gentil américain,*" she said. "Come in, Mademoiselle Toklas is expecting you."

She ushered me into a vestibule of paintings, and through that to a high-ceilinged white room with tall shutters. The major painting on the wall was the well-known *Jeune Fille aux Fleurs* from Picasso's Rose Period, a young nude girl holding a bouquet of flowers.

I looked around — Picabia, Juan Gris, Matisse, more Picasso — the major part of Gertrude's overwhelming collection. I sat down, and then suddenly realized I was on the famous shabby old horsehair sofa on which Gertrude used to curl up, directing the chatter of her salon, counseling, advising, listening — but mostly talking, in that deep warm golden voice which would not ever again call me a "silly bashful boy." It was a haunted room, and ghosts were talking.

There were fresh red roses in a white china vase upon the table, and I laid my bouquet beside them. It was quiet here; the clatter of Paris was stilled. I heard Alice saying something to Madeleine in the kitchen, a little noise, and then more silence. A huge ornamented silver tray with tea things was on the table in front of the sofa. Through the ceiling-high French windows I looked out upon the chimney pots in the quiet enclosure formed by the tight-pressed houses — the open shutters, a few window boxes of plants here and there; and the flat roof on which the aging deaf and blind old Basket went to do his little duties, and from which he had recently fallen fifteen feet at midnight. Alice had written about it, and suddenly behind Alice's chair by the window I saw the dog lying. I got up and went to pat him; he sniffed my hand and tried to wag his tail. I passed my hand over his back, feeling the sepulcher beneath the old stiff white hair.

There was a rustle in the dining room, and Alice came round the corner — frail, wispy, tiny. She stretched out her arms, and I bent down to her small height to kiss her on each cheek.

"Dear boy," she said, "dear, dear boy." She held my hand a moment without speaking, and then pushed me away at arm's length, looking up. "It is really our Sammy, after all these years! Sit down, do." She went to her chair by the window, arranged herself, and I sat again on the horsehair sofa.

I remembered all our little conspiracies of the past and how she had kept from Gertrude the fact that I had left a manuscript on the garden wall overnight. Somehow she had gone on being fond of me, through all the years and departures and deaths. I did not know why. I was continually disappointing her, I was lazy, I was not especially decorative to have around. But she liked me, and went on liking me, perhaps in the way she loved faithful old Basket. She was a woman of great generosity and intense loyalty and tenacity in her affection. Only once had she ever suggested a reason for her fondness toward me. We had been speaking of the novelist Julian Green, and she said: "You are much like him — quiet, gentle, and almost angelic — and yet there is so much beneath we do not know . . ."

She had not noticeably changed. Her eyes were still luminous and quick, her short hair fell somewhat over her forehead. The patrician hook of her nose was still the same; her shoulders still bent forward.

She rang a small silver table bell, and Madeleine appeared with the steaming teapot, which she put on the ornate silver platter. In her other hand she had a plate of delicious cookies that Alice had baked.

"And how have you been, Monsieur?" Madeleine asked.

"Splendid," I said, "and I congratulate you for having lived through the war."

Madeleine shrugged. She was a healthy woman, about forty, with brown hair and lively eyes and the ruddy peasant complexion of southeast France. "It was hard now and then," she said, "but most of us made it." And then as she realized what she had said, she quickly went back to the kitchen.

I looked at Alice. She was staring out the window at the chimney pots and the rooftop on which she walked when there was sun.

The atelier had ceilings about eighteen feet high, and the walls were almost completely covered with paintings. Alice poured the tea and we each had a few sips with some cookies. Then she said, "You've never been in this room, have you?"

"No," I said, "it was only four weeks at Bilignin."

"Ah, yes," she said, and that faraway look came into her eyes again. She sighed. "Well, I will show you what you don't recognize," she said, and with that began a tour of the room, starting with the Picasso *Jeune Fille* that dominated all. "Imagine," she murmured, "Gertrude paid twenty-nine dollars for it about fifty years ago."

"And priceless now."

She went around the room — about fourteen Picassos, several Matisses, many paintings by Juan Gris and Picabia. Included in the collection was one by Sir Francis Rose. "Gertrude left too soon to make him really famous," she said, "and besides, neither of us was ever really sure of his talent." Then she showed me the famous Salon des Refusées, which contained paintings they had grown tired of, or come to consider poor; it was a long corridor with canvases stacked against the wall. I saw several by Francis Rose there, a Picasso, and a few by Pavel Tchelitchev. "Sometimes an artist went bad and Gertrude then lost interest in him and I too — bad in his work, not his life necessarily," Alice said.

"Gertrude's testament said that I could sell a painting now and then if I were out of money," she said, "and I have, and when it is all over, Allan Stein — he's residual heir, with his children — will get the collection and they can hardly wait to get the paintings to sell them. Allan has a small perfume business here in Paris, you know, and every Christmas his Armenian wife, Roubina, sends me three quarts of bad cologne, which I either pour down the drain or give to Madeleine . . . or you, now that you're here," she said, looking at me narrowly as if to determine whether I liked poor cologne.

"Never for me, thanks," I said. "I'm always overweight with luggage."

Alice looked thoughtful for a moment. "It really is the

most wretched cologne ever," she said. "I think it's distilled from the urine of Armenian peasants."

It took two seconds for her remark to hit me, and then I whooped with laughter — and a little shock, for Alice rarely said anything not couched in the most elegant gentlewoman's language. All of her annoyance at the Steins' efforts to get an early hand on Gertrude's collection of paintings was contained in that one sentence.

After I wiped the tears from my eyes, she said, "Perhaps you can give it to someone over at the Récamier."

"Yes, perhaps Mademoiselle Sartre might enjoy it. The concierge."

Alice opened her eyes wide. "A relative of Jean-Paul?"

"No, but she's nice."

"The first time you came here, all those years ago," Alice said, "you stayed over on the rue des Beaux-Arts in the very room where Oscar Wilde died. And then we found you a place at the Récamier. Do you like it any better?"

"Much," I said, "except they had *punaises* the other night, bedbugs, and the *patronne* insisted I had brought them, but the maid told me they had been there a long time."

"Pity," Alice said. "But that's Paris for you. They're everywhere."

"You'd think the Pasteur Institute would come up with a remedy, the way they did for the ants at Bilignin," I said, remembering how one night Alice had poured some magical sweet stuff on the windowsill, and the next morning we blew the shells of the ants' bodies away.

"They're too busy with heart disease and cancer," Alice said.

No moment could ever have been right to mention what I had on my mind, but I decided to get it over with. "I visited Père Lachaise yesterday and took a small bouquet of flowers," I said. I had seen the single grave marker, monolithic and simple, with the name of Gertrude Stein on one side with the dates of her birth and death, and on the other side Alice B. Toklas, with an empty space waiting.

Alice studied the rooftops of Paris outside the window. "That was nice," she said, "a very thoughtful gesture."

There was a moment of awkward silence.

"I miss her, Sammy," she said simply.

"I know, I know."

"Really, no one can know," she said. "It is only I who can know. But you have a great deal of empathy and that lets you partly know."

There was another silence. Basket stirred.

"We all loved her," Alice said, "but nothing will bring her back. It is only that this room is so empty without her laughter and her voice."

She was silent again. From that very first meeting with her, and in all those afterward, she gave the impression that she was waiting — the way one waits for a slight sound at the window, or in the next room. But she did not break, this tiny iron woman, in all the long years that she survived Gertrude — or if she did, alone in the great empty apartment at night, no one knew.

We talked that first day, talked and talked. She had just sold an article on cooking and had been "hideously overpaid" for it. On the proceeds she was going to take a month in Spain and another in Cannes, and had already out of the money taken a trip to Switzerland to see Bernard Faÿ — still in exile because of his suspected collaboration during the war — and had bought herself a dress of pure rayon, of which she was much enamored. The Exposition of International Culture had been a flop, enlivened only by an American journalist (nameless, male) slapping an Italian journalist (nameless, female) in the face. Dozens of well-known names zipped through the air and then vanished. And all the time Alice, who had picked up a pillowcase from a pile beside her chair, was basting infinitesimal stitches with red thread into a hem.

She listened eagerly to the news of what women in America were doing, and I told her what I could remember of new female tricks — such as the mechanism of a new hair-tinting shampoo with a mystic vegetable catalyzer that stopped the action when the hair was done and the proper color achieved.

During the next fifteen years I managed to come over to Paris again for one entire summer and fourteen Christmas visits with Alice. There were always flowers and a note of invitation waiting for me at the Récamier, and I always took flowers or gadgets to her. Between us there sprang up a very deep affection, but there was something added to it, for I really loved this woman with a mind as sharp and witty as that of her beloved companion — perhaps in certain areas even more brilliant.

Alice always sent me a copy of everything of Gertrude's that was published posthumously, as well as of her own books. In 1954 it was the American edition of her own sprightly *Cook Book.* Omited from it — although included in the British edition — was the famous recipe for hashish fudge that had been sent to her from Brion Gysin in Tangier. In the year the cookbook was published in America, Harper had been reluctant to include this recipe, although six years later it was contained in the paperback edition. I took the book to Paris with me at the end of 1954.

"Alice, my dear," I said. "There is one thing lacking in this edition — the recipe for hashish fudge. How does it happen it's in the British edition and not the American?"

"Well," she said slowly, "for one thing, the British are braver. Harper thought it not politic, since the drug culture has not yet really begun in America, and marijuana has been illegal there for a very long time."

"I'm sorry they left it out," I said. "I should love to have it."

Alice smiled, sitting in her low chair, into which she seemed to sink deeper and deeper with each passing year. "Why don't you just leave the book with me, Sammy, and I'll copy it out for you."

I was suddenly shocked with a consciousness of my temerity. "Oh, that's too much work for you," I said. But she insisted I leave the book, for her eyes were still good and she had no trouble reading or writing.

"I can't see you tomorrow," she said; "there are some dull people calling. But come the day after, at four."

Alice's invitations always sounded faintly like royal commands, and I was a loyal subject. You would break any engagement when she asked you to be free, and it happened often.

When I went there on the day after, she handed me the book. On the last endpapers, in her thin tiny writing, she had copied the recipe together with the amusing comments that had appeared in the British edition. I kissed her hand — so old, blue-veined, with paper-thin skin — and then pressed it. "I am deeply touched," I said.

During the years when she could still walk, there were many excursions. One summer we went down together to a crossroads hamlet at La Régie in Cher and took rooms at the house of the lady mayor who ran the village. Or we went shopping at La Samaritaine, where the clerks mistook us for British and because Alice carefully examined the merchandise she bought whispered that we were certainly mistrustful ones. We walked the streets looking into bookstores, and checking to see if they had on their shelves the French translations of Gertrude's work. One day our photograph was snapped by a street photographer, irritating her greatly: "Invasion of privacy!" she snapped at him in French, but I took the card and ordered several prints. Again, we went calling on a young couple she knew — the wife working in the American Embassy and the husband struggling to be a composer. "She's a great beauty," said Alice, "but he'll never make it. His stuff is too derivative." I agreed with her after hearing some of it. After all, one seldom disagreed, any more than with Gertrude.

Often during those years, Alice took me to lunch at expensive places she could not afford. One of her favorite restaurants was Les Porquerolles, where they prepared a wonderful bouillabaisse in front of your eyes. For a small woman Alice could put away an amount of food that far overreached my own capacity.

A year after Gertrude died, in 1947, I managed to stop drinking entirely — with the help of a tough-minded hard-bitten AA group in Chicago that met at the lakefront and Chicago Avenue and called itself the Water Tower Group. It included a lot of radio announcers and some genuine intellectuals, and its leading spirits were the mother and father of Marlon Brando.

My stopping pleased Alice a great deal. "But the trouble, Sammy," she said in the early 1950s, "is that during your creative years you got lost in the bottle the way so many did."

"I know," I said shamefacedly, "and there I stayed and nothing came out."

"Why did you drink, really?"

I made a hopeless gesture. "Why, indeed? Maladjusted? For the reasons the drunkard gave the little prince?"

"I don't remember them," she said.

"The drunkard said he drank to forget. To forget what? That he was ashamed. Ashamed of what? That he drank . . . It all left the little prince very melancholy."

"Do you realize, Sammy," she said, "that when Gertrude talked to you about being surrounded by drunks, and mentioned a lot of them, that she was talking directly to you?"

"Yes, I think I did."

"Both of us saw your problem but all we could do was give a little warning. How you ever managed to hold down a university professorship for so long is a mystery."

I laughed, rather hollowly. "I suppose I'm one of the few teachers who actually fell asleep once — very briefly — while lecturing. Usually it's the students."

Alice chuckled deep in her throat. "We kept worrying about you a lot," she said. "Gertrude was of the opinion you'd never write again unless you stopped. She said it devoured all passion, and yet for writers life has to revolve on passion. But a drunken writer's passion is false. It is just the counterfeit sense of power that alcohol gives."

After a moment, I said, "When Gertrude told me to stop teaching and be a butcher if I wanted to be a writer, she was right. You do use up all the word-finding part of your brain while you're lecturing. But add another strike against me that stopped the writing: if you're smashed, drunk, all the time you're not teaching, how can you write? You can't even see the typewriter keys, let alone think or find words or create."

"Well," she said, "it may begin to come out now. Look at me — I've done two books already, mostly to pass the empty time."

"It may be too late for me to begin again," I said. "I lost seventeen years."

She looked at me archly. "You really are a silly boy," she said. "I'm over thirty years older than you are, and if I can write at my age you can at yours."

She liked to live well, but there were problems. Some money came from a group of her old friends who could afford it — Virgil Thomson, Carl Van Vechten, Doda Conrad, Thornton Wilder, Donald Sutherland, and Janet Flanner. Once in a while one of the pictures in the collection disappeared; the royalties from her books were certainly not enough to keep her in the grand style to which she had long been accustomed. The old story of the shopping bags from Fauchon's, the expensive greengrocer, has often been told; the empty bags would be filled with produce from the cheaper street markets — an underhanded trick to play on her, but a necessary one.

As the years passed and the Christmas visits grew to be traditional, our relationship grew deeper, warmer, and more profound than it had been before. Much has been said of her malice; such statements seem false to me, for I saw but little change in her personality from beginning to end. She started gradually to tell me little secrets, which I always promised not to tell; and she engaged in moments of self-criticism, such as the time she confessed she had almost committed a *bêtise* — "and at my age too, Sammy," she said, chuckling quietly.

It is true that she was sharp-edged about certain things: she could not endure stupidity or gaucherie. There was a deep humor — sometimes black — to her "malice"; you laughed at what she said — it was hard to take offense. It is true, too, that there were quarrels and "Byzantine intrigues" between Gertrude and the others, or between Alice and others — but there was always a good reason for the complete break, and the cause usually lay on the other side, not Alice's. It was likewise true that she was not more or less human than any of us: offend her deeply and that was the end of your relationship with her. In the last years especially, her heart was open and giving, and the charities she performed for her friends were widespread and sincere, although they could not involve money.

Obviously there were things she did not like and could not ever stand — drunkenness being one of them. The great fight with Hemingway is traceable to the night he showed up completely intoxicated at Gertrude's salon and had to be forcibly ejected by two men, one of whom was my own professor, Clarence Andrews. Hemingway publicly vowed he would get even with Gertrude and Alice for ordering his departure, and he tried to get his revenge in *A Moveable Feast,* but she survived his slanders well enough. As a matter of fact, she had the last word: in the 1960s Alice was interviewed by German television for a special program devoted to Sylvia Beach's Shakespeare and Company. During the interview, Alice was asked about Hemingway's remarks about her in his posthumous book. "That is a private matter," she said. The interviewer persisted: "The world says that Gertrude Stein influenced Hemingway a great deal."

And in one of the classic lines of insult, with an inflection of boredom and indifference combined in her own special way, Alice replied, "Oh, Hemingway was a horror." No more was said on the subject.

To protect and preserve this deep friendship which existed between Alice and me, I did everything I could for her, and she reciprocated by loving me in the gentle fashion that a woman in her eighties can bestow on a person three decades younger.

Often, in the years that passed, I thought of these two women and their influence on me. Certainly when I was young I was grateful for the gift of their friendship and affection. The glow that came from knowing them surrounded me in my teaching days and I did little to dispel it. My university students considered me glamorous because I knew Gertrude and Alice, and I did nothing to upset the legend that grew around me, helped along by a facile tongue and innuendo in class, a jokingly cynical attitude toward life and myself, and a past which suggested the darkly mysterious. When stories were created about me, I smiled and let them run their course.

But it is surely not true to say that I ever traded on — or *used* — my friendship with Gertrude and Alice in any way. I honestly loved them and loved them honestly. And as we all grew older and the friendship turned to love and deepened, they became a very real part of my life — more important to me than my diminished family. A friend once said that my relationship with them had a kind of Greek balance to it, always with the human qualities in the foreground. After

Gertrude's death, when the great warm heart was stilled, Alice and I came closer because Gertrude drew us together; our love for her found a new reality in our mutual affection. I was one of the "welcome old ones," as Gertrude called those from the days before the war of the 1940s.

Nothing in my life has ever had any more real meaning for me than my knowing these two, and to the end their presence will still be tenderly and happily alive for me.

Once during the late 1950s Alice invited me to lunch at the Méditerranée, one of the great restaurants of Paris in the Place de l'Odéon, not far from Sylvia Beach's bookstore. The time set was one in the afternoon; I was a little early, and Alice late. The maître d'hôtel, learning that I was waiting for someone, showed me to a small bench with a table, close to the outer door, and closer even to the area where the food was being prepared. His manner was courteous, but to him I was a stranger not to be overly pampered.

It must have been fifteen minutes before the door opened and there stood Alice, dressed in a long heavy black fur coat that must have weighed half as much as she did. On her head was a pointed fur hat, very sleek, so that she reminded one somewhat of a mountain troll.

"Ah, there you are," she said, and came toward me. The maître d'hôtel saw her at the same time and rushed in her direction. "Ah, Mademoiselle," he said, "how good of you to grace us with your presence once more." His manner toward me changed instantly when he realized that we were together.

"Shall we sit inside, Sammy — or here?" she asked in English.

"Wherever you want, my dear."

"Let's sit then where you were sitting," she said. "It's cooler, and I won't have to take my coat off."

Workmen had been running around with planks and fixtures. "They're adding another room — business is good," Alice said, drawing off her black kid gloves. "This is really a very famous restaurant. All of us used to come here — Pablo, Bébé Bérard, Lord Berners, Gertrude, and all the rest. They then had the best seafood in town."

From our position we could watch the intricacies of the

food being prepared. Alice watched the chef. "He's fairly good," she said after a time. "Very skillful with the mechanics — crêpes and that sort of thing."

She turned to me. "And what have you been doing this morning?"

"I got up very late, had my croissant and coffee — that's all. And you?"

"Oh, I've been all over town, shopping. So many things to get for so many people." She picked up the menu. "What shall we have to eat? Seafood . . . oh, they have jugged hare! It's usually delicious here."

Jugged hare it was then, for both of us. Meanwhile the workmen passed back and forth. "I suppose it can't be helped," she sighed. "They have to work."

The hare arrived, and Alice relished her first taste of it. "Ah-h," she said, with a tremendous sigh of approval.

At that moment the foreman of the workers approached her, beret in hand, and started to speak to her in French.

"Mademoiselle," he was saying, and with that she extended her left hand with the tremendous oval ring set with gleaming topazes for him to kiss — which he did lightly. "Mademoiselle, I am only a humble worker but I have seen you here many times and at the opera and elsewhere, and I hope that you will permit me to thank you for bringing to our city the luster that you and Mademoiselle Stein brought for so many years. And we thank you for living among us." He bowed his head again over her hand, and was gone.

"Wh-what was that all about?" I stammered.

"Ah," said Alice, "he was remembering the old days." And the hare cooled on her plate while she looked off into the distance, beyond the chef, outside the windows.

Suddenly it was too much. The whole world coalesced, drew down to a point, and I realized that I was sitting here beside one of the historic figures of the century. I started to weep silently, and Gertrude was in my tears as much as Alice. I did not want her to notice my lack of control. Soon she picked up her knife and fork and started once more to eat, still silent. I did the same, but I could not see what I was cutting or eating. I kept turning my face away from her and wiping my eyes with the handkerchief in my breast pocket. It took me a full five minutes to get hold of myself, and the taste was gone from the food for me.

Finally she slid her hand over mine, beneath the table. "Sammy," she said, "now stop it this instant." The gesture nearly wrecked my hard-gained control. "There is nothing that can be done about it," she said, "and we who are left behind can only wait."

"Well," I said, "it was one of the nicest tributes that anyone could give."

"Yes, it was nice," she said.

It was a long leisurely lunch, ending with crêpes, and afterward I took Alice back to the rue Christine with her bundles. She asked me to return the following day.

I arrived at four o'clock, the appointed time. Madeleine cheerfully let me in and showed me into the room. Alice soon appeared.

It was chilly in the salon. I looked at the nonflaming heater that burned kerosene. "I believe it's gone out," I said.

Alice shivered slightly. "Yes, it does seem so," she said. "Would you mind terribly filling it? The kerosene is in the Salon des Refusées in front of that stack of Francis's pictures. Madeleine should have done it."

"I'll do it," I said. I got the kerosene and carefully poured it in. "It's a wonderful contraption," she said. "It works like those hand warmers that you take to football games in the States, and when you go hunting."

The heat soon made itself felt in the room, along with a faint odor.

"And now," she said while I lighted a cigarette for her, "I have some things for you." There were several objects on the floor beside her chair.

"First of all, this," she said, handing me an embossed silver box, rather tarnished, with a rose decoration on one side of it. The bottom fell off as I handled it.

"Ah yes, you'll have to have it fixed," she said. "It was Gertrude's stamp box." Then she held up a tie-dyed scarf of orange beige color, with a geometric and flower design. "And this too — it was her favorite scarf. And also —" She held up an ancient picture frame that seemed to contain a sheet of blank paper. "We found this frame — it's double-glassed, you see — one day on the *quais* along the Seine. It dates from about the middle of the eighteenth century.

"And what is that inside it?"

"You have to hold it to the light," she said. "It's a pinprick portrait of Voltaire with his little dog behind him. It was done by the nuns of Cirey in the eighteenth century before they discovered how anticlerical Voltaire was and what things he was going to say and write about them."

"Haven't I seen this reproduced in *Paris France?*" I asked, holding it to the light.

"Not exactly the same one," Alice said. "This was our treasure."

She was quiet for a moment. "Francis always wanted it," she said, "but the door is no longer open to him. It just got to be too much," and she recited a long list of his escapades, ending with, "and so he is banished, and is now designing wallpaper somewhere in England, Brighton, I think."

"Things might have been different had Gertrude been able to make him famous, as she helped Picasso."

Alice sighed. "Who can say?"

Then something began obscurely to worry me. By 1958 the eight volumes of the Yale edition of Gertrude's unpublished work had appeared — and now Alice was giving away the treasures. She had always said she would stay alive until the final publication of Gertrude's work, and one rarely gave away mementos except when death was anticipated.

". . . er . . ." I said. "How's your health in general, my dear?"

Again she looked out the window. "It's perfectly all right," she said. "Do you think I'm giving you these things because I think I'm going to die?"

Sometimes her candor, even her bluntness, was disconcerting. ". . . uh . . . the thought had crossed my mind," I said, being equally blunt.

"Nonsense," she said. "When it's time for me to go I'll go. But I wanted to be sure you got these things instead of those . . . Steins. Especially Roubina."

"Aren't families awful?"

"Necessary, but almost always awful," she said. "How's yours?"

"There aren't many left," I said. "I'm closest to my sister — and that only because we live far apart."

"It's the best thing to do," she said, nodding slowly.

"How can I ever thank you for all these things?" I asked.

"Just go on being Sammy," she said. "Our 'silly bashful boy' — although you're not a boy any longer. When was it we first met?"

"Nineteen thirty-seven," I said, "although we began to write in nineteen thirty-three."

"Did you send all of Gertrude's letters to Yale, as I asked you to do?"

"I kept some of the postcards," I said, "but the rest went, and all the cards will eventually."

Alice laughed. "My, hasn't the talk grown morbid! Let us turn to something a bit gayer."

For the life of me I couldn't think of a happy thing to say.

But she did. "How are the bedbugs at the Récamier this year?" she asked. "Are they all gone?"

"Every last one of them as far as my room is concerned," I chuckled. "The people over there are always very nice to me, probably because you and I are friends and you and Gertrude first sent me there. They always give me a room with a view of the square."

"And the bells of St. Sulpice bounce you out of bed every Sunday."

"At least three feet," I laughed.

"How does it happen you always come over at Christmastime?" Alice asked. "You used to come in the summers and just settle down into the life of Paris."

"Well, there's no business in my shop at Christmas," I said, and shifted uneasily in the chair.

"Your shop — what do you mean?" she demanded. "Aren't you still teaching at the university?"

"No," I said, "I never wrote to you about it because I wanted to tell you face to face."

"Well?" she said.

I was uncomfortable. "Well, I . . . uh . . . saw the . . . about nineteen fifty-four, that is . . . I saw the student revolts coming and I didn't know how long it would take for them to explode but I didn't want to be there when they did. So I studied under one of the old masters and opened a shop where I give" — I could hardly say the word — "tattoos."

I must say that nothing in the world bothered Alice. "Cocteau experimented with them for a while," she said. "Do you make much money at it?"

"On the day my weekly take equaled my monthly salary at the university," I said, "I tore up my Ph.D. diploma."

"Now that was silly," Alice scolded. "You might want to go back some day."

I shook my head. "Never."

Alice harrumphed. "Never say 'never,' " she said. "A day might come . . ."

"I'd stand in a bread line first," I said emphatically. "Higher education has failed in the States."

There was a silence. "The first of the . . . dropouts," she said, by chance using an expression that would not be current until much later.

"I suppose so," I said.

"Were you terribly unhappy teaching?"

"Yes, toward the last," I said. "Gertrude told me many years ago that I couldn't write and teach at the same time."

"Ah yes," she said, "and now do you find that you can produce?"

"A little," I said. "I sold my first story a month ago."

"Gertrude might have been disturbed if she knew about your shop," Alice said.

"A lot of persons were," I said. "All my colleagues at the university were shocked, and even the unshockable great Doctor Kinsey said, 'Oh, Sam — be careful!' "

"What kind of clients do you have?" she asked.

"Mostly young navy boys from Great Lakes Naval Training Station," I said, "and then the lower-class city boys with that terrible blinding beauty of the uneducated. I kept a journal for Kinsey and for two years after he died, a total of eight years, beginning right when I started . . . the business — about a quarter of a million words."

Alice said, "My! that's a lot of writing!" Then she thought a moment. "Why do people get tattooed?"

"I found thirty-two motivations," I said, "everything from an assertion of masculine status to Sartre's 'forever-act.' "

"On second thought," Alice said, "I think Gertrude would've been fascinated."

"It might have depended on how orthodox she was."

"Completely, but of course she didn't practice it at all."

"According to Leviticus," I said, "a Jew cannot have any marks on his body. It's tied up with the mark of Cain. And if an Orthodox Jew dies and has a tattoo on him, the rabbi has to cut it off before burial."

Alice shifted in her chair. "Are you sure about all this?"

"Yes," I said, "I did some research. But what amuses me most is the young Catholic sailors who say they'd like to have one but their religion forbids it. Then I quote the New Testament to them, the place in Apocalypse or Revelation where the angel of the word of God appears and says, 'For I have on my vesture and on my thigh a name written: King of Kings and Lord of Lords,' and then I say 'If it's good enough for the Angel of the Lord, why not for you?' and that always confuses them a great deal."

Alice chuckled. "I should imagine. It even confuses me. The whole thing is wonderful. My," she said softly, "I do wish Gertrude could have heard this."

"But," she added, "you sit up very straight in that chair, and tell me exactly why you abandoned literature for tattooing."

I made a helpless gesture as I straightened myself. "You ask me a very complicated question I'm not even sure I can answer exactly."

She looked at me severely. "Is it a part of the self-destructive urge you seem to have?"

"No, no — I hope I don't have one of those. It's just that . . . well, after twenty years teaching became really unbearable. The last five years were loathsome. I sometimes had to take half an amphetamine tablet in the mornings before I could face the classes. The students got progressively worse as the years went by, and without alcohol I had to keep looking at the ugly pimpled face of reality all the time. I used to give little oral quizzes when I had to teach freshman English — they didn't even know they were being quizzed. But I'd ask humanities questions and then . . . mechanical or technical ones."

"Were you testing backgrounds?" she asked.

"Yes. And finally one year there came a class in which not one person had ever heard of Homer . . . but three fourths of them knew how to change a sparkplug."

"That's hardly reason enough to throw away a lifetime's work," she said, frowning.

"Alice," I said, almost desperately. "Hadn't I justified my existence? In the first ten years of teaching I'd come in contact with about five thousand students, and I hope I helped some of them to see light. Then I worked on rewriting that encyclopedia for two years, remember — and those new articles, soundly critical and done from a modern point of view, were going to be influencing kids for the next twenty years. Then I taught for ten more years — five thousand more students. Couldn't I stop something I had come to hate?"

"Yes," she said. "But . . . tattooing! It seems so far away from . . . from teaching."

"As far as I could get from *Akadēmia,*" I said. "A new world. A sleazy fascinating new world. Profitable, too. My own boss. I deliberately looked for the most outrageous occupation."

"Self-destruction?" she asked.

I laughed. "Why say that? I was answering very real needs of inarticulate people. And having more fun than ever before. I actually liked going to work every day. It was a continuing theater. And I really helped a few in the process — advice and all that. Besides, I was cautious enough. I overlapped tattooing and teaching for two years until I saw that I could make a living at it. Furthermore, the students were getting restless —"

"So you said. In what way?" she asked.

"An example. Once I announced a quiz for the next day. A young smart aleck said, 'Doctor Steward, since we live in a democracy, why don't we take a vote on whether we want one?' I looked at him, called him by name, and said: 'When you enrolled in this university, certain of your democratic rights were automatically suspended. There'll be a quiz tomorrow.' "

"A hard man," Alice chuckled.

"So it was really to save myself that I quit teaching. Going on with it might even have started me drinking once more."

"On that note," she said, "we'll stop. I'll never complain again about anything you do. I guess you know what you want."

In the late 1950s I asked Alice if I might bring along a friend of mine, Rudolf Jung, the English editor of a trilingual magazine that had taken some of my stories and essays.

"By all means," Alice said. "I should be delighted to meet him if he's a friend of yours, despite the fact that he's German."

"His geographical home may be Germany," I said, "but he's either British or American in spirit — more the latter. He was a money courier for the German resistance against Hitler."

"All the more reason to see him then," Alice said. A date was arranged.

Rudolf had a very pleasant personality, and could spread honey expertly. Alice received us graciously.

Rudolf spoke of his admiration for Gertrude until I gave him a warning glance; Alice could take just so much mention of Gertrude at one time. Then Rudolf shifted his talk and started to comment on the paintings, showing so much sensitivity and appreciation that Alice was thoroughly delighted.

She finally turned to me. "I had a manuscript for you to read, Sammy. It had a lot of material about tattooing in it, but I swear I have lost it somewhere, and haven't the *weeni*est notion where it may be."

I have never had any experience of a psychic nature whatsoever, but at that moment I *felt* the book behind my back, in the huge heavy Spanish table — with doors beneath — that was in the room.

"It's Madeleine's day to go shopping," Alice said, "so if you will excuse me a few minutes I'll brew the tea and fetch the cakes." She left the room.

I quickly leaned back to open the lower door in the table, and there was the manuscript. Rudolf was aghast at my boldness.

"But how are you ever going to get her to look in there?" he asked.

"Trust me," I said, "I'll find a way."

Alice came back with the tea and the miniature fruitcakes she had made. We sat and talked for a while longer, and then I said, "My dear, have you ever tried the dowser method to find that lost manuscript?"

"The dowser?" Alice said, puzzled. "You mean finding water with a twig? Ah, but there isn't a twig within a kilometer of the rue Christine."

"No," I said, "there's another way, using the same principle. You tie a string to the middle of a pencil and then your subconscious tells you where the object is."

"I never heard of such nonsense," Alice said. But she was rummaging through the papers on her table for a pencil. "Will a bit of yarn do?"

Poor Rudolf was turning red in the face to keep from laughing.

"Of course," I said.

She found both pencil and yarn. I tied the yarn to the middle of the pencil so that it hung horizontally and kept the end of the yarn between thumb and forefinger. "And now," I said, "you must put your hand on top of mine, and think very hard about the manuscript and where it might be."

She did, and with a slow imperceptible movement I twisted the yarn ever so slightly until the pencil was pointing directly toward the Spanish table. Then I looked at the furniture. "You see?" I said. "It's there. May I open it?"

"But of course," Alice said, extremely interested. I opened the door and pulled the manuscript from the shelf. "There," I said, "the lost is found."

"Well, I never would have believed it," Alice said, peering at the manuscript. "Yes, you're right — this is the one I wanted you to read. Now how in the world did that happen?"

Rudolf was seized with a fit of coughing and choking, unable to contain himself any longer. I looked at him solicitously. "Shall I beat you on the back?" I asked. He shook his head.

Alice looked thoughtful for a moment. "Sammy," she said, "if it worked for the manuscript, I wonder if it would work for a check for fifty dollars that I lost some time ago?"

This time Rudolf was really seized with a fit of strangling.

"Where did you see the check last?" I asked Alice.

"It was right here on my table." I saw the pile of papers, and the wastebasket just beside the table.

"Well, we can try," I said. Rudolf was making so much noise between coughing and strangling I thought he might have to leave the room.

We fixed the dowser again and she put her hand on top of mine once more. With a bit of manipulation I managed to get the pencil to point toward the wastebasket, and a little downward.

"That's evidently where it went," I said, "into the wastebasket. You'll just have to tell them the check is lost and ask for another."

"I rather imagined I'd thrown it away," Alice said reflectively, and the talk turned to other things.

When we got outside Rudolf said, "How could you have done such a thing to poor Alice?"

"Well, no harm done, was there?" I said. "And I really did want to read the manuscript."

"I thought the end of the world had come," Rudolf said, still laughing, "when she asked you to find the check she'd lost."

"So did I," I said. "It was all I could do to keep from confessing on the spot."

"Well, you're right," Rudolf said. "No harm done, and a lovely afternoon."

Rudolf Jung was involved, too, in another episode with Alice during the fateful winter when she went to Rome. She was spending some months in a convent run by the Canadian Sisters of the Adoration of the Precious Blood, and the Stein family succeeded in having Gertrude's collection in the rue Christine declared a national treasure left unprotected. They obtained the legal papers necessary to confiscate it, and moved it in toto, first to the Palais de l'Elysée, and then to the vaults of the Chase Manhattan Bank. Of course, none of this legal maneuvering was known to Alice at the time, and it was characteristic of her, when she returned to the bare walls of the apartment in Paris, to say: "Oh, well, my eyes have grown so bad I really could not have seen the paintings anyway . . . but I keep them in my head."

And it was true that her eyes were bad. Her handwriting had become large and sprawling, instead of the delicate spidery stuff she used to spin. A note from her in Rome reached me in Chicago toward the end of 1960, so that Christmas I did not stop in Paris but went straight to Zurich where I met Rudolf, and together we set out to spend a couple of weeks in Rome. We established ourselves in a middle-class hotel and went wandering that first day, a Sunday, loving the fountains that confronted us at every turn, the mingling of the classical with the new, the ocher color and beauty of the city, and the Roman sun.

Our ramblings took us to the foot of the Via Veneto and we started the climb up the street, on the side of the Hotel Excelsior. A few cafés beyond the hotel we decided to sit down for coffee, relaxing lazily in the sunlight and inhaling the good odors of Rome.

"I must really give Alice a ring," I said, "and tell her I'm here, and make an arrangement to see her."

"She doesn't know yet you're in Rome?" Rudolf asked.

"No — I didn't tell her when I'd arrive, just that I'd be here."

Suddenly a Roman taxi stopped directly across the sidewalk from our table, beyond the grass plot that edged the street. The driver hurried around to open the door, and out stepped Alice.

I was more than dumfounded. "Come," said Rudolf, "she sees us."

I threw the appropriate lire on the table and hastened toward her. She was wearing, even in that weather, the same heavy black fur coat and pointed fur hat that she had worn at the Méditerranée in Paris.

"Alice!" I hollered, just as she was about to turn. Rudolf had been wrong; she may have looked in our direction but she had not seen us, not with her eyesight as poor as it had become.

At that moment I reached her and we kissed on both cheeks, Rudolf standing a respectful distance behind me. I said, "You remember Rudolf, don't you? I brought him once to the salon in Paris."

"Ah, yes," she said, extending her hand, and Rudolf bent over it.

"For heaven's sake, when did you get here, Sammy?" Alice asked.

"Just last evening," I said, "and believe it or not, I had just finished saying to Rudolf, when your taxi drove up, that I must give you a ring today."

"Well, you wouldn't have found me there," she said. "I was just across the street buying a pot of flowers for the John Browns. He's the cultural attaché here, you know, and a dear friend."

I couldn't help saying it, and immediately wished I had not. "You mean . . . you took a taxi just to cross the street?"

She laid her hand on my arm. "My eyes, Sammy — they're not all they should be."

"Well, you have a couple of seeing-eye dogs now," I said. "Where do you want to go?"

She pointed to a café a door or two away. "I must buy two boxes of sweets for the Brown children," she said, leaning heavily on my arm as we started. "They make the best candy in Rome here."

The café entrance to the street was one door; inside it were two entrances, the candy shop on the left. But Alice turned to the right, to a narrow glass-enclosed sidewalk café filled with people, a row of tables on each side of a narrow aisle. Puzzled, and wondering if she wanted coffee, I nonetheless said nothing for I imagined she knew where she was going. She started down the narrow aisle with me behind and Rudolf following. To my dismay I saw that she was heading straight for the blank wall at the end of the aisle.

She saw it then too. "Oh bother," she said. "We've gone the wrong way."

The Romans clustered at their tables were fascinated with our strange procession, and the remarks they were making were not very nice. How to get out of the aisle was a problem. Both Rudolf and I found ourselves squeezing between the tables so that Alice could go first, and go she did with serenity and great dignity. She gave no sign she had heard any comments.

We finally freed ourselves from the cul-de-sac, and I was sweating. Alice saw the door to the candy shop and started toward it, while I assisted her up the two steps.

Her appearance in the heavy black fur coat made one or

two of the female clerks behind the counter giggle, until I glared at them.

Alice spoke in English with almost an attitude of "Be damned to you if you don't understand it."

They didn't. There was a hurried consultation and finally an older woman came forth, to ask in a heavy accent what she could do for Madame.

"In the first place," Alice snapped, "you can call me Mademoiselle." The trip through the café had evidently irritated her more than she showed.

"Yes, Mademoiselle," said the clerk politely.

"I would like to send two boxes of sweets to the children of John Brown," and she gave the clerk their names, which were dutifully written on cards.

"And the address, Mademoiselle?" asked the woman.

Alice fumbled in her purse and then looked stricken. "Oh," she said, "I left it across the street at the flower shop." Then rallying, she said, "But you must certainly have a street directory here."

Two young men had suddenly appeared, very elegant and wearing carnations. "But of course, Mademoiselle," said one of them who must have been the manager, and snapped his fingers. Another young man went running and returned with a huge directory.

"And the name is —?" asked the bright young man.

"Brown, John Brown," said Alice, and spelled it. By this time the manager had rushed somewhere and got a chair for Alice, a huge episcopal armchair like a bishop's throne, with a tall back. Alice sat down gratefully.

There was a hurried consultation. Another young man appeared with a telephone directory.

"I am sorry, Mademoiselle," said the manager. "There is no John Brown listed in either volume."

"Perhaps it will be under the embassy," I suggested hopefully.

"No, he has his own villa," said Alice, her irritation slowly growing. "I do know he's here in Rome. I just sent a pot of flowers to him and his wife."

Then a thought struck her and she turned to me. "Now you can do something," she said slowly and deliberately. "Go to the flower shop across the street, Sammy, and ask them for

John Brown's address. Tell them I just sent a pot of flowers to him and the Signora Brown."

The outside air was decidedly cool on my hot face. I crossed the street and located the flower shop. A buxom red-faced woman, looking like the Widow Roux at Bilignin, let me copy down the address, and sweating, I hurried back across the street with it.

This time there was such a crowd in the candy shop, nearly all of them thumbing through directories, that it was hard to find Alice. But Rudolf stood guard beside her chair and I pushed through the crowd.

"I have it!" I hollered above the racket, waving the piece of paper.

"Let me see it!" the manager cried, pushing through. He took it from my hand. Then he struck his palm against his forehead and said, "But of course! I know exactly where it is."

"A lot of fuss and feathers," said Alice calmly. She opened her bag, took out a ten thousand lire note, and paid for the candy. Gradually the underlings and clerks faded away, until only the manager and ourselves were left.

"We thank you, Mademoiselle," the manager said, bowing.

Alice descended from her pinnacle a little. "You have been very gracious," she said, "and after all, your sweets are the best in Rome."

"Thank you very much, Mademoiselle," the manager said, and we escaped into the open air.

There were other adventures in Rome with Alice. In 1958 she had returned to the Catholic Church, surprising a great many people. In her letter announcing this to me she said that there had been no trouble at all, and that the nice young priest in Paris assured her that when the moment came, she would be able to talk to Gertrude again.

In the winter of 1960 I squired her to Saint Peter's and then for a slow walk through parts of the Vatican Museum, all the while feeling that perhaps it was for the last time, a feeling I am convinced she shared.

John XXIII was then Pope, and Alice had known him well while he had been apostolic nuncio in Paris, before his elevation.

"Do you know," she said in her slow way, "that after John

became Pope, someone came to him and said, 'Are you going to keep up the practice of Pius XII and bless the multitudes twice a day from the balcony?' said John said, 'Indeed I am not' — twiddling his fingers at them — 'what do you think I am — a cuckoo clock?' "

We both laughed aloud until a guard near the door of the Sistine Chapel (for we were in the long tapestry-hung corridor that led to it) put a cautionary finger to his lips. We went into the chapel and looked at the ceiling together. I rented a mirror for Alice, who found it tiring to bend her neck to look up. Just how much of it she was able to see with the cataracts clouding her vision, I do not know. And after the Sistine Chapel, she had a desire to see Michelangelo's naked Christ standing beside the cross, so we went to the Church of Santa Maria sopra Minerva for a look at it. But since it was the Christmas season the nuns had draped a piece of purple cloth from the hip across the genitals, an absurdity that both Alice and myself found ludicrous.

Then there was a jet-set party for her, lionizing her as much as Gertrude had ever been. I was uncomfortable among all the handsome young men of Rome with their skinny shoes and narrow ties and silk suits — a *marchetta* here, a *marchetta* there — the too-beautiful young men too young for the middle-aged women they escorted, but after dinner I took a position at Alice's feet and did not move the whole evening. We left at two-thirty in the morning.

"Oh, oh, I'll be in trouble," Alice said as we taxied under a full moon down the empty Roman boulevards. "I'll have to ring and get poor little Sister Clothilde out of bed to open the gate."

I stood at the outside iron gate until she was safely in the convent. The taxi bill that night was enormous, but her footman paid it willingly.

She wore very well the mantle of royalty and graciousness. Those in Paris who recognized her bowed in the streets, or kissed her hand. Her smallness made me bend nearly double sometimes to hear what she was saying. Perhaps toward the end she grew hard of hearing, as Gertrude had been. Old age was wrecking her physically, with her arthritis and her dim eyes, but she never complained about her ailments — it was not the thing to do, and she was always a gentlewoman.

I had become acquainted in Paris with Jacques Delarue, the liaison officer between the Sûreté Nationale and the Préfecture de Police, who had written a serious book about prison tattooing, *Le Tatouage du "Milieu."* Delarue one day was to take me to his home in Le Pecq to meet his wife and children. A conflict of appointments made it necessary for him to call at Alice's apartment for me. This he did, saying when he met Alice the only sentence in English he knew: "I do not speak very well the English."

Wherewith Alice launched into a long laudatory account in French of Bernard Faÿ, still in trouble over his alleged collaboration during World War II. Monsieur Delarue was vastly embarrassed, I think, because his sphere of influence did not extend to the freeing of political prisoners; I was a little embarrassed too, feeling that it was hardly the time or place for her exculpation of Bernard Faÿ — but it did show the bulldog tenacity and loyalty of Alice when her friends were concerned.

As the years passed and the end drew near, many of Alice's stories began to take on what in America is called the "shaggy dog" quality — endless stories with many small details leading nowhere, or to a point that made a listener silently groan; and her speech yearly grew slower and slower.

Here is one of those stories, set down almost verbatim from my notes:

"There was a man in Chicago, Sammy," she said. "No, I won't tell you his name because you might know him or run into him and let something slip sometime. Anyway, he had often heard of the numbered Swiss bank accounts, and he wanted one, not to cheat the government so much (although he didn't like the taxes any more than anyone over in the States does) but because he hated the Internal Revenue Service and he thought his money was being taxed twice — once when the taxes were withheld from his wages and then again when the bank interest was taxed. Well, he got together ten thousand dollars in hundred dollar bills — you see, he wasn't really a very rich man — and then he took a dollar bill for measuring purposes down to Marshall Field's department store in Chicago and went to the imported candy counter and found that a block of dark chocolate called 'Térésina' (it's delicious — have you ever tasted it?) which is made by I think Tobler in Switzerland just exactly fitted the size of his dollar bill, so he bought two bars of the candy and took them home and carefully unwrapped them and ate the candy, I suppose, and then fitted his hundred dollar bills back into the wrappings for the Térésina bars and sealed them ever so carefully again and put them in his suitcase.

"Well, he was going to stop off in Paris for a couple of weeks and he was staying at a small hotel on the rue de Four where the *patron* did not look very honest and the chambermaid less so, so he decided that they might want some chocolate and take his precious Térésina wrappers and find out what was really in them and he couldn't think of anything to do except rent a safe-deposit box, a *coffre-fort,* at the Crédit Lyonnais, the one on the rue de Rennes I think, or perhaps the rue Madame. So he took his candy bars and his passport and went over and applied for a safe-deposit box. The *garde* was one of those typical old Frenchmen with a huge handlebar mustache, and there were endless forms to fill out, even including things like I suppose was your grandmother left-handed, but after about an hour all the forms were filled out in quintuplicate or however many there were, and then the *garde* said to the man, 'And now, Monsieur, I must see three pieces of identity,' and the man was astonished and said, 'But is not the passport enough? Look, there is my picture, my signature.' But the *garde* was firm about it and said no, so the man went away and back to his hotel and rummaged and looked and searched and he finally found a social security card and a hospital card of some kind, neither of which is any proof of your identity but he took them back and the *garde* was satisfied then and said, 'That will be six thousand, six hundred francs a year,' and the man was surprised and said, 'But I thought you said it was only six hundred francs a year' (which was then about a dollar and a quarter or a half or some ridiculous amount like that because it was in the days before the franc was revalued). And the *garde* smiled and said, 'Ah yes, but the six thousand is a deposit on the key and will be returned to you when you return the key, so you must guard it carefully,' and the man looked at the key which was very old and intricate with many wards, and it was still not very much money and the man paid it, and then the *garde* pressed a button and they went downstairs to the safe-deposit boxes which were in a twenty-foot-high room, and the *garde* moved a stepladder with wheels over to a row of vaults and climbed up and opened one, and it really was a vault, big enough almost to contain a body, and then the *garde* climbed down and the man climbed up and the *garde* watched while the man pulled his two candy bars out of his pocket and dropped them on the floor of the huge vault and then locked the door and climbed down. The *garde*'s eyes were almost popping out of his head and he said, 'But is that all that Monsieur wishes to deposit?' and the man said yes, at the moment it was all, leaving the *garde* mystified and muttering something about 'these mad Americans.'

"And in two weeks the man went back and saw the *garde* again who said, 'Ah, it is the American with the candy bars!' and the man smiled and said yes, he wanted them now, and so the *garde* went downstairs with him again and moved the stepladder again and the man climbed up and got the candy bars and the *garde* said, 'But Monsieur has the rental for a full year,' and the man smiled and said, 'Well you can rent it to someone else again or else keep your lunch in there,' and the *garde* this time was really convinced that the man was crazy because the man gave him a five hundred franc tip, which was then about a dollar."

There was something almost biblical about her slow rate of delivery in those last years.

"And I suppose he lost the candy bars on the way to Zurich or wherever he was going," I said.

Alice's eyes sparkled with delight. "No, not at all," she said. "He got there with the money, only to discover that in that year the Swiss had so much money in their banks that they charged him one percent per annum just to hold it for him!" And she laughed deep in her throat.

The whole story must have taken her forty-five minutes to tell, but when you are sitting beside history, you do not fidget.

After the apartment at 5 rue Christine had been stripped of all its paintings, Alice was eventually evicted from it in 1964, and friends found her an apartment in what she called a "hideously modern" building in a quarter on the Left Bank where it did not seem proper for her to be at all — 16 rue de la Convention. I visited her last on a bleak December day, and a small Spanish girl came to the door to let me in.

"Mademoiselle is not feeling well today," she said softly. "May we ask Monsieur not to stay too long?"

"Of course," I said. The huge dark heavy Spanish furniture had been moved from the rue Christine; it was so large that it filled nearly all the place, leaving you about twelve inches to squeeze by. The maid showed me into Alice's bedroom.

I was more than shocked by her appearance — her eyes sunken, her face emaciated. But the indomitable spirit was still there — and she was sitting up in bed, clothed in a blue bed jacket.

"How do you like the new place?" she asked after our greetings.

"Superb," I lied.

"You do not," she said briefly. "Nor do I. But you can look down from the bedroom window at the chapel. I've never been in it, but a charming young priest brings me communion every day."

"That's nice," I said uncomfortably. "By the way, I think I didn't thank you for the copy of *What is Remembered*. It was very moving, and I liked it a lot."

"It should have been better," Alice said. "But I was . . . so tired when I wrote it, and I forgot so many things. And let's face it, Sammy, there isn't much more time, and almost everything has been said."

Her face brightened for a moment. "Do you remember the first kitchen gadgets you sent us? Gertrude kept them in the most precious of all places — in the atelier on top of her manuscripts. Did I ever tell you that?"

"No, you didn't, darling. But I'm glad to know it. It's proof enough to the world that Gertrude's writing meant everything to her and you. You said 'the most precious place.' "

"The world no longer thinks of her as a . . . faker," she said slowly.

"Not for one moment, ever. There is too much in her, and there still is, and it will take generations to get it out, just the way the physicists will be busy for years explaining Einstein's equation of the universe."

"I hope that her memory . . . stays green," she said. "Will you help?"

"All I can," I said. I saw the Spanish maid beckon silently, and I rose, leaning over to kiss her forehead. "I cannot stay long today, but I will be back."

"Yes," she said, her voice a little dulled. "Yes, Sammy, do come back." And then with a characteristic flash of her sometimes black humor, she said faintly, "Or do come visit both of us. You can stay with us — there's room for three. We'll all be together again."

That was in December 1966. On March 7, 1967, she moved to Père Lachaise, where she and Gertrude lay head to head.

Gertrude Stein lunching at Aix-les-Bains, 1937.

Alice B. Toklas at Aix-les-Bains, lunch under the grape arbor, 1937.

The front gate to the chateau at Bilignin.

View from the garden at Bilignin over the valley of the Ain River.

Gertrude Stein in her tomato patch, 1937.

Samuel Steward in Gertrude's tomato patch, photo by Gertrude Stein, 1937.

Gertrude Stein with Basket and, Pépé, 1937.

At Bilignin, left to right, Madeleine Daniel-Rops, Alice B. Toklas, Gertrude Stein, Henri Daniel-Rops, 1937.

Gertrude Stein with Basket, and Pépé standing on her favorite Roman column, New Artemare, 1937.

Samuel Steward on Roman column, photo by Gertrude Stein, 1937.

Henri Daniel-Rops and Père Bernardet at Hautecombe, 1937.

Basket and Gertrude Stein ponder bread at Bilignin, 1937.

Henri Daniel-Rops, Gertrude Stein, and Alice B. Toklas enjoy a shooting gallery at a country fair at Virieu-le-Grand, 1939.

Bilignin, 1939. Yves Tanguy and Alice B. Toklas at far left, Mme. André Breton, center, Gertrude Stein talking to André Breton at right, with Roberto Matta closest to camera.

Gertrude Stein and André Breton, Bilignin, 1939.

Bilignin 1939.

To Sammy

On his birthday.

For which is what it is
That which is that Sammy is
With us with our love
On his birthday.
Bless little Sammy
Which he is
All little Sammy
What he is
Which is what he is:
With us which he is
With our love
On his birthday.

Gtde.

Bilignin, 1939. Birthday poem "To Sammy" from Gertrude Stein.

Thornton Wilder in Paris, 1939.

The American Hospital in Paris where Gertrude Stein died in 1946.

Gertrude Stein's tombstone at Père Lachaise.

Alice B. Toklas at Bourges, 1950.

Samuel Steward, Basket, and Alice B. Toklas on the terrace at 5 rue Christine, Paris, 1952.

Paris, 1952. Left to right, Luis Rose (son of Francis Rose), Francis Rose, and Samuel Steward.

Paris, 1952. Esther Wilcox.

Alice and Basket at La Régie, at Soye-en-Septaine.

Samuel Steward and Francis Rose, Paris, 1954.

Samuel Steward and Alice B. Toklas on a Paris street, 1954. Photo by a street photographer.

Alice B. Toklas on the way to La Samaritaine to shop, Paris, 1954.

The Letters

Note

THESE LETTERS from Gertrude Stein and Alice B. Toklas, numbering somewhat over a hundred, have been arranged chronologically. The first ones, from 1933 until her death in 1946, are all from Gertrude Stein (one is signed with both their names), with the exception of a few letters from Alice Toklas regarding "business" matters during their tour of the United States in 1934–1935. The remaining letters, from 1946 until her own death, are from Alice B. Toklas.

Both Stein and Toklas use their own forms of punctuation, Stein usually employing commas liberally and Toklas using a short dash to separate sentences. In the Toklas letters, a small "x" sometimes marks the end of a paragraph, but some paragraphing has been done according to sense.

Parentheses where they occur in the text are Alice Toklas' own insertions; she sometimes uses (?) when she herself is not sure of a thing. Some words that are entirely indecipherable are indicated by blank spaces between brackets; dubious words are shown within brackets but are followed by a question mark, e.g., [alone?].

Minuscule in the early years, the handwriting of Alice Toklas grew gradually larger and sprawling as her eyes dimmed. Toward the end there are many omitted words and lapses; these again have been indicated by blanks within brackets.

14 December 1933
27, rue de Fleurus, Paris VI

My dear Steward

Yes I do remember Professor Claire Andrews, I often wondered what had become of him. We corresponded a long time ago for a short time and then he stopped writing, he meant a great deal to me because he was I think the first man connected with the teaching of English in an American University who took any interest in me. As I remember I saw him, did he not come over once and was he not a rather stocky shortish man with a very square head, that is at least my memory, but I am not at all sure.

I like what you have to say about the autobiography, I feel more or less that way about it myself and I will like from time to time to have a Sunday letter. When I was young I was always firmly convinced that the sun always shone on Sunday, perhaps it still does, anyway in America.

Best of the season's greetings to you
Always
Gertrude Stein.

a rather stockish shortish man: Gertrude Stein's memory was at fault here. Andrews was lean; his face drew down to a point, he had a mustache, and he was one of the two men who ejected Hemingway from Gertrude's salon, when he was drunk.

a Sunday letter: I had told her that I wrote business letters during the week, but used Sunday to write to those I admired; I had also in some detail praised *The Autobiography of Alice B. Toklas.*

19 December 1934
Deshler-Wallick Hotel
Columbus, Ohio

My dear Steward,

I had your letter last night and I was pleased and I would have been more pleased if you had been there yourself but anyway I was pleased. I liked your Columbus a lot, it is an xceedingly pleasant Columbus, and I am glad the first University understanding I ever had came from there. My address in America is always Random House 20 E 57 Street, and I am sorry you were not there last night. I cannot say that too often, but anyway we met before and we will meet again.

Always
Gertrude Stein

we met before: In letters.

20 February 1935
The Roosevelt
New Orleans, Louisiana

My dear Mr. Steward,

Your letter of the seventh of February to Miss Gertrude Stein has been following her about and only reached her yesterday. It is I who am answering it at the moment, Miss Stein will answer you as soon as she has a moment free, because it is upon me that the arrangement for her lectures has fallen.

She is more than eager to lecture at Helena, she wants to go to Helena rather than anywhere else. It is something she has never seen, something she has never seen anything like. She says this has been a visit where she does everything she has never done before. And so Helena is a possibility. But I will need some help, perhaps you will be able to help, perhaps someone you know will be able to.

We do go to California in April. The dates are still a bit vague, we think of the seventeenth as the day we planned to go back to New York. Now if we go to Helena and it is possible for you to arrange three lectures between Helena and Butte, still it is a long journey and it would have to be broken by lectures at Portland and Seattle. It has been understood that a lecture at the State University is arranged before one at a Club or Society. If that can be done for these two states why then Helena is easy. Do you know any means of approaching the English Departments of these two universities?

Perhaps it would be best that I should give you the conditions of the lectures.

The audience is strictly limited to five hundred, if tickets are sold it is not to be for the benefit of a fund or of a cause, there are no introductions, the fee is one hundred dollars for universities, colleges, and schools, two hundred and fifty dollars for clubs, etcetera.

Of course if you don't know how to reach Washington and Oregon, please don't feel that you have failed Miss Stein, something may turn up that will help, though for the moment I don't quite see from where or I should not be bothering you.

I am very sincerely yours,
Alice Toklas

5 March 1935
The Midway Drexel Apartment Hotel
6020 Drexel Avenue, Chicago

My dear Mr. Steward,

I was just about to answer your letter of the twenty-eighth when your second one came this morning.

It does look as if Miss Stein and I would make Helena, thanks to all your efforts. Miss Stein is still excited about the idea of Helena, Montana, as she calls it. And she wants to see the gold mine, the ghost city, and the Hangman's Tree. And it may all be possible. I am going to use your very good introductions at the universities of Oregon and Washington at once and see what can be done.

For a moment we will talk business. Will Carroll College sponsor a lecture, fee one hundred dollars? Will the good ladies of Helena sponsor another one, fee two hundred and fifty dollars? Two separate and distinct lectures, you understand. We want your college and I would like the ladies to cover air tickets to N.Y. Now as to the dates I must have made myself very little clear. We leave here to go to Texas on the seventeenth, we go to California for the end of the month, we stay in San Francisco until about the 16th of April. I am therefore proposing a lecture at U. of O. for about the 18th (if this is not the end of Holy Week of Easter, I am writing without a calendar), about the 20th to the U. of W. and about the 24th to Carroll College. Will you let me hear from you about Helena and C.C.

About the objection of Mr. Hughes to no benefits, I think I

may be able to win him to a purer point of view, and those of Mr. Onthank concerning limiting audience can no doubt be arranged. I hope to have answers before we leave concerning a definite date at Carroll.

G.S. is enjoying her course here enormously, four lectures and ten conferences. One lecture already and two conferences. She has written four new lectures of course:

The American Language and How It is Made
Narrative in Prose and Poetry
Is History Narrative
Is History Literature

And then there is one other How Writing is Written that she only gave once before coming south and west and has not given since. These five are what she will give for Texas and California, and let us hope Oregon, Washington, and Montana. I have always so much wanted Miss Stein to see the Northwest, where I spent four happy years.

I hope I have made myself a little clear, there is much noise about me. And please believe me very appreciatively,

Very sincerely yours,
A. B. Toklas

P.S. G.S. sends you kindest remembrances.

Hughes . . . and Onthank: Richard Hughes wanted the Stein lecture to benefit his local United Charities; Onthank wanted a huge audience at $5.00 per person.
four happy years: Alice graduated from the University of Washington.

15 March 1935
Drexel Apartments,
Chicago, Illinois

Mr dear Mr. Steward,

Thank you so much for your letter of the ninth and for all you are doing. I might be more exact and gracious if I said "have done." Missoula, U. of M[ontana] have already written and of course we go there; arrangements quite satisfactory for everyone more than probable. U. of W[ashington], likewise. And Carroll definite, is it not. Please do not be a miserable man about my dullness, U. of M. pleases GS. ever so much more than any ladies, even those of Helena, new pronunciation included. And please do write to Portland about a club lecture. GS. prefers men in the audience to only women if there should happen to be such a club in Portland.

The lectures and conferences ended here yesterday, they went off very well. GS. had a furiously good time with the students here, she will tell you all about them and their work. The Prex. has asked her to come back next year. We leave Sunday for Texas, until the 20th c/o The Hockaday College, Dallas, and then c/o Mrs Maurice McCashan Jr., 3376 Inwood Drive, Houston until the 24th, after that???, I'll send you one before Calif. as soon as there is one.

Please don't let Carl's habit of mixing up over enthusiastic admiration with friendship mislead you, the only part you can count upon is my presence of all the extravagances he wrote.

GS. will write you from Texas, but sends you warm greetings in the meantime.

I am ever yours sincerely,
A. B. Toklas

new pronunciation: Stein and Toklas had always said Hell-EE-nuh; I corrected it to HELL-uh-nuh.

24 March 1935
Houston, Texas

My dear Mr. Steward,

Alas, alas, all our plans for a northern trip have gone wrong. I had a wire from U. of W. saying they did not see their way to sponsor a lecture, U. of O. does not answer, and nothing from the U. of M. So the adventure of a visit to the northwest is not for us. And most of all we regret the excitement of seeing you, Carroll College, and Hel'ena Montana as an unrealised dream. I had wanted GS. so very much to have seen all that northwestern country, perhaps another time, for in the beginning that is when we first landed I said I wanted to stay on and not go back to France, and GS. said umph, later she said, if we come back and more lately when we come back. So perhaps we may and then the northwest and Carroll College, which means you for of course she won't lecture again. Please do not take on my disappointment unless doing so diminishes yours, for of course you did want to see and talk to and hear GS.

And now there's only time to say how deeply I appreciate all you've done and how touched I am ~~to suspect the~~ with your reason. We are off tomorrow to Oklahoma City!

Ever yours,
Alice Toklas

Western Union wire — San Francisco, California
16 April 1935

SO VERY SORRY NOT TO HAVE WRITTEN YOU REASON WHY NORTHERN TRIP WAS IMPOSSIBLE STOP WE LEAVE HERE FRIDAY FOR NEWYORK WHERE GERTRUDE STEIN HAS ENGAGEMENT ON TWENTY FOURTH OF THIS MONTH STOP SAILING FOR FRANCE MAY FOURTH STOP MANY THANKS FOR YOUR WIRE AND MANY KINDNESSES WARMEST REMEMBRANCES

ALICE TOKLAF [sic]

Postmarked 10 June 1935
Bilignin par Belley, Ain

My dear Steward,

We did everything xcept meet and it would have been most awfully nice to meet, but we will meet and then it will be most awfully nice to meet and to have met, we are back here and liking it but with many regretful thoughts about America which I am afraid we even liked better, we did, we certainly did like it even better but anyway we will meet

Always
Gertrude Stein

Postmarked 2 September 1935
Bilignin par Belley, Ain

My dear Steward

Yes I have read your book, and there are spots in it that I like very much, the beginning and the end are the best, you see I am bothered much bothered by the necessity of content without form, creation without intention, and most of the writing today has that trouble, when the content was included in the form and the creation in the intention that was one thing but now it is the other thing and if the intention is the intention, it is a mess, in your beginning and in your ending you do realise something of this thing and then the intention is intention and it gets wrong. It would have been nice seeing you and surely we will get there again and then we will meet and that will be a pleasure,

Always
Gertrude Stein

Alice Toklas wants to be remembered and do go on telling me about yourself I like to hear

G.S.

your book: A collection of short stories written in Claire Andrews' class and called *Pan and the Firebird* (Harrison: New York, 1930).

Postcard, 28 November 1935
27, rue de Fleurus, Paris VI

It was nice getting your letter we were awfully troubled that you had been swallowed up in the Helena earthquake and now you write from the State of Washington as calmly as if the Herald had not been full of panic about your late abiding place. We are settling down to a peaceful Paris winter untroubled we hope by revolution, but that is as it will be, at present it seems more favorable than it was going to be, and today is Thanksgiving and we have a turkey and all complete.

Always
Gertrude Stein

earthquake: A series of severe temblors rocked Helena shortly after my departure; Carroll College was gravely damaged, as were many other larger buildings.
Herald: The Paris edition of the New York *Herald-Tribune.*

Postcard, postmarked Paris
24 March 1936

My dear Steward,

We are pleased to hear that one thing did not overwhelm you and now there are so many others, one never knows whether it is worse than the newspapers say or not so bad, and do come come and see us in the country and that will be nice, I am working very hard, after the lark in England lectures seem to be out of my system, I am enjoying working at plays and have done two that I like, well anyway let me see your novel, we will be at Bilignin then, and good luck and lots of love.

G.S.

overwhelm you: The earthquakes in Helena.
lark in England: A reference to her lectures at Cambridge and Oxford universities.
your novel: My novel, *Angels on the Bough,* was to be published in late May 1936.

16 June 1936
Bilignin par Belley, Ain

My dear Sam,

The book came and I have just finished it and I like it I like it a lot, you have really created a piece of something, by the way how old are you, I have just finished it and I am not sure that I am not going to read it again. It quite definitely did something to me. There are things I might say but it is not that, I have to read it again to know what it is, the first 25 pages did not do it and from then on it did, something came into xistence and remained there, I have to read it again to know more just what, it has something to do with the way you have met the problem of time, as I say I will read it again and then I will write again, you have succeeded in reaching a unity without connecting, I often think that the American contribution is making anything dead, nobody else in writing xcept Americans ever made a thing xist without life be without life and you do that but you do do something else it is a certain level that is there, well anyway I will read it again and write to you again, and with that level you do make it and it is all that, it will be nice meeting some time and don't worry you can eat just what you need and nothing else and so we are looking forward to your coming, that was a funny story about Time, that is not part of the weekly newspaper is it, because if it is, I do not know them but it is strange that they would do that, things are very mixed up in Paris just now but here in the country everything is relatively peaceful xcept the weather, there is snow where there should be no snow and consequently there are other things that are not, I will read the book again and write again and I can tell you that I like it and that it did something to me

Always
Gertrude Stein

The book came: Angels on the Bough.
how old are you: Twenty-seven.
story about Time: The March of Time, a weekly radio program, had quoted Stein on the possibility of war; I had written to them complaining that the voice they used on the program was hardly that of Gertrude Stein, and that the quotation from her was in error.

26 October 1936
Bilignin par Belley, Ain

My dear Sam,

How are you and where are you and what are you doing there, we are having a lovely autumn after a not so lovely summer it was cold and you were hot, but cold or hot I do like weather, we are staying a little longer and then we go to Paris, it will be nice seeing you next summer, but tell me about yourself now and always a great deal of affection for you

Gertrude Stein

Postcard, postmarked Paris
22 November 1936

My dear-~~Steward~~ — Sam,

Merry Christmas and Happy New Year to you and many more of them, I like your writing about the lake and the cold because when we were there it was like that, write again soon, and do another book and lots of love

Gertrude Stein

the lake and the cold: A lengthy paragraph in one of my letters had described Lake Michigan during a winter storm.

3 February 1937
27, rue de Fleurus, Paris VI

My dear Sam,

They did do you well in the Bulletin, it was clearly and well done and they were right it was a good book and do do go on and do another; you are coming over are you not, there is going to be an xposition in spite of the rain they have at last started and though they won't be ready to begin they will be ready not so long after as we all thought, I am working a lot, I am doing the American part of the second volume of the Autobiography and I am almost at Columbus Ohio, I am wondering how you will like it, I sometimes think it is simply good and sometimes I think it is simple without the good, well anyway it is going on. But that is inevitable that it should go on, I liked your remembering my birthday, thank you, the performance of they are wedded to their wife goes on the end of March in London, Lord Berners who has done the music is also doing the décor, we are quite xcited, and otherwise everything is calm who wrote the thing about you a great deal of affection always

Gertrude Stein

in the Bulletin: The report on my dismissal from the State College of Washington was in the *Bulletin of the American Association of University Professors,* Volume XXIII, Number 1, for January 1937. The report was written by R. E. Himstead, General Secretary, and Carl Wittke, head of Committee A on Academic Freedom and Tenure.

Postmarked 26 August 1937
Bilignin par Belley, Ain

My dear Sam,

I am so pleased that you are there and going to be here, we are very near Switzerland so it might be nicest for you to come here at the end of the Paris visit, stay with us a bit and then we will take you to Geneva and leave you there for your Swiss time, so when do you want to come, you take a morning train around eight and go to Culoz where we call for you, it will be nice

always
Gertrude

you are there: in Paris.

Postcard, postmarked 29 August 1937
Belley, Ain

My dear Sam,

Culoz Friday 15.29, and please are you on a special diet of any kind, let us know, we are quite accustomed to that and do not mind, it will be a pleasure meeting, a real one

Gertrude:

a special diet: My food allergies were for milk, eggs, wheat, potatoes, and all their products, a real challenge to Alice's cooking.

Postmarked 12 September 1937
Bilignin par Belley, Ain

My dear Sammy,

Just to say happy day, and any number more happy days, in other words bon voyage, your letter just came and we were pleased to have it, we liked you before hand and we liked you a lot more after, we have not had nice weather since you left, but now it is clearing up, we did get 30 écrevisses which we would so willingly have shared with you, and the detective story, I gather it is a sweet one, more allegory than detection, because happily there is no corpse just doors and windows, and I like doors and windows even when they are or are not. Anyway a great deal of affection from us all, and very soon

Always
Gertrude

écrevisses: Crayfish.
detective story: In Gertrude's style of writing, I composed a series of instructions about the wallpaper in my bedroom, which—if she followed them—would lead her to a medallion in the center of which I had written "I love Gertrude and Alice."

Postmarked 25 September 1937
Bilignin par Belley, Ain

My dear Sammy,

Here are the photos and a few taken the other day, everybody asks after you and I think the Rops are a little dispirited at not hearing from you do write them. Rops xplained to me that his idea is to get you the job for next winter that the Lycée usually prefers an Englishman because they think that accent better but they have an Australian and they could therefore seemingly take on an Ohioan, but anyway do write to him nice letters, they leave next Wednesday, we have seen them quite often and they talk of you they think you are quite angelic in appearance which seems rather funny to me, but that is the way they feel about it, and did you leave a pair of shoes behind you, if you did sometime Thornton will take it or them back to you did you, they were found in the room that opened from your bedroom, and each shoe was in its little case so Alice thought most likely it was you, otherwise no news, it rained from the time you left until yesterday but now the sun is shining pleasantly again, we are going to look for mushrooms wish you were with us,

Always
Gertrude

shoes: I had left them in one of the hidden recesses. The spare bedroom had several secret cupboards in it, wallpapered over and with no seams, so that unless one knew their location they were quite invisible.

Postcard, postmarked 26 October 1937
Belley

My dear Sammy,

The photos are nice particularly the shooting and the bread, we are on the eve of departing, helas. The Rops write that someone is going to be at your place who is a friend of theirs but you will know about this by now, we are very fond of you and you are a very awfully nice Sammy.

Gertrude

shooting: A candid snapshot of Gertrude at a shooting gallery at Virieu-le-Grand, with Alice Toklas and Henri Daniel-Rops looking over her shoulder.
someone: Charles Du Bos, a French theological philosopher who gave a course of lectures at Notre Dame University, in Indiana.

Postcard, postmarked 10 November 1937
Paris, Rue Dupin station

My dear Sam,

Thanks for your letter I liked it and I liked the parts you liked and I like about the pigeons particularly the pigeons again, and do get time to write more much more, you should, there was something that really meant something in the novel. And the five was a sad five, we knew it, it is a sad number, I am writing a lot and I will write and tell you all about it and anyway do write

Always
Gertrude

pigeons: I had described the way pigeons walk, saying that now I knew why there was the expression "pigeon-toed."

Postmark illegible, Nov? 1937
27, rue de Fleurus, Paris VI

My dearest Sammy,

Delighted with the telegram Alice is delighted with the gadgets she keeps them on a shelf on the best Italian furniture in the atelier with the best treasures, and she shows them with so much pride, they are so useful and so beautiful and so pale blue and we are so pleased with our Sammy and so much to tell you, we are leaving rue de Fleurus, we have a new and lovely address 5 rue Christine, everything is lovely and we are so happy about it, it is a long story and we will tell it to you quietly in Bilignin or in rue Christine, and here is a bit that will please you and we saw the Rops and we talked endlessly about you and I am writing a life in french of Picasso for the Floury edition and we are so busy we move the 15 of January and we love you a lot and you are a sweet Sammy

Gertrude

gadgets: From a large department store in Chicago I sent about twenty kitchen gadgets to them: a "beast" thermometer, an egg whipper, a garlic squeezer, a lid opener, and many other things not available at that time in France.

Postmarked 12 January 1938
~~27 rue de Fleurus~~ 5, rue Christine, Paris VI

My dear Sammy

Here I am writing to you with a Christmas pen, it is a monster, but does not write very well, I was so successful with my 35 franc camera I bought the same sum fountain pen, perhaps when I get used to it it will be alright, and we were all at dinner at the Rops and we spoke and spoke of you without end, and they said if you were sad all you needed was Paris and they are not without hope, but he said he did not want to say anything until he knew, and so perhaps something can still happen, and I have meditated a lot about your letter perhaps it is better but you see I think the trouble it certainly was with Hart Crane, the question of being important inside in one, read the original Making of Americans, you see the difference between inside and outside, well it is a bother, I do not think [frightful? pursuance?] of living crowds it out, but disproportion between yes and no, it should be all no or all yes but one at a time, well we are moving and we have not moved for a long time, we are taking it calmly, that is we are not, but it seems so, everybody is so pleased with you, Alice's joy in the gadgets is as lively as ever, and now she is to have a refrigerator and there is a cover to that for things in your collection, it seems to be a regular Swiss Family Robinson collection, and Rops is so touched with his wife's photo and his own little Christ, and everybody says how Sweet is Sammy and he is perhaps he will be sweet enough to be happy that is our wish

Gertrude

Postmarked 16 May 1938
5, rue Christine, Paris VI

My dearest Sammy,

The Daniel-Rops were here yesterday afternoon and naturally we talked about Sammy, they are upset about your not getting the job, we all seem to want you over here and they all seem to want you over there anyway it does seem to be a very popular Sammy and that is very nice for everybody including Sammy, and now now everything is getting cheaper over here, won't you be coming, you are always welcome at Bilignin that you know, and the Père Abbé says you are always welcome at Hautecombe, and the Rops having completely hated the Midi are going to be our neighbors again and they say you are always welcome there so welcome

Sammy come, I wish you could come too while we are here we would love to show you our home we love it completely and entirely and I don't know but we have been awfully busy ever since we have been here, I don't know, but it seems very occupying this our new home, and then I am writing an opera did I tell you with Lord Berners a new Faust and I think a good one, I have done the first act and I am quite moved by it, well if you come and perhaps you will come it will be fun talking it over, the Picasso book is going very well, they have translated the Autobiography in Italian and are now going to do some more, and perhaps, well there are so many perhapses, and you are going to see Thornton soon, it would be nice if you came over together well well I don't seem to know just what to say xcept that although it is a rainy day we love you Sammy

Always
Gertrude

not getting the job: Daniel-Rops had suggested that I apply for a scholarship from the International Institute of Education, but his proposal was made after the closing date for applications.

Postcard, postmarked 14 June 1938
Bilignin par Belley, Ain

My dearest Sammy,

What did happen to you and where are you and will you be here and how much we will be pleased to see you and so much to tell you and Sammy where are you

Gertrude

This postcard is in neither the Bancroft nor the Yale collection; it was donated for sale in the San Francisco public broadcasting auction of KQED in May 1971.

Postmarked 25 June 1938
Bilignin par Belley, Ain

My dear Sammy,

Whenever anybody says Sammy somebody says he is a darling or somebody says he is an angel, that is the way somebody always seems to feel about Sammy. The Rops are going to spend two months here, and how we will talk about you. Père Bernardet and another one of the fathers the very tall one blonde and with a good big nose a young one, were here the other day, they had not quite had permission to come they hoped the Père Abbé would be gone before they had to tell him but we had an amusing time, I told them the theme of the Faust, by the way I will send you a copy, Alice is going to make more pretty soon, and they were very xcited about its theology, Père Bernardet was a little worried about it, but the other one he was convinced he thought it was good theology alright, it will amuse me to know how you feel about it, and as to Wordsworth and Coleridge, it is funny about Wordsworth I had not read anything for years, and the other day here I had a volume of it by chance and I read the ode on the intimations of immortality and was disappointed. It is not very fresh, but on the other hand the revolutionary things like the telling of lies about the windmill the things that were really revolutionary then have the charm still of being revolutionary, I think that is true if a thing is really revolutionary and underneath was then the things that were that have the charm of that however much that revolution has become a past thing. Coleridge is different, that is just simply that, in a kind of way he and Poe are very much the same, their narrative poetry is so simply poetry that the narrative and the poetry are really one, the owl who hoots or the raven who speaks or the albatross who does not do either it is really the only thing I know which is really disembodied poetry, so simply so, there, that is more than a sentence but you can make a sentence of it, or perhaps it only is a sentence well anyway I am awfully pleased that the warmer sun has made peace come, and next summer it will be all our sun, and Alice sends lots of love and Pépé and Basket and everything does it sends lots of love to Sammy, we were at Culoz the other day meeting someone and to us Culoz is Sammy and naturally we only talked of him

lots of love
Gertrude

Wordsworth: Since I was teaching a graduate course in the early Romantic poets, I had asked Gertrude for her opinion of them to convey to the class. The only reference to windmills in Wordsworth occurs in *The Prelude*, Book 10, lines 364–374; she may have been mistaken about this, because the lines referring to a child's toy are relatively unimportant.

Postmarked 11 July 1938
Bilignin par Belley, Ain

My dear Sammy,

Have anything you want now and always but my dear the Guggenheim prize people never listen to me xcept to go the other way, I once made fun of them in something Henry McBride printed and anyway they wouldn't listen to me even if I hadn't, but if you want me even so I am yours to command now and always, but if you can get somebody with a pull do do so, because I do think that is the way it is done, how about Thornton though I believe they don't like him either because he once did something, but if you want me I am yours, the Rops are coming to lunch on Thursday, do come too, we do love you, and make everything go well and please us all

Always
Gertrude

Guggenheim: Wendell Wilcox and I both wanted to apply for a Guggenheim grant and asked Gertrude among others to recommend us; neither of us got it.

Postcard, no postmark [May? 1938]
Paris[?]

My dear Sammy,

Greetings and then some, no Madeleine Rops is very well and they are coming down in July and we are here and you are there and there is so much to say, but happily lots of time to say it in. Send us another postal card and lots of love.

Gertrude and Alice

No date [probably August 1938]
Bilignin par Belley, Ain

My dearest Sammy,

Yes we know, du Bos had told Rops and Rops told us and I told Père Bernardet, and everybody is pleased, don't you worry Sammy, whatever you do there is always one thing that is sure and certain and that [is] we all think that you just can't help being a sweet and angel boy, you are, you know and everything you do always has that as a background and we all love you. We were at Hautecombe yesterday, Bernard Faÿ who has not been well is staying there, and we all had a happy day there, and I have given Wendell's mss. to my London agent and he has just had a favorable report from his reader and I am pleased and here is the *Faust* and the Rops are coming back today, they are where they were Roltinod par Belley though I imagine only Belley would reach them they are to be here six weeks and there is lots to tell you but that will be very nice, and lots of love oh lots and lots and lots

Gertrude

Yes we know: I had been going through a difficult period with Catholicism: first a communicant and then not. Gertrude refers to the fact that I had finally decided to be one.

Bernard Faÿ: Gertrude and Alice had first met Faÿ in 1924 when he was teaching at the University of Clermont-Ferrand. In 1941 he became director of the Bibliothèque Nationale, appointed by Pétain, and so was able to help Gertrude and Alice secure extra rations. He was arrested in 1944 and accused of collaboration, spending many years in "exile" in Switzerland. Alice continually tried to get him cleared of the accusation. Faÿ wrote a preface to the abridged version of *The Making of Americans* (New York: Harcourt, Brace, 1934).

Wendell's mss.: Wendell Wilcox had first met Gertrude and Alice during their visit to America in 1934–1935.

Faust: A carbon copy of *Doctor Faustus Lights the Lights* by Gertrude, with several corrections in her own handwriting.

Postmarked 23 August 1938
Bilignin par Belley, Ain

My dear Sammy,

We were all with the Rops to-day, they took us to Chaubotte and Mont Rénard and lots of places and we had a beautiful time and incidentally we talked about Sammy, and Rops suggests that he could get Maurois to write a letter to the Guggenheim people strongly recommending you, will you let him know just as soon as possible, if it is really urgent telegraph him the name and address of the person at the Guggenheim to whom Maurois should write, I think it would help a lot, and Rops can do it without difficulty so do attend to this at once and now I will write you a lot soon but this must go off right away lots and lots of love

Gertrude

Maurois: André Maurois, French novelist, biographer, and essayist.

Postmarked 25 December 1938
5, rue Christine, Paris VI

My dear Sammy,

Happy New Year to you Sammy and be a happy boy, I am hoping for some result for you and Wendell, anyway we are all pulling all our strings, and perhaps, but anyway you will come about that there is no doubt and that will be a pleasure to us all. We have been very busy getting Francis Rose ready for his London show, we are always very busy with something and the weather has been cold really truly cold, Alice and Pépé sit by the radiator, and I am working well at least I am going to be working at the novel, and yours is it good, tell me more about it and go on being fecund, just as fecund as possible, and happy New Year, and the Rops are very well and nobody forgets you no not ever

Always
Gertrude

Postmarked 28 January 1939
5, rue Christine, Paris VI

My dear Sammy,

That is a funny coincidence because it was Florence Sabine who was at the Medical School with me to whom I wrote for the two of you right in the beginning, I am a little cheered because I never had a candidate who got as far as you two, 700 to 100 is quite a reduction, and I hope it is a success, good luck and more good luck, Madeleine Rops was just here to see our Baby Basket, we went to Bordeaux to get him a most xciting trip, and he was scared of everything stairs and stores and everything and he had a terrific time but now he is beginning to get used to the world and he is very lovely and you will see him this summer, come to us first and think about Artemare afterwards and that was an xtraordinary thing you sent me, the mixture was so characteristic of what makes Germany be Nazi, and there will be so much to say, and here are some of the Francis Rose catalogs give one to Wendell and all of you all my love

Always
Gertrude

Florence Sabin[e]: A member of the selection committee for the Guggenheim awards.
700 to 100: Both Wendell Wilcox and I had been informed that we had passed the preliminary hurdles for the Guggenheim award and were currently in a group of one hundred persons instead of seven hundred.
Artemare: After visiting Gertrude and Alice I had planned to stay in a small hotel in Artemare and write for the rest of the summer.

Postmarked 31 March 1939
5, rue Christine, Paris VI

My dearest Sammy,

I am awfully upset, not so much about you as about Wendell, your sister is right the time will come, but the Wendells did so desperately need a change, oh dear oh dear what awful people, they do make one feel race prejudicial, yes they do, and of course come and stay with us as long as you like which will not be longer than we like, you are a sweet boy, and we will tell you everything and you will tell us everything, my child's book looks as if it was going to go well, babies do seem to cry for it, we hope big and little babies, and the Rops will be in Paris when you get here but we will be already in Bilignin, for you to come, bring your story along, oh dear I wish Wendell had got it, horrible people, lots and lots of love

Gertrude

I am awfully upset: Neither Wendell Wilcox nor I received a Guggenheim award.

Postmarked 7[?] July 1939
Bilignin par Belley, Ain

My dear Sammy,

Madeleine Rops says that you are a nice fat little Sammy now, I am so glad that you are well and happy, you said you were staying three weeks in Paris, when are those three weeks up, perhaps the Rops would like you to drive them down here, as Madeleine is not very strong yet, we would be glad to have you until the 30 of July when others come and perhaps you could arrange with Hautecombe, or just settle down in Belley and that would be nice, let us know as soon as possible your plans, it will be nice seeing you, it is nice and hot now lots of love

Gertrude

nice fat little Sammy: A temporary cessation of smoking had added about eight pounds to my weight.
Paris: This letter was sent to me in Paris; I had already seen the Rops.
30 of July: Sir Francis Rose and Cecil Beaton were to arrive on the day I left for a stay of about three weeks in Algiers.

Postmarked 9 July 1939

My dear Sammy,

August would be far away, and 15 to 20 July or 16 to 20 would suit us well, but of course we want you to do whatever pleases you, seeing you would please us bien entendu, and are you still on your diet Alice wants to know and you and you can let us know as soon as you can just when, just what day and when, but if you want to go to Algeria first, it is nice to have you there anyway, because sooner or later we will have you here. My novel is getting on, I don't take much stock in novel writing but it is getting on lots of love, let us know right away which

Always
Gertrude

15 to 20 July: I arrived on the fifteenth and at their insistence greatly overstayed my visit, leaving for Algiers later, and then returning to Bilignin.
your diet: The same food allergies were still with me. Gertrude was shortly to write, during the war, her book called *Alphabets and Birthdays,* in which under "S" she made such fun of Sammy and his ailments. (See Appendix II.)
August: I was already in Paris; she wrote to me there.
my novel: Ida.

Postcard, postmarked 21 July 1939,
round robin to Steward's aunts, the
Misses Elizabeth and Minnie Rose.

Dear Sammy's aunts,

He has told us so much about you that it is quite natural to write to you and to tell you how much we like having him with us, and how well you brought him up to be pleasant in the home. We spent some pleasant days in Columbus Ohio, I am so sorry we did not know you. Always Gertrude Stein.

When they ask but why did you want to go back to U.S. I always say because I want to see Columbus Ohio again — and now there would be another reason. A warm remembrance. A. B. Toklas.

And so from the three of us comes this little message bearing greetings, and from me lots of love! Sam

Note from Gertrude Stein to Picasso
n.d. [July 1939]

Cher Pablo,

Ce mot va introduire le M. Sammy Steward, il est charmant, fais gentil avec lui.

Cher Pablo: this note will introduce le M. Sammy Steward, he is charming, be gentle with him.

Postmarked 17 November 1939
Bilignin par Belley, Ain

My dear Sammy,

Over these roads you bicycled so splendidly, Basket and I at night walk darkly, well we walk in the daytime too but even that is more or less darkly, it is lovely, the country, we have had summer, and now autumn, and pretty soon it will be winter but so far not too cold, lots of new friends, the English Bigges and the french Jacquots beside all the rest who are still here, not the ménagerie, Onslow Ford went to England to die for his country but instead he got appendicitis and is in hospital, the Spaniard has gone to Buenos Aires, and the Chilean and his wife have gone to New York, they wrote to ask if I knew anybody who wanted to see them over there but somehow I didn't. André Germain is in Switzerland taking a cure, Francis [Rose] and Cecil [Beaton] in England, the Balthus in Switzerland, and the Leyris still in Champrovent, and you and the eleven, are they still eleven, or are they a round dozen now, Basket got under an automobile but nothing happened but a stiff neck which is over now, the Rops in Bordeaux their mother still here and lots of love Sammy

Always
Gertrude

Bigges, Jacquots, et al: New friends and acquaintances of Gertrude and Alice.
the ménagerie: The group of *surréalistes* surrounding André Breton.
the eleven: I had told Gertrude that I had barely escaped marrying eleven times.

(Typed letter, signed "Alice" regarding a second lecture tour for Gertrude. It exists in two nearly identical copies, one sent by surface mail, the other by air. Both letters are at Bancroft Library.)

26 November 1939
Bilignin par Belley, Ain

Dear Sammy,

We were very surprised to receive your wire forwarded from Paris yesterday. Gertrude answered it at once. [Probably because of the war, I never received the letter.]

Gertrude would like to lecture in U.S. but a lecture agency never seemed possible because they leave so little freedom and peace for the lecturer to be calm and comfortable in. Friends who have undergone the trial have come out of it surprised and scarred. Of course nothing like this must happen to Gertrude. Can it be that your friends are not like all the others. Could they produce a contract that could satisfy Gertrude's continuing her usual quiet life with the perfect freedom to do what she wants every minute of the day and night except give say three lectures a week. And where would they propose that they should be given. And what happens to the several places where she would want to lecture because of her attachment to her audiences in '34 and '35 and who could not afford the agent's price. And how could it be exclusive management if these places were included. (Exclusive management, you wouldn't think Gertrude would want two agencies.) And what kind of an audience would an agency find. And just what does a minimum fee mean if they guarantee the fixed sum mentioned in your wire. And what would their advance fee be.

You see how many questions your wire has suggested.

As for Gertrude you know how much she enjoyed lecturing in U.S. in '34 and '35 and what a good time she had doing it. But I did all the arrangements and she had time free to work and radio and for all kinds of things.

I didn't suppose I'd ever be writing this kind of a letter to you, but here it is, with my love.

Always yours,
Alice

your wire: The cable — one of the few things Gertrude did not save — suggested the agency of Ford Hicks, who wanted Gertrude to lecture for a $375 fee, of which he would take 20 percent. Hicks, as we later found, was a second-rate man who handled only second-rate speakers. Gertrude would have been sadly disappointed with him.

Postmarked 22 December 1939
Bilignin par Belley, Ain

My dear Sammy,

No no no, no Mixer, $25 is not cheap it is a helluva lot of francs, and other things are to be done with them, and besides in this particular moment, everybody has time enough to mix by hand all the mixing that needs mixing, so keep all information till later when we are there or you are here or something, but thanks all the same and besides it does look quite large, but anyway money is money, and not now to be spent on mixers. You do not say anything about the Eleven, are you not writing, you can always have a sequel when the Eleven becomes Twelve, and now about Hicks, he does not really answer the questions, he does not say what the ewers [?] are as the french comynes[?] so fondly say, the space to be occupied, he does not say anything about an advance, and as we are paying our own xpenses these are capital questions, and he seems to think we would prefer 30 dates at 250 to twenty at 375 which naturally we would not at all, in fact his letter is more conversation than statement of facts, my book on Paris, France is finished you were its first reader but enthusiastic as you were the editor is more so and has all kinds of projects, we hope they will come off, and here we are spots cold spots warm, but after all we are on the Southern slope of the Massive Centrale although Alice and Pépé do not always feel that way, and we are starting a foyer des soldats, much xcited thereat, we are turning the barn into a sports center and another little place next to the bread oven into an indoor place and Alice and I are doing it all and we are very busy, we just are busy but not so busy as to wish all dear Chicago merry Christmas and a happy new year particularly the Wendell Wilcoxes and Sammy

Always
Gertrude

Postmarked 13 February 1940
Bilignin par Belley, Ain

My dearest Sammy,

That's a nice letter it sounds like the nice old Sammy and I guess it is just as well not to be catholic any more, of course you will have attacks and relapses but I like the idea of a Junior college for you, I think it is much more sensible and will make it possible for you to write more, anyway enough is always enough, and enough said, and for the mixer it has not come yet but we will love it when it comes and we would have liked the record but we have no phonograph and we take the will for the deed, and perhaps Wendell is right well anyway now you will be a rich boy you will come over soon and often.

Better write on a new page that one would be too difficult, why should not Wendell write all the Meditations of an Unpublished Author, he could make that a beautiful book, but bless him, he like all of us has to do what he pleases. Now about Hicks, he doesn't sound so bad but he is foolish like all good business men, it is the business way, say I hear he had to do with movies, could he not arrange that The World is Round, or the Autobiography of Alice B. Toklas be done by Hollywood, if he could he could be our agent and we could go and sit out there for large sums and lecture for him leisurely also for large sums and everybody would be happy, do have him do that, I like him and I would like him so much better if he could do that, the Autobiography would make a swell film, so would The World is Round, either or both, do tell Hicks to do so, he ought to be able to, well let me see, the Rops are still in Bordeaux, Béon is alright, the lady of Clemelieu [?] has just sent me photos of her paintings and says she is going to America, we have gotten to be very dear friends with the Bigges, Francis is sad in England, write to him, Ruan Minor, Helston, Cornwall, and lots of love to our own Sammy

Gertrude

we have no phonograph: I had planned to send Gertrude a birthday greeting on a phonograph record, but could not at this time send a package to France.

perhaps Wendell is right: Wendell Wilcox had said that he had got it psychically that Gertrude and Alice were not coming to America.

Now about Hicks: We were just beginning to discover that Hicks had no Hollywood connections at all, and that he was not a very successful agent.

Béon is alright: The aged Baronne Pierlot and her sons, the comtes d'Aiguy, who lived there.

the Bigges: Richard and Emily Bigges, who were neighbors, had decided to live in France during the war rather than return to their native England.

Postmarked 25 March 1940
Bilignin par Belley, Ain

My dearest Sammy,

The Mix master came Easter Sunday, and we have not had time to more than read the literature put it together and gloat, oh so beautiful is the Mix master, so beautiful and the literature so beautiful, and the shoe button potatoes that same day so beautiful and everything so beautiful, and now how much do I owe you Sammy dear because we are very happy to have it here, bless you Sammy, Madame Roux said oui il est si gentil, et en effet he is dear little Sammy, Easter morning, what a spring, lovely as I have never seen anything lovely, wish you could see us in the spring, but perhaps, well anyway lots of love and lots of thanks and tell me how much we owe you, Alice all smiles and murmurs in her dreams, Mix master

Gertrude

tell me how much we owe you: It took several letters because of the delays in mail service during the war to convince Gertrude and Alice that the Mixmaster was a house present.

Madame Roux: Their ever-faithful housekeeper, who had been with them almost since the beginning of their stay at Bilignin.

Postmarked 4 April 1940
Bilignin par Belley, Ain

My dearest Sammy,

Day and night Mix master is a delight, it was so sweet of you not to accept my countermanding order, first we had to work it together but now Alice works it all alone and it saves her hours and effort, she can write a whole advertisement for Mix master she is so pleased and Sammy please let me know xactly how much we owe you transport and all, please, I can't tell you how happy Mix master makes the home, we do not know whether Basket and Pépé know the difference but all the rest of us do, otherwise life is continuing peacefully, we garden we work and we sit in the garden and we see a great many people one might not think but we do, by the way not by name but all the same you are mentioned in Paris France, now I am thinking of doing a companion work of it about America, it might be rather fun to do, come back to doing portraits as I did in Geography and Plays, I suppose that is inevitable, I have also done Superstitions into English and I am hoping that they will do it, so far we have not been homesick for Paris yet but I suppose by next fall we will be, are you coming over this summer now that you are all rich and to be professors, I suppose the Eleven who are probably thirty-four by now never got to be any more, lazy, and love to the Wendells and thanks again and again and again for Mix master, three long cheers, neither war nor anything could stop it, bless Sammy

Always
Gertrude

are you coming over this summer: It was a curious naiveté on Gertrude's part that permitted her to think civilians could travel freely in wartime.

Postmarked 4 April 1940
Bilignin par Belley, Ain

My dearest Sammy,

I just wrote you miles about our love for the Mix master and how happy it makes us and what a love you are and how much do we owe you including the postage, and it's a pleasure to pay for anything so perfectly lovely and which moves so wonderfully around and around, perhaps we could write a series of adds for Mix master and get rich that way, I am glad that the eleven marches, it might be a very good book, and now about M. Ford Hicks, it does not sound so bad, if we could go over in the fall and when the cold weather came do our movie, and there we could garden and take exercise, while it is too cold to do the same thing in the East, they are doing a show at the Yale Library in the fall, but would they come to hear me talk about Paris France and the United States of America while they were electing a president, I have not had any cable from Mr. Hicks but really until he knows what he can do and what he can offer it does not seem worth while cabling, the Bigges I think you saw him a thin Englishman at the Ménagerie where they painted and where we took you away but perhaps he was not there that day, anyway that is who they are, god bless Sammy and the Mix master and perhaps M. Hicks

Always
Gertrude

the Bigges: The Bigges came with André Breton and his *surréalistes* to Gertrude's afternoon party, but she was confused about taking me away from the *ménagerie* for I was never there.

Postmarked 1 May 1940
Bilignin par Belley, Ain

My dearest Sammy,

Your letter arrived just the first of May and here is a *muguet,* Dear Sammy, the Mix master, Alice just can't tear herself away from the Mix master to tell you how she loves it but she will, it makes spoon bread, it makes mashed potatoes which are a dream, and Alice cries but what can Sammy eat that the Mix master makes what what and the motor answers What What, Dear Sammy, and it does seem if we ever are to be in Hollywood it will be the work of Sammy Dear Sammy, wouldn't it be nice it they wanted us and gave us so much money we could buy a car and drive a car we and Sammy at the wheel, we did not make the Chartreuse but we might make Hollywood, bless Sammy, I had a lovely letter from Wendell, and I will be writing soon, they never did send me the Poetry number nor have I had your article about the mix master, send it send it lots of love

Gertrude

muguet: Gertrude enclosed a pressed and dried lily of the valley in her letter.

Poetry number: An article by Wendell Wilcox entitled "A Note on Stein and Abstraction" was published in the April 1940 issue of *Poetry: A Magazine of Verse.*

article about the Mixmaster: June Provines, a columnist for the Chicago *Tribune,* devoted one of her columns to the adventures of the Mixmaster.

Postmarked 16 May 1940
Bilignin par Belley, Ain

My dearest Sammy,

Oh dear, well it is just oh dear, and the only comfort is the Mix master, who is so at home that it seems just like home well to us and the Mix master, otherwise well otherwise, Yale University is making a show of my ms. this fall the Yale University Library and I imagine they might like to add to their collection the print you did of my hand, or did it get lost, Thornton is arranging it all so you might ask him if he would like it, and I am working on my new child's book, and Basket and Pépé had worm medicine today and so they are both resting, and Alice is knitting socks and I am writing to Sammy, and it is not winter any longer it has suddenly turned summer. Well well well, and we have lots of pansies [?] we are kind of worried which is natural but François d'Aiguy says it is alright and I guess it is and lots of love

Always
Gertrude

Oh dear: I had been hospitalized as the result of an auto accident, but there was not much damage.

print of my hand: This is in the Bancroft Library.

pansies: According to an old French superstition, a profusion of pansies meant bad luck.

Postmarked 8 July 1940
Bilignin par Belley, Ain

My dearest Sammy,

Here we are the Mix master and us have all weathered the storm xcept that just the last day, Alice dropped the big Mix master green bowl and it fell into little pieces on the kitchen floor, such lovely green little pieces, and some day will you send another bowl and we will well some day, and that is really all there is to say, and here we are and loving Sammy dear Sammy dear Mix Master and dear Bilignin, bless you

Gertrude

Postmarked 18 November 1940
Bilignin par Belley, Ain

My dearest Sammy,

Yesterday came a letter written in November and to-day one written in July that stayed and stayed in occupied territory and just came out now, apparently the Mix Master bowl was already busted then, alas there is not much to mix these days in the Mix master but when there will be it would appear that there is a metal mix master bowl and that we must have, Alice says she would not like it at all she wants the one she broke she does not want anything else, we are hoping that mixing will mix soon, you see you can use other bowls but they do not twirl around in that lovely green mix master way and when they do not twirl their contents instead of staying down rise up and spill and therefor the mix master will have to be a mix master still. I am glad you like predictions, the one we are all loving now is St. Odile, who said the war would end in the eternal city and also that the germans would leave France being overtaken by a mal étrange, I like that very much and there are 11 butchers in Belley including charcutérie and they were wicked too, so you see you are pursued by the number 11, we are hoping that the butchers will begin again November 24 but to-day they said not, that they had been called to Lyon, but I do not think that is true, you see everybody has now to stand in the market and wait their meat turn instead of pleasantly being inside the butcher shop and waiting for contrebande. Mrs. Balthus announced the other day that she lived two days a week *hon-*

nêtement and the rest of the time she lived by contrebande, anyway we have a raw fish and poultry shop in Belley and that makes up for something, poor Sammy you would suffer, no rice, so little meat, Basket II has taken to bread there is lots of bread, and we still have cake not Mixmaster cake not much but Peycru[?] cake, and when you write to Francis tell him to write to me by you I have already written to him by Thornton but has he had it, I would like news of him if nothing more than fish and chips, they are covering themselves with glory, the tight little island and fish and chips I suppose helps, lots of love and lots of love from us and everybody

Gertrude

St. Odile: A fifteenth-century saint noted for her predictions and visions: early in the war Gertrude forsook Nostradamus for her.
Mrs. Balthus: A neighbor in Bilignin.

Postmarked 9 September 1941
Bilignin par Belley, Ain

My dearest Sammy,

The letter did come they do seem to come once they are written, and, do send some of those daily mystères, nobody seems to know how I suffer for them, I am now reduced to reading the old ones for the third and fourth time which makes them just a little not, so be a good boy, and send them along, two at a time but send them and the Bowstring murder but really any and all of them will do with or without my name in them, I cry aloud for books but nobody answers me, at least the books don't answer me, I have acquired 4 Dickens and Uncle Tom's Cabin from a Chanoine at Belley, and the Vicar of Wakefield, but no mystères, you always come through with gifts Sammy even if not with letters so come, now perhaps having got the habit you will know what I like. You are right about our staying, it is the most xciting and fascinating xperience, the conversations I wish I could tell you any day's conversations and each day has them, the Rops are here, more Ropsian than ever, so many things to tell you about them, it would be nice if the navy brought you to us, we could spend hours and hours, we eat lots of luxuries, but your specialties alas n'xiste pas, but since we like luxuries it is alright, lots of love, tell Wendell I will be writing soon, but naturally since you se faire rare you are answered at once, lots of love

Gertrude

The letter did come: One of the most annoying things about our correspondence during the war was that Wendell Wilcox's letters always seemed to reach Gertrude, whereas at least half of mine never did.
daily mystères: I told Gertrude I had fallen into the habit of reading at least one detective story [*mystère*] a day; after her plea, I sent her several packages of paperback detective stories.
Bowstring Murders: Gertrude's name was mentioned in *The Bowstring Murders* by Carter Dickson.
the navy brought you to us: I had enlisted in the U.S. Navy, but my food allergies soon got me discharged.

Postmarked 13 January 1942
Bilignin par Belley, Ain

My dearest Sammy,

The second nice little package came bless you, the snow is snowing and the cold wind is blowing, but we have plenty of wood and everything is alright, Bennett Cerf sent me by request War and Peace and it's a wonderful book to read just now, now when Russia is so real and war is so real and peace well there is not much peace in war and peace which is a way it has, and we wonder every day about you all, are you taken now now that they think they need you more than they did, I can't tell you how near you all seem now that our country is in trouble, we have nice new friends here now, a half Scotch half mexican wife and a french husband and they are mighty nice neighbors and they keep turkies and cows, all of which makes naturally nice neighbors even nicer, the d'Aiguys are in Tunisie eating dates, the Chaboux are here and busy as usual as indeed we all are, there would be, there will be so much to tell you some day, and thanks so much for the books, they are so pretty as well as so interesting, and they are such a comfort, but you always are Sammy in spite of your neglectful ways, take care of yourself and lots of love

Gertrude

The Rops were in Aix en Provence for Christmas so we could say how do you do. Paris France in french is a great success.

Chaboux: Gertrude's doctor and his wife, great good friends of Gertrude's and Alice's.

Postcard, postmarked 1 April 1945
Paris
[censored by military]

My dearest Sammy,

Here we are in Paris, glory be, your brother-in-law seems to have gone but if he comes back tell him to come. We heard a lot about you from a stoutish officer who knew you in Loyola [University in Chicago] and who helped buy the Mixmaster and we showed it to him and we were all happy. To be sure it would be nice to have you [here] but you were certainly not made to be a soldier, but could you not be a correspondent or something where your tummy could feed itself, and Wendell, love to Wendell love to you all, I am putting your new address (yours is the same) into my address book, bless you all, and do not drink, no do not do not drink but come to Paris, lots of love

Gertrude

a stoutish officer: Arthur Kogstad, a former student of mine at the university.

Postmarked 7 May 1945
5, rue Christine, Paris VI

My dearest Sammy,

I am awfully upset at your sad news and I telephoned to the Rops and they were very upset. Will you tell your sister how sorry we all are. Rops you know is not teaching any more, he is living entirely on writing and lecturing, it is a little wearing for him and not so certain, but these days in France things are as they are. Spring has come and never have I seen Paris so lovely, abundantly warm, soft skies and lovely buildings and the American army, it was sad not to be a soldier bold but there are compensations, lots of love to you always

Gertrude

your sad news: My brother-in-law, Lieutenant Arthur E. Ury, was killed on March 4, 1945, during the drive across the Rhine in the last days of the war in Europe. He had seen the Rops in Paris in February 1945.

Postmarked 27 October 1945
5, rue Christine, Paris VI

My dearest Sammy,

It's a long time between drinks but there is so much to do these days and then there is still more, there always is still more, what can we tell you, first is the Mixmaster still re-created that is can one get spare parts, we could do with the two twirlers our two got busted in the country and the bowl in which the twirlers twirl, would it be too much bother, these days one asks for what one wants, since you cannot buy you have to ask and asking works such is the way of life, my we have been busy and hoping we can go to Biarritz for my play, Yes is for a very young man, and after that well anything is after that, the Rops are still in the country and guarding le silence, just why I do not know, but they are, sure some day you will come back, there are lots of new ones but you will be a welcome old one, you bet, and Wendell he's had a book, but we haven't, how about it, lots of love

Always
Alice and Gertrude

twirlers twirl: I finally sent them a green bowl and two twirlers, as they requested.

Wendell he's had a book: Everything is Quite All Right. (New York: Bernard Ackerman, 1945).

22 August 1946
5, rue Christine, Paris VI

Sam dear —

Your wire did me good because at once there came back to me the really good time you had given Gertrude — so many times — who always said she liked your specialties including the allergy — but it was your telephoning and just having a casual conversation that pleased her most and she constantly spoke of it — so like Sam and nobody else. Gertrude was the happiest person that ever was but you found a way to give her a new pleasure — and so I will always love you. Basket and I stay on here alone — so if you come over we'll try to welcome you prettily in Gertrude's home.

Always affectionately
Alice

it was your telephoning: On January 20, 1946, I called Gertrude and talked to her for twenty minutes, about nothing in particular and everything in general. The bill was enormous.

Postcard, postmark illegible October [?] 1946
Thouars, Deux Sèvres, France

This is where Basket and I have been for a fortnight. Not exactly the country but nice and quiet and calm and restful. The air is delicious — the sky incredibly beautiful — the lonesomeness extreme — but we stay on for another fortnight. Are you being a good boy. Or are you like Basket — perfect with an occasional lapse. Have you seen Thornton. He wrote me that he expected to see you — he thinks you should teach — he's a firm believer in teaching. He is of course the best example of the benefits it is possible to achieve from learning and teaching. Well, tell me what you're up to now, Sam dear.

Love
Alice

31 December 1946
5, rue Christine, Paris VI

Dear Sam — A happy New Year to you and many more of them. Basket and I made up our minds we'd write to you this year — that is I did and Basket accepted going to bed temporarily here in the sitting room. I found a sweet snap of him with you I think just from the waist down leaning in a doorway at Bilignin — it seems not to be possibly any body but you — I'll send it to you some day. I'm just a bit wanting it a while longer — when I first came back here alone I destroyed all the photos and negatives of all kinds of photographs over the years and so when I find a snap (All of them went to Y[ale] U[niversity] L[ibrary] so I thought) it has an enormous value to me — but eventually all the drawers and chests will be empty. I really get on very well — as well as any one does who is halt and blind and deaf and dumb and in perfect health does.

The Sparrow article delighted me — thanks so awfully for sending it — it had that Sammish impishness that pleased Gertrude so much — she would have laughed out [loud]. What a time you had of it — but what made you leave Loyola. Oh, Sammy, aren't you good at all any more. I'll begin to worry terribly about you if you're just adrift with an allergy (is that what it's called when it comes to be an adverb) in the wilds of Chicago. Be careful, very careful. Best hurry up on the simplification work and make enough to come to France — that is Paris — soon. For all our sakes come soon.

When I've finished sending things to Yale and done some typing and cleaned the flat and caught up with darning and patching — well then it will be spring and Basket and I will take walks and be in excellent form for when you do come. It's [the rue Christine] a nice quarter right across from the Pont-Neuf and four American blocks from Notre Dame and just full of Gertrude. She used to wander all about it and at all hours — except the mornings — before noon she never got out and so she always knew the leisurely afternoon life of the population when they could talk endlessly which she and they did. When you come you'll like them better than ever you did because I think the liberation loosened them up beyond what they were when the Germans first came. There are lots of picture shows too more than there were. And the Petit Palais has all the treasures from all over France gathered together like the exposition of '36 and they say it may last for years. This is the highlight because the Louvre wont be ready for years. It has just a few rooms opened.

Do you remember Francis Rose? He remembers you and sent you his greetings. He has completely reformed — strange to say it is quite becoming though he has lost his looks — married a quite poisonous Frederica who has done him a world of good and paints beautifully — surer and firmer than when you knew his pictures in '39. He spent the summer in France near Lourdes where he went for a pilgrimage and he painted three or four pictures of it — quite masterly. And now he is doing a big picture a *Hommage à Gertrude.* He lives in London where he can sell his pictures. Frederica writes. It is all so different than it was. Francis has kept his sweetness and pretty ways, but has lost the eccentricity and exotic color of his youth.

Madame Pierlot died during the occupation when she was 92 years old from a cold she caught in the attic going over old papers and letters. The family went completely to pieces after she was no longer there. Bob d'Aiguy became impossible and Gertrude rowed with him as everyone did eventually — François was always gaga — Diane I don't think you met.

It will in an hour be the New Year so I'm going to bed so as not to know anything about it but once more all my best wishes to you always

Affectionately yours
Alice

The Sparrow article: From September 1943 to October 1949 I wrote a monthly article of about a thousand words for the *Illinois Dental Journal,* a most unlikely vehicle. The articles were on a diversity of topics having nothing to do with dentistry and were done under the pseudonym of Philip Sparrow. The one to which Alice refers was entitled "On How to Write an Encyclopedia."

simplification work: I had forsaken teaching temporarily to be a department editor for a rewriting of the *World Book Encyclopedia.* All editors followed the "readability formula" of Rudolf Flesch.

picture shows: Alice was of course referring to art galleries.

Madame Pierlot: The grande dame who lived at Béon with her sons, the comtes d'Aiguy, and daughter, Diane.

Postcard enclosed in an envelope with a snapshot of Basket.
Dated probably January 1947,
and sent from Paris.

Dear Sam,

Why dont you write to me. Didnt you get a tremendous long letter I wrote you. Amongst many things I said my very prettiest thanks for all the wonderful things the box held. Tell me — did you never get the letter or perhaps this won't reach you. Have you a new address again.

I've just packed the *Angels on the Bough* for Yale. Gertrude's library — it has been decided — goes to Yale U.L. It's a satisfaction to know it's going to be together — that is books and mss and letters. It's a deep regret that the rest wont stay together after me. Sometimes I think the objects on the table — the chairs on the rugs — the pictures — will refuse to be separated and will perish when one forces them. Ah — they're after all the things Gertrude touched.

It's warmer — the sun has shone for five consecutive days — one thing Basket leaps about. Isnt this [the enclosed snapshot] a part of you and the other Basket at Bilignin in '39. Write to me at once or I'll think I've lost you.

Love
Alice

tremendous long letter: This is one letter that never reached me, either because I had a new address in Chicago or the postal system had failed. The "box" to which she refers was filled with an assortment of new kitchen gadgets. The snapshot was of Basket and myself from the waist down.

31 July 1947
5, rue Christine, Paris VI

Sammy dear,

All these weeks since your precious letter and article and the adorable snap and your lovely out of the blue voice on the telephone have gone and if I think of you with love and gratitude how do you know — how can you suspect. But I've been so tormented — so miserable for so long now that it just took this three weeks old heat wave to do me in completely. But since the heat is to continue indefinitely according to the man who runs the weather in France, I got up during the night and did my housework and I'm all settled to write to you with Basket sheared *en lion* for the first time — trilletted[?] and more beautiful than ever next to me.

Well to begin with your article — it was perfect and Gertrude would have been very pleased with it. It is such a warm faithful portrait of her humanity and variety. But Sammy — I am ashamed to think that you have no better souvenirs than the thorns from Bilignin — you who gave so continuously — so generously. But I can make amends — there will be some one going back some time who will take the real souvenir to you. I'll manage so that you wont have to wait until you come over. And how I wish you'd make it soon — it would mean so much to have you in Paris — do be a really good boy and save your pennies. I dont think you'd have any trouble to get a position at the American school by applying well in advance. They dont pay handsomely but probably enough to live on quietly. If you dont like the idea dont hate me. I'll try to think of something else. But if you want to teach you'd have to be awfully good which might be a bore. Living conditions are quite possible — every thing except keeping warm — heating adequately just doesn't exist. But do make plans to come.

The snap is so like you — often when I look at it it is a good moment before I realize you are in costume so natural does it seem. I am sending it on to Yale with the article on Gertrude. You havent asked my advice but Donald Gallup — Yale University Library would be very happy to have a word from you saying that Gertrude's letters to you will eventually go to Y.U.L. Of course you will do as you think best about this. Then I must tell you about the comfort it was to hear your voice on the phone but you really mustnt. The Kiddie was here at the time and he said it was absolutely astronomical and though it did me a world of good and I loved it just the way Gertrude had you musnt ever repeat it. You must put the money in your *bas de laine* to make coming over sooner. It is quite strange — your voice when I heard it was so natural — so Sammy — And I was pretty low in my mind. The horrid administrator in Baltimore — his name is Edgar Allan Poe! — is doing every thing he can to retard Carl Van Vechten's work on the unpublished manuscripts. Carl and I want to see the work started at once — naturally — and he goes on delaying with one excuse and another. It's unbearable — unthinkable that what Gertrude wanted is not being done. I've been trying to find the money here but how to get it over to U.S. in dollars with all the French *office d'échange* is more than any one is ready to undertake. My last hope here has vanished and I'm sick with it all — there is nothing to do now but wait until October which is the earliest the horrid creature puts as his earliest date. I'm really telling you my worries but you will please forget that I have done so and dont mention it to me or to any one. It's so hot I get foolish in the head.

I havent told you that Francis Rose designed a very simple but beautifully proportioned headstone for Gertrude's grave. I've had some photos taken and will send you one as soon as I get them. Precious — precious Gertrude out there alone — she who was always so surrounded. Sammy are you still *practiquant* — what a consolation it must be. Forget this weakness it's fatigue and the heat — and I never tear up or censor my letters so I'll let it go *telle qu'elle* [*est*]).

The Kiddie of the Autobiography was here in Paris for a month — he's doing his souvenirs of Gertrude, they're quite alright. A New Englander looks at Gertrude Stein — of course that is not its title but that is what he's done — it may be liked — it's hard judging. Francis Rose is doing his memories too — and he and his wife are coming over in two weeks to spend the rest of August and September in the south of France. He painted some beautiful pictures near Lourdes last year — he works tremendously at everything — frescoes and designs for stuffs and wallpapers and book jackets and illustrations — he and his wife are madly extravagant. They require so much merely to get up and go to bed with — oh dear no ribaldry was intended — anyway they both work hard and manage to pay their bills — and I'm as fond of him as ever.

To Do isnt printed yet I'm not sure that it will be for Darantière tells me that Dufy is very very ill — in any case there is no immediate question of it. Dufy's illness has also upset the book Darantière was to do with some colored plates of Dufy and a text by Gertrude on Dufy. It's one of those strangely entangled French situations that become crystal clear one day and are all but accomplished before you catch your breath. The French are wonderful but I wouldn't change my nationality — nothing would suggest the necessity — really one doesnt want to complain about them more than one allows oneself as a foreigner to do. But come over and see them and

Your ever affectionate
Alice

snap and your lovely voice: I had sent her a snapshot of myself in costume as a "super" with the New York City Ballet and telephoned her one day.

your article: One of the "Philip Sparrow" articles in the *Illinois Dental Journal* (February 1947) was devoted to Gertrude Stein.

Gertrude's letters: These were given to the Beinecke Library at Yale in the late 1950s.

are you still practiquant: Are you still a practicing Catholic. The answer was no.

Francis Rose . . . memories: His autobiography, *Saying Life* (London, 1961), was a vast tissue of inaccuracies; for example, while he was supposed to be in Germany with Goering et al. during August 1939 he was actually at Bilignin with Cecil Beaton and myself.

18 April 1948
5, rue Christine, Paris VI

Sam dear,

What do you think has happened — there's a nice man from Farrar Rinehart named W. Raney who knew and admired you in Montana in '35 when there was a question of Gertrude's lecturing at the university. He was fifteen then and you were proposing the most heroic sacrifices to see that she got there. Can you imagine my pleasure in hearing him tell all about you. It's a very real pleasure — like nothing I've had in months. Raney is a friend of Carl Van Vechten's and it was he who accepted the volume of Gertrude's that Carl had prepared — *Last Operas and Plays* — that will come out in autumn. He's just here for two weeks and though he has lived in N.Y. for some years keeps a nice Western freshness and enthusiasm and so it's nice to talk to him about you — wasnt it nice that he should have known you. He and Donald Sutherland from Boulder (U. of C[olorado]) are the most enjoyable of the deluge of visitors to Paris. D.S. is doing an admirable book on Gertrude's works — it will be for some years to come the most important one to be written — he hopes to finish it this summer.

I've been seeing a little of Wendell's friends the Andreases

— they are fresh and unspoiled — I guess the West is best. Perhaps Chicago isnt so awfully west — but it is west of N.Y.

Basket had rheumatism but is now happily cured — when there is spring weather we walk over to the Madeleine and back and twice we have spent the day in the country. If it can be managed we will go to the country for at least August.

This is my news now we will talk about you — as a friend used to say — you were a dear to send me your articles — they are so much you that they bring you very near — the one about the broken radio I liked best and [knew least?] — its subject is not one that has ever caught me before or ever will again unless you write about it some future time. It has all your best whimsy and pretty lightness and it carries one along with the tempo you set. The one about your friend was revealing and so became passionately interesting though it disappointed me considerably that you recognized him under so many names — getting orthodox — you'll say. Perhaps — especially for others. It would be nice to know spring was really spring for you.

You are an angel to leave your letters — fifty years hence because it isnt necessary to be a witness to the wonderful old man you'll be then — from Gertrude to the Y[ale] U[niversity] L[ibrary]. I'd no idea there were so many — which only makes your gift more marvelous. Are you still at the plush-carpeted oak-staircased encyclopedia — and do be patient with the Devil as an old Spanish friend tried to teach me when I was young in California. Do I preach to you too much — Virgil Thomson said not to profit *trop de mon âge* — but it's a temptation. France isnt quite China but you know how age is respected here (to be sure they love killing their grandmother if she has some money put away — a few years ago two girls killed theirs because an antique dealer had been in their village and the only thing he wanted to buy was her 18th century porcelain soup tureen so they did away with her to get it). Well one cold day I had to go to the *mairie* and I was in the queue when a man said — *La veille grandmère se passe d'abord* and I did — you just better believe I did. Age is the next best thing here after pregnancy — ah ça — otherwise it isnt our week so to speak — one has to admit that

Americans arent loved in Europe — except Mrs. Roosevelt in England.

I'll be writing to you again Sammy dear — good luck and love to you always from

Alice

your articles: Two of the "Philip Sparrow" articles—"On My Poor Old Radio" (August 1947, *IDJ*) and "To a Chance Acquaintance" (December 1947, *IDJ*), a quasireligious one.
oak staircased encyclopedia: Compton's, in Chicago.

22 July 1948
5, rue Christine, Paris VI

Sam dear,

Isn't it just too commonplace always to be telling you that I think of you so much and so warmly — that your letters are the greatest comfort to me and then — *silence absolue.* It's not possible to describe to you the way I've been shoved about — just like the G.Is and not liking it any more than they did. There have been a lot of things to straighten out — and most of them still look very crooked — and an avalanche of American friends — children of friends — grandchildren of friends — acquaintances and their descendants — friends of friends and theirs — but no you can see the effort and the futility — now they are in London or Switzerland and in September Basket and I may go to the country. An inn in the Dordogne has been recommended — the patron is an ex-chef — there is a woods not far away and a hot bath daily — the three requisites — and very cheap. Perhaps it is dirty. *Tant pis.* Basket needs some country runs and a change. To leave here will be a wrench and it will be lonesome down there but it's all been arranged — just a letter from the patron.

Now enough about myself — let's talk about you. It is not for me to tell you for you know it by now that it's all one to me how you achieve your salvation as long as you do. Whatever makes you happy — the Church or Alcoholics Anonymous or anything else. I'm a good Jesuit — any means that suits you — why even what Francis chose — a strong wife. It was difficult to accustom oneself to her at first but in spite of obvious and hidden faults — it's because she's not so simple as she first seemed that one likes her — she gradually impresses herself on you as being altogether respectable. So if a goodlooking female a very few years older than you are says she wants to marry you and you think she really is in love with you — why just let her have her way. Francis is really happy and it is she who has induced this. And don't talk about the love of a good woman — for though she may not be bad she's certainly not what one would call good. Is there anything like her in the offing for you. For you and Francis are not so awfully unlike. And she would give you every chance to work and the way you want to.

Aren't the tapestries too beautiful — to live with *La Licorne* — imagine waking up and finding it there before you again. Here there have been many shows but nothing exciting like the tapestries — the painters paint stupid abstractions that dont achieve becoming pictures and are too pretentious for decorations. Picasso is in the south avoiding an issue by making or rather designing and decorating pottery. The only person who keeps his early energy is Jean Cocteau — who is ageless and agile. He has kept the unfashionable virtues of generosity and loyalty and makes they say good films.

They are translating into Italian *The Making of Americans* unabridged — if Gertrude could only have known this — and they are doing four others — they propose doing all of them eventually. Mondadori the editor is an enthusiastic admirer. *The Makings* was passed about amongst the resistance — they considered it liberation literature — how much Gertrude would have loved all this. It was the translator [Fernanda Pivano] who was here for a few days who told me all this — such a nice warm sympathetic person. The French translations are continuing — the last *Three Lives* is just being placed. The book of *inédits Last Operas and Plays* that Carl Van Vechten has arranged with Rinehart is postponed from October to January. The Kiddie's book is out — it is not the manuscript I saw — *n'en parlons pas.* Père Bernardet from Hautecombe is now at L'Hay la Rose and gets into Paris lately more frequently than before. He came to see me the other day.

Did I tell you that the Daniel-Rops have bought a *domaine* on the Lac de Bourget — his life of Christ for adults — for young people — for children — illustrated — unillustrated — with notes — without notes — *de luxe* — without luxe has sold a million copies. Likewise under the same and varied conditions his story of the Old Testament. He says he will write no more novels not even the lives of the saints — nor the martyrs — nor the mystics. There never was a more enterprising salesman than he — and Madeleine [Daniel-Rops] remains an enigma to me — of how much is she conscious — does she know all or nothing — she's a fascinating subject.

Do you know the Andreas — but of course you do — because I asked them and they said that they'd only met you once or twice. What is the answer to her — she's a complete enigma to me. I like him a lot but she remains embarrassingly unsolved. They are bringing a young Chicagoan to see me on Saturday. Do you remember Cecil Beaton — he's desperately in love with Greta Garbo and the Duchess of Kent equally so with him. Do you like my gossip — everybody tells me a little — eventually I hear it all — none of it holds my attention long enough to follow the plot. Do you remember Madame Giraud — she is living at a convent near here — she is having a sad end for she does not at all like living with the *bonnes soeurs* — but her grandchild has married (she has three children) and there is no room in the flat any more for her. Do you remember Christine née Jouffray — she was and is so very pretty.

The sentence of Bernard Faÿ has been reduced from life to twenty years so that when there is an amnesty for political prisoners he will be freed. If de Gaulle comes in and he may he'll declare an amnesty before the end of the year. If not perhaps some one else may — but not so likely.

I have just learned a delicious French usage. On wedding invitations when they say the mass is at noon they mean one o'clock — when they say at noon precise they mean half after twelve and when they say at very precisely noon they mean noon. Are they not the most delightful children. It's their aged childhood that makes them so surprisingly naive later.

But now to the kitchen. You know Wendell Wilcox

taunted me once with cowardice because I was afraid to use yeast — so here I am off to it now — *nous verrons ce que nous verrons.* My love to you always — my dear — do forgive me and write to me again.

Alice

Alcoholics Anonymous: Alice knew of my problem with alcohol.
in the offing for you: Emmy D. Curtis, a Chicago widow.
to live with La Licorne: Alice enclosed a brochure illustrating a show of medieval tapestries.
The Kiddie's book: Alice was horrified at the end result of W. G. Rogers' memoir of Gertrude, *When This You See Remember Me* (New York: Rinehart, 1948). During her lifetime Alice approved of only one book about Gertrude, Donald Sutherland's *Gertrude Stein: A Biography of her Work* (New Haven: Yale University Press, 1951)
the Andreas: Osborn and Miriam Andreas, of Chicago; he was author of a book on Henry James, *The Expanding Horizon,* as well as a philanthropist and patron of James Purdy's, whose first work was published through his generosity.

8 September 1949
5, rue Christine, Paris VI

Dearest Sam,

It is seven o'clock — it is full daylight — Hitlerian hour still — and finally I'm telling you why it is only today that there is a free hour ahead for what I've longed to do — to tell you about everything. Basket has been sick off and on since July — desperately so more lately. He's back now at the vets again — better than he has been but not cured. He's not been in pain but twice for a day each time. It has been a bad time for me — he's been the sweet companion I've needed since Gertrude went and to have to accept his not being well again doesnt come easy. Now that you share my troubles it is easier and you'll forgive me for this and so much else — wont you — dear Sam — and so I've never written to you to tell you so many things.

But first of all to thank you for the beautiful beautiful basket and all the treasures it holds. You can't fancy what the fragrance of the sweet grass did to me as I undid the package. It's one — indeed the most precious of my perfume memories — sweet grass and heliotrope are more my mother to me except the smile in her eyes. When I was a little girl we spent the summer at Lake George where I fell off a log into the river and was promptly taught Our Father — and my mother bought endless baskets made of sweet grass for her friends and herself — and when she died there was one in which she kept her best handkerchiefs which I kept until I left San Francisco and always wondered afterwards why I had. And only you would have answered and understood the need now to have something to connect me with my childhood. And so you see how many things there are to thank you for — you and your letters — the adorable basket and all the marvelous things it holds — of course the needle threader and the adjustable measure for hems and so many other things that were unheard of and the greatest eye-openers and savers one could imagine and such time savers — down to the last pillow slips — a hasty decision to cut what was left of the great sheets from Bilignin and make new slips was quickly achieved but sewing one was endless hours until you came to the rescue. And the quantities of sewing cotton and darning cotton and wool are more than I will need for the rest of my days — and the tape measure in honest inches —

Interrupted — so a day later. You do see how delighted with all the marvelous provisions I am and though I do appreciate all your pretty thought and do thank you from the bottom of my heart I want you to promise me that this is the last of your overwhelming generosity to me. *Please* write and tell me that you promise — your word would calm me — for it upsets me that you should be so madly extravagant. You know very well that it would have kept you here for a week — and a year of Alcoholics Incorporated [A.A.] would mean a new fund for the trip. That is what you must be doing — isnt it — I would so love to see you. Does that clinch it.

The weather has been exceptionally mild — spring came early and it is going to be a lovely one — the chestnuts and peach blossoms and wild daffodils are all out. It's impossible to get into the country for a day — to go in the train with Basket now is impossible. It would be too fatiguing for us. But I hope to take him mornings into the Luxembourg [Gardens] — only ten minutes from the flat. Gertrude always did.

My household work seems never ending — always increasing for some mysterious [reason] — but the long projected cookbook has to materialize — *nous verrons ce que nous verrons.* Years ago when I spoke of it to Thornton Wilder he only said — but Alice have you ever tried to write. Not since I was ten or eleven years old was the answer — so perhaps one has to have some experience of writing for even a cookbook. But cant one count and build upon conviction — prejudice and passion — my inadequate equipment.

When Thornton Wilder was here he took me to hear music — rather badly played — and Jacuetz [?] in *Don Juan* — excellently played and beautifully staged — décors and costumes by Bérard whose death was a great shock to me. We were very fond of him though Gertrude had years ago tried his painting and found it wanting. She had preferred Francis Rose his friend. Francis' painting has developed marvellously — he brought some of his pictures over during the winter — most of them for a very large triptych of the Crucifixion — he's going to have a show in London in June and one here in autumn. His marriage is very successful.

My best news — and the best thing that will happen to me is that the first book of Gertrude's unpublished work has appeared — *Last Operas and Plays.* I devoutly hope you haven't gone and bought a copy because I've had Rinehart send you one. Don't ever buy a book of Gertrude's because I'll always have one sent to you. There are some completely lovely things in it — some of them with Bilignin and its landscape as their subject. There is still unpublished enough material for nine or ten more volumes.

Have you seen Andreas' book on Henry James — *The Expanding Horizon.* It is a bit dry but should prove excellent propaganda amongst the young. They said they knew you a bit — she's a strange creature. And their friends the Knapiks — do you know them — he's a great cook and she's smashingly beautiful. She takes her supreme good looks so quietly that they become veiled and only come to light slowly — but I've seen nothing like them for years.

Do you know Capote — his success a bit overdone — excellent climate and good landscape — too many butterflies — his and his characters' sexual life boresome. Faulkner's last interesting but mistaken. Is there no one writing better than these two. Here they're mad about Steinbeck and dos Passos. Sartre discovered them and though he's beginning to be oldfashioned his Americans continue popular. I have [met] a just twenty year old youth — precocious graduate of Harvard and at work on his fourth novel — aside from this quite pleasant.

Do you still work at the opera — it's the nicest way to hear it — if you can't get to rehearsals which is perhaps more comfortable. But the ballet sounded even more exciting — wasnt it. I've kept off the subject of your teaching again — fearful that you had once more thrown it over — I do hope not. You always made me feel that you were so exceptionally good at it — making things come alive to the dullest of impossible boys — they are of course no duller than girls — who know how to make themselves look so. Dont you find subjects galore among their strange relationships. You ought to be able to do a smashing novel about them and no one has in U.S. (They do it all the time in England — do try it.)

Oh by the way — about brilliant conversations when under the influence of — Jo Davidson used to say the same thing — in fact used it as an excuse — it made him brilliant and gave him courage. Gertrude used to tell him it was just the contrary — he lost his usual easy native wit. Well one afternoon we went to see the Davidsons and a friend of Jo's was there completely *parti* and quite a bit maudlin. Jo took Gertrude aside and excused his friend and Gertrude said she didnt much care for it and added — You see Jo why I say what I do when you are like that. Like that — never — said Jo indignantly and wouldnt believe her so Gertrude said why not let me be the judge — you see how little your friend is capable of weighing his wit. Gertrude always said that liquor only improved the *déséquilibrés* and my dear we hope you are not that.

Yes the Kiddie's book was frightfulness extreme — the pang it gave me is over and he is fading gently away. Of course he couldnt have had any pure feeling for Gertrude to do such a thing. What's this — who was comparing him to you.

And here's Francis address (I remind you he's a Bart — like

this 'Sir F.R. Bart' ((he doesnt mind it and his wife can eat it with a spoon and not be a snob!)) 2 Bassett House — Flood Street Chelsea — London S.W.III and I'm sure he'd be delighted to hear from you.

And now to thank you for the lovely medallion — so perfect — Gertrude and her flag — it is going to make things come true for her isnt it. But how did you make it — how *did* you — it leaves one breathless — what a Sam — what a country. Bless you both. All my thanks — appreciation and love to you

Always yours,
Alice

I've just telephoned to the vets. Basket is getting well again. T[hank] G[od].

the Knapiks: Virginia and Harold Knapik were friends of Alice's from 1948 until her death in 1967. Virginia worked in the American Embassy; Harold was a student at the École Normale de Musique and a composer. Both the Knapiks died in 1975, she of a heart attack, he a suicide.
the lovely medallion: An aluminum circle with a flag in the center and writing stamped around the edge, made on machines you find in penny arcades; I had stamped "Gertrude Stein" around the edge.

27 May 1949
5, rue Christine, Paris VI

Sam dear,

Here is a quiet Sunday afternoon and here is the news — the sweet grass sweet Sammy's basket — is more than ever my delight — it has cheered me through some dark days. Basket was desperately sick — the vet didnt think he could cure him. For a few days he didn't recognize me and then the treatment commenced to be effective and so at last he came back and we were both pleased. He is as thin as a hound at the foot of his master on a gothic tomb and isnt as gay as he used to be but he's here again and for the moment that is everything. Then I had what one might call a household accident. In an excess of zeal I took the large cover off the radiator to wash the woodwork in the back — it's a tricky operation — having succeeded in lifting it into the air the radiator fell on me and one foot and ankle were pinned under it — and I had to wait forty minutes to have Gabrielle come and rescue me. It was just painful for a day — arnica did the trick — but as it wasnt possible to walk — out came the lovely basket and all my mending and darning done. I commenced some fancy sewing — neckerchiefs — and now every day it is scenting the room and inviting me to do what I like most to do — a little fine foolish sewing. One gets so bored with doing useful things — necessary things. *Vive l'inutil — la périssable!* And the lovely sachets are acacia — but definitely Gertrude's favorite scent — acacia in France and iris in Italy — and saffron in Spain. And saffron reminds me I'm so glad the allergy has been thrown overboard. Dont you think A. Anonymous has something to do with it. I do. I'm all for it since it has done so handsomely for you. The program is sensible and generous and for Gods sake take it as yours and *doucement allez doucement* as they used to say in Bilignin.

Painting as a diversion for you is perfect — the trouble with Picasso was that he allowed himself to be flattered into believing he was a poet too. Gertrude and he had quite a scene but she told it in *Everybody's Autobiography.* The only person who did both not equally well though equally charmingly was Max Jacob — do you know either his poetry or his painting.

The dental journal articles are gay and personal but if you're going to really get to work on something really your own you're right about giving them up — they'd be getting in your way. It will be the deepest satisfaction to me if you pull off something of your real quality — you know Gertrude expected it of you and in all your fancy there is evidence of a direction — a choice that makes me long to see what will have been accomplished two months and ten days hence.

Do you know an irrepressible youth named Don Roscher. He sent me a photograph of himself — no this is not the first — his teeth always exposed to a favorable light and in a new position. But this one was different — there was another person in the picture and a damned distinguished one at that. And then on the back he had written who it was — Wendell Wilcox. And I was so pleased to see him and to renew my memory and correct it — of our simple brief meeting after a class at U. of C[hicago]. And he looks in so much better health than I had hoped for — not a bit frail or wispy. His life with his cats seems as strenuous — as occupying — as harassed as mine with Basket who offers new pleasures and new worries every blessed day.

It is naturally days since I commenced to write to you — interrupted by photographers who came to do a picture or pictures for an illustrated book on Picasso — one a month appears. A Swiss editor came to see what he would choose for his book — *Picasso before Picasso*(!) There's a little café scene he did in '02 or '03 and a friend gave me in '08 — one of the rare ones under the influence of Toulouse-Lautrec which I produced with considerable pride. Ah yes said he looking at it a little cockeyed — just what I want but unfortunately not the right proportions for the format of the book I envisage. Then there is the lady who is organizing a loan show for charity and who wanted the blue nude with the basket of flowers. The title of the show was *The Mother and Her Child*. But said I — she is not a child with her mother — would she not be just a shocking *fille*. She was ready to overlook the nude's lack of reference. Then there has been a deluge of musicians — executants and composers and one or two concerts which frankly bore me. I would have preferred *The Marriage of Figaro* by Vienna opera which unfortunately I didn't hear. If you're really coming over next year I'll try to hang on for it — there will be so much to hear and to do — so go quietly until then and make it.

Francis Rose has just sent me a large photograph of a new homage to Gertrude he is doing — this is of a wash study for it. His pictures look very different than they did two years ago but they're a reasonable development from any of his old works. There is really no one here doing anything as important amongst the men of his age — he is having a show in London in June and one here in November.

Do you know the Knapiks — she is very refreshing — a strong wind off the lake — and ever so goodlooking. They have republished Gide's *Oscar Wilde* — did you ever read it. Gide has become a worried Victor Hugo — that's what the French feel. And Sartre is out of fashion — like Dior — the new look is no longer new.

Now I must get this to the p.o. — air mail in the pillar

boxes it seems goes by boat mail so Basket and I will trot up to get it into its proper box. Sammy dear I send you my grateful love.

Alice

Don Roscher: A Chicago acquaintance of Wendell Wilcox's.

29 January 1950
5, rue Christine, Paris VI

Dear Sam,

There were two or three things in your letter that I've been wanting to talk to you about. Three weeks ago already there was Wendell's arrival and I let that slip by but now your package has come and I'm so cross with you that there's no delaying any more — for I'm really very angry with you indeed. You know you have no right to do any such thing — indulging me in all kinds of mad luxuries. How ever with such *extravagances* are you going to put *pennies* aside for your trip this summer — how ever I ask you are you going to be able to manage. Oh Sam — you are just a mad boy still. Though I adore my transparent raincoat and apron — the first I've ever possessed — I'm still very upset — even when I look at them in all their beauty. Will you ever be *rangé* — reasonable — provident — practical — careful — if not all at one time well two at a time in turn. It is a delight to possess the lovely objects but I'm distressed even when I thank you so many times for your thought of me.

Then your last Philip Sparrow's modest proposal — what a thunderclap — what beats me is their having printed it — however did they not notice its deadliness. You left no one thing unsaid — they had to be told how effective your new broom had swept all before it. Of course you knew what was coming — it wouldnt have surprised you. In a way it is too bad — it did give you an outlet. Where will you find anyone who will let you so gracefully resent becoming forty and the other things you wrote about — so amiably — without propaganda or an ax to grind. And who else is doing it — you were quite alone. Are you finding a new market — are there no weeklies or monthlies that are not filled with screen radio television or atomic bombs as their by products. Is there nothing between such subjects and the academic life. Is there no quiet sensible living any more.

The stray Americans over here — those who have come over on scholarships are frightfully dull — with no exceptions and they are young and precocious — and leave one exhausted after a short while. Their weighty complacency cant be shoved about. Wendell [Wilcox] doesn't take them on — his liveliness finds distraction in less commonplace subjects — even to the extent of a kind of irregularity — I suspect. He is so like his letters that it is as if I'd really known him — which of course was not at all the case — for we'd only met at the university for a moment. He is living quite near here and that unfortunately doesnt mean I see him often — but he has a number of friends here. He meets some casually on the street whom he didn't know were in Paris. To this extent he is at home in Paris. He was seduced I suspect by the Italians but likes the French. As you know he came over with Miriam Andreas — but she flew home after depositing him here. Their friends the Harold Knapiks whom I like a lot have moved into this quarter. It sounds like a small town life and if I were younger I'd enjoy it too. It is very nice just knowing it is there.

There will be two events to mark Gertrude's birthday — a large show of manuscripts and first editions at the New York Public Library and a half hour's radio performance in which T. Wilder — who is going to be here this month — Carl Van Vechten — who came over in the autumn — Virgil Thomson and Rogers are to take part. *Three Lives* is to appear in French and *The Making of Americans* *un*abridged in Italian — an early *conte* to be printed in a limited edition (hand press) and a copy has been ordered for you. When Carl was here we went over the future publication of Gertrude's inedited manuscripts and the means are guaranteed. Thank goodness — it's a great relief to me. There are still one or two things for me to do — if I'm not too hopelessly ineffective. Always so optimistic in the beginning — the new *tuyau* will do the trick — and then when it fails — fussed beyond words until the next *tuyau* turns up. It some times works but mostly not.

Isnt the Sadlers Wells technique superb — quite breathless — did you see Gertrude and L[ord] Berners' ballet *The Wedding Bouquet* and did you see Margot Fontaine [*sic*] dance. The Paris ballet is amateurish by comparison and the de Cuevas' ugly. Carl took me about to the ballet and to see a very brilliant Jean Cocteau adaptation of *The Streetcar* etcetera. I'm a little fed up with the Columbus Mississippi School of Writers.

Basket was frightfully sick but is in good form now — a little too fat but as it's very cold it wont do him too much harm. And he's very handsome — having achieved a fine new coat after having been bald and shaven! I'm well and jog on. Dear Sam — I'm surrounded by your gifts — the sweet grass work basket filled with its treasures is on the table beside me and with my gay transparent apron I'm going to work. Thank you — thank you — thank you — write to me soon that you've gotten to work and that soon I'll be seeing a manuscript if not a book.

Love to you always
Alice

raincoat and apron: Such plastic articles had not yet arrived in Paris.
modest proposal: A "Philip Sparrow" article suggesting that the South quietly secede from the North on the next anniversary of the ending of the Civil War. The article had such a divisive effect on the national dental convention that the Illinois state association passed a resolution and disclaimer against "Philip Sparrow," asking him to resign, which he did.
Miriam Andreas: The wife of Osborn Andreas was christened Marian, but to what she called her "disreputable" and most intimate friends she was always "Miriam."
an early conte: Things As They Are. (Vermont: Pawlet, 1950).
tuyau: One of Alice's rare uses of argot; she does not mean "pipe" or "tube" but "confidential information" as employed by a "lead."

15 May 1950
5, rue Christine, Paris VI

Sam dear,

Your *mea gulpa* [*sic*] pleased me so much that I felt I ought to telephone you and then I remembered how I'd scolded you when you once and with no such excuse — so madly rang me up. But gulpa is delicious and now don't go and tell me it's just an insane typewriter (are there typewriter psychiatrists now in my poor native land).

Well gulpa isnt the only reason I wanted to write to you. There is first of all your actually being here on the twenty-eighth of next month and the pleasure it's going to be — and that you are not to worry about the *G. Washington* — it's a sturdy old tub — it was the fault of the pilot boat's instructions — very English he or it on a frightfully foggy night. I had the story from a passenger — he said it was a superb example of the English genius which first requires a muddle and then muddles through. The *G. Washington* being an American boat complicated things — there was more trouble creating the muddle than if it had been an English boat — which would have been more adaptable — more sensitive to what was expected of it. He made out a good case for the pilot and the staunch resistance of the *G. Washington.* Anyway it is nicely mended now and will bring you over safely.

Now have you made any plans for hotel reservations. You must — it's holy year and the hotels are enjoying the first advantages. Would you like me to do something. There's a nice hotel in the Place St. Sulpice — just in the corner and opposite the side of the church — a room giving on the square with balcony — running hot water and elevator for five hundred francs a day — breakfast and baths extra. Would you like me to do something about that — or do you want to go back to the rue des Beaux-Arts. Wasnt it the hotel where Oscar Wilde died — de Nice or what — or Wendell's which he says is alright. The landlord is *impayable* and the landlady his and his and his and his. But something must be done because by the end of June everything will be full up. The provincials have already commenced pilgrimmaging to N. Dame. On Saturday a friend of Virginia Nabick [sic] who has a car took V.N. and Wendell and me to the forest of St. Germain where we picked a few last hyacinths (spring has come late but with undue heat), had a picnic lunch and then went on to Versailles. It was absolutely inconceivable that Wendell should return to Esther [his wife] without having seen the Palace inside and out. There were thousands of visitors — the palace had more people than on that awful day when they stoned the gates and forced their way in. To be sure it was a Saturday that we went but that is the day the amiable young lady with the car is free. So let me know at once about the hotel and anything else whatsoever that may occur to you.

Your being a 1950 Winslow Homer is delightful — but are you can you or anyone else be a W. Homer. He is the American painter — unique and so far beyond all the others as to really be a painter without the limitations of nationality and time. So go on being a W. Homer and without date.

Did you know that the Picasso portrait of Gertrude has finally been returned to the Met (after a considerable struggle) and is now hanging in one of the rooms of French paintings with a Rousseau.

I'm so glad you have no more *régime* to follow because I make a number of dishes without much exertion which are quite edible and amusing. We get everything in Paris we did in '39. But there is one thing in the way of household utensils I would very much like to have — it's a series of measuring spoons — tea and soup size — the teaspoons marked for halves or perhaps it's a separate spoon. I have seen them in an American kitchen and they would be a help and a pleasure but not take up too much room. But *nothing* else — I have all the lovely things you sent me and they are wonderfully useful.

You mustnt think that Paris is tempting — it really isnt. There's nothing seductive about the French or their country — charming and in spots beautiful but not seductive. And anyway you know what Gertrude used to say — temptation wasnt tempting.

Did I write you that the first thing she ever wrote is being printed — unfortunately limited edition — to be called *Things As They Are* — a copy has already been sent to you. The raincoat is a dream — quite out of this world as you say in U.S. It fits perfectly and you were angelic to send it to me but at the same time very naughty. I created quite a sensation by carrying it into the drawing room at a lunch party quite unconscious of what I was doing but not at all displeased — there is nothing like it in Paris.

I havent said anything about the pleasure seeing Wendell familiarly has been to me but we will soon be talking about this. Francis Rose was here — he is going to have a show here in the autumn. He is painting beautifully and interestingly — what Gertrude expected. His wife is able — handsome and intelligent — and I forgot charming — and I'm devoted to her. Basket is better than he has been but not as well as he was — alas — we're getting old.

Of all the things you left at Bilignin for us to keep against your return I find alas only the guide to Paris. What became of everything else — especially the Henry Miller — which I remember still at Culoz. It wasnt amongst Gertrude's books — which one of his was it?

À très bientôt happily — don't forget to let me know about a hotel or anything else.

Love from
Alice

Did you remember Béon and Madame Pierlot — she died in '41 aged 92.

the G. Washington: One of the United States Line ships was driven by heavy seas into the dock at Southampton and badly damaged.
Francis Rose's . . . wife: Alice sometimes changed her mind. In December 1946 her initial opinion of Frederica Rose was that she was "quite poisonous."
Henry Miller: Left behind at Bilignin during the hectic days before World War II were a number of books, among them the Obelisk Press first edition of *The Tropic of Cancer.*

30 May 1950
5, rue Christine, Paris VI

Dear Sam,

Well — no wonder — the Hotel des Beaux-Arts — rue des Beaux-Arts — didn't answer you. There aint no such animal. You're so plausible — when I read your letter immediately it was familiar — I placed it at once. (After the other afternoon's excursion I found the one I'd in mind — it's the hotel d'Isly — rue Jacob). The hotel de Nice and the hotel d'Alsace are the only two hotels on the rue Jacob [*sic:* Alice means rue des Beaux-Arts] — they refused to acknowledge any acquaintance with your name — [though] I did persist with poor Oscar's. So I went to the Récamier which looks cleaner and ever so more respectable (I take it you intend to be good on this trip — or dont you — remind me to tell you a sweet story about [Myras?] and her reform). So there you are — room with balcony giving on the Place St. Sulpice — no. 3 bis — for June 28th — quite definitely being held for you *sauf avis contraire.* (Is a plastic fib one that can be seen through and doesnt hold hot water). As for your photograph — my dear Sam — did you think I needed one — the only thing that has changed is your nationality. Everyone who has seen it when I put the question answers French — not a bad idea — it will make you more welcome to the casual stranger.

No you musnt bring me anything more than the measuring spoons — they are absolutely all I need. Was it a Chinoise that you weren't given in '39 — that's my memory of the last hectic days before you left — just ahead of the mobilisation. Life hasnt been the same since.

There are no gadgets in France though there's great talk about them but they still make and use eighteenth century things — that dont get housed very well in more modern sized kitchens.

Things As They Are was written in 1903 — and in '05 became *Melanctha.* I'll tell you the rest when we meet — too long to write and especially now for I must fly. Wendell has not been overly well — he calls it a cold but it's a *dérangement* to which he is susceptible — more's the pity. He's leaving on the 6th — you'll be seeing him before you leave. It was too nice really meeting him.

I'll be writing you soon again

Love from
Alice

Hôtel d'Alsace: By chance I stayed at the Hôtel d'Alsace in 1939, and equally by chance learned I had been given the same room in which Wilde died. I had confused its name with that of the street, rue des Beaux-Arts.

Place St. Sulpice: Gertrude and Alice were fond of the Hotel Récamier and placed many of their friends there.

Postcard, postmarked 3 August 1950
La Régie, Soye-en-Septaine, Cher

Dear Sam,

Pleasant trip down. The good K's [Knapiks] and Louise B.[rooks] personally conducting. The place here charming —

everything hoped for and more. The hostess active intelligent amiable — the only guest a young Swedish girl — dumb dull deadly — but with the body of a 12th century angel. The only rub — and that not because of herself but she occupies the only spare bedroom besides mine — but she leaves around the twentieth — perhaps before. As soon as it's decided I'll let you know and you'll come down for two or three days — yes? Save time around then. The walled garden is sweet — Basket is unleashed and wanders about. The three small *caniches* are sweet and leave him alone. I read a book a day — write five letters — and today raked the garden paths. Such a relief to be beyond hearing of Gabrielle — and beyond yours is a deprivation for your loving

Alice

Keep well be good and enjoy yourself

Postcard, postmarked 7 August 1950
La Régie, Soye-en-Septaine, Cher

Dear Sam,

It is now decided that the Swedish girl leaves on the twenty-first so would you like to come on the twenty second and stay to the twenty fifth. There is a train at seven in the morning — another at noon — I'll write you the exact hours. It is probably the Gare d'Orsay but all that later. Life here continues to be very quiet and agreeable — both Basket and I will be spoiled for Paris and Gabrielle. The return to them is not an alluring prospect. No word from the Nabiks [*sic*] — I hope nothing has happened to them. There is a little dog here very like Jane B[owles] but not at all like Miriam [Andreas]

Love
Alice

11 August 1950
La Régie, Soye-en-Septaine, Cher

Dear Sam,

Well then it is all fixed for the 22nd. The train leaves from the Gare d'Austerlitz — not as I wrote the Gare du Quai d'Orsay — at two o'clock. It is either a Micheline or a *rapido*.

Your ticket is to Bourges where you arrive at 2:30 and where Madame Debar and I will meet you in her car. Soye etcetera is eight kilometers south. The Swedish child (frightful) will have left — we had to wait for that — but you may still find her — though I hope not. A schoolteacher from Vernon who has an early eighteenth century laugh — the rest is best forgotten — or better still never remarked.

The days are very agreeable here but there is no distraction of any kind. But you will bear with it until the afternoon of the 25th when we will take you back to Bourges for a six o'clock train. And we will have had a chance to see each other quietly.

It is so calm and the air so alive that Paris with the hectic and torrid nights is quite forgotten. It rained the purest most direct from Heaven rain yesterday I've ever seen — with not as much as moving a leaf — each drop knowing its place went directly to it and all day they fell with precise regularity. It was English not French poetry. As it hadnt rained for months today was dry in the garden but poor Basket got rheumatism. I am giving him aspirin which usually does the trick.

I am reading Balzac after years of abstention — he is *la gloire de la France* — not Monsieur Gide.

And now I am going to bed. Dont say it would have been better to have waited until morning to write to you.

Love to you Sammy dear from

Alice

This letter is not in the Bancroft Library collection, but was donated to the KQED public auction (PBS) in May 1971.

Postcard enclosed in envelope

29 August 1950

La Régie, Soye-en-Septaine, Cher

Dear Dear Sammy,

It was sweet of you to come here and sleep away the days — as Basket and I do — and sweet of you to take the spotted suit to Paris. Sweet yes — but are you good. *Ah cela* as Madame Pierlot said when she was asked if a cousin of hers had as much charm as she had. *Ah cela* she answered. And not for a minute do I believe you saw the ghost of the curate — whom I didnt see — on the steps of the cathedral (for all the evidence I have he never did exist even in Bourges to say nothing of in the rue Christine). It was not in the Marines but in the *services de Santé* we activated ourselves in the other war — the one before the last as the English say. It rained most of yesterday and all of today — the plums are sweet — the tobacco leaves are enormous — they are of the size those of the banyan tree must achieve. Muchette [one of the three poodles] has been shaved à la cow-girl — bathed — and Basket has gathered in the fleas she has shed. A p.c. from Virginia saying they are calling for me at 8:30 A.M. so we wont say goodbye yet for surely I'll be back at 5 rue Christine to telephone you. Be a good boy. All my young friends are so naughty and the worst of them writes me Dear Wicked One and ends Do be good!!

Love from
Alice

spotted suit: Alice asked me to carry a soiled suit of hers to her Parisian dry cleaner.
ghost of the curate: We had teased each other about a local legend of Bourges, and I had written that the curate's ghost had followed me to the dry cleaner.
the Marines: Another part of our private teasing, but she took this seriously.

5 September 1950
5, rue Christine, Paris VI

Dear Sammy,

Louise Brooks was only twenty minutes late but they enjoyed Madame Debar's hospitality and saw the pups and we got on the road finally at ten o'clock and though we took a shorter road than we did to go down it was six o'clock before we got to the flat — Louise Brooks being not only a cautious but a slow driver. So it was too late to say goodbye to you but you did know didnt you that you had all my good wishes for the voyage and for everything that is to follow. Are you having a pleasant crossing with plenty of sunbaths. Are your cabin companions not too impossible — is the boat arriving on time.

It was a jolt to leave Soye and come back here — though the weather down there was frightful after you left — absurdly cold and stormy (equinoctial yes in Europe). Madame Debar was kind and attentive to the end and with Marguerite's efficient attentions the return here has seemed a doubtful pleasure. But Gabrielle had had a great attack of energy and devotion during her two weeks of convalescence (the two weeks of illness she was prostrated by the pain five different maladies caused her to suffer) she washed all the woodwork of the flat (which means the salon walls) and is now ready for a spell.

Basket doesnt like the terrace any more — he considers it squālid as the English pronounce it — but the streets excite him.

Everybody is out of town except Max White — who had telephoned before my return and came to see me at once. He had not received my note (it hasnt yet been returned to me) and had no feeling about my not having followed his advice — he says he gives too much to expect all of it to be followed. So thank goodness I havent lost him. But I have lost the cap of a tooth and must go to the dentist.

Now I am going to the kitchen and use all your lovely things and then I will sew and use more of your lovely things — as if they were necessary to remember that you arent here but in Chicago. Let me hear from you soon. It was good to see you but it would be better to be seeing you more.

Be a good boy or I wont love you — you are the only person I want good. Do I love you now

Alice

Max White: An American novelist whom Gertrude and Alice had known since 1935. He had contracted with Holt to help Alice produce her memoir: *What Is Remembered* (New York: Holt, Rinehart and Winston, 1963). But personality differences arose, and Max suddenly stopped working with her. A letter from him instructs me to explain the matter this way: "I hadn't joined in collaborating on the proposed book with the intention of manning Alice's homemade wind machine, and as I gradually began to find out that was how it looked, my enthusiasm began to cool." He destroyed the notes he had made up to that point and four days later left for Madrid, without further communication with Alice.

15 October 1950
5, rue Christine, Paris VI

Dear Sam,

It was high time that your letter should have been answered and then unexpectedly there was the most incredible exciting marvellous news — the Yale University Press has accepted to publish all the *inédits* of Gertrude and *with enthusiasm.* The news came a week ago and has left me limp and overwhelmed — bathed in the light of having beheld a vision. And as a nun said to us on the day of the armistice of '18 — And to think it was done by human means. You remember that Gallimard had accepted Donald Sutherland's book on Gertrude's work — well a month ago Yale Press accepted it too — so there was a reasonable but still faint hope that they would do as much with one of hers. But all the *inédits* never suggested itself. They will make nine or ten big volumes. Carl is to have the first ready for next March — publication for next October. You — dear Sam — more than most will appreciate what this would have meant to Gertrude and what it does to me. If she only could have known it. Of all the books over the years only three were accepted enthusiastically — *Picasso* and *Paris France* (both ordered by the publishers) and the *Autobiography.* And now this. It has been a worry that in these four years there had been published but one — the two limited editions couldn't count. Isnt it too wonderful. Your answer isnt necessary but will be ever so welcome.

Otherwise there isnt much news nor need there be. The benefits of the Régie still persist though Basket rather handsomer than usual was a bit under the weather. Gabrielle had fed him too much bread (Remember her medical (!) training and experience). There's a word occasionally from Madame Debar — she seems not to yet have sold (a split infinitive because of the *malaise* it produces in T. S. Eliot) the puppies. I am trying to persuade the Knapiks to go down to La Régie next year — as if there is a guarantee that there is to be one. They enjoyed their trip in three or four countries with Louise Brooks but were exhausted on their return — nothing like the intolerable energy of a slow person like Louise. The Knapiks in excellent form — and Virginia in great beauty — were at the ballet (execrable) with Max White. The youngest of the

Fulbrights took me there. Francis' flat is nearly done and looks nice and fresh — except the best room which has a dark ruby plushy paper which offends me. He himself seems refreshed and let us hope nice. Frederica handsomer than ever came through on her way to Corsica and again on her return. I become more and more devoted to her.

Entre nous I dont think Carl is a bit well — indeed a photograph of him in a newspaper was alarming and a friend of his who came here lately confirmed the impression. He is drinking too much — he is seventy years old and for some ten years was a total abstainer (Surely you would never revert — promise yourself that nothing would tempt you to. You know Gertrude said temptation wasnt tempting. You dont mind my saying this because you know I care) So perhaps it is just as well you didnt see Carl — all this news of the present state of his health came after I told you to go see him — about three weeks ago.

What kind of painting does Scherer do — pictures surely are exciting and great company.

No *dont* send me *anything* please — not until there is a little gadget that will pry Gabrielle out of the house — then please send two because she's an extra tough subject — but *nothing* until then. All the lovely things you have given me are wonderful and I used the Sunbeam [Mixmaster] yesterday when I had Max White and Ed Livingood for lunch. And now I am going to write two lines to tell Wendell the good news and then I am going to patch and darn with Splendid Sammy Threads Splendid Sammy Apparatuses. For them and so many others and so much else all my grateful thanks. Love to you always

Devotedly
Alice

Gabrielle: Mlle. Gabrielle Delarue, an elderly white-haired housekeeper from Brest, whose strong opinions and personality frequently clashed with those of Alice.

22 November 1950
5, rue Christine, Paris VI

Dearest Sammy,

The Yale Press' enthusiastic acceptance is still a very active comfort — it will never be an accepted commonplace. They went down to see Carl [Van Vechten] in New York and agreed upon the conditions. The first volume is to contain all the unpublished portraits of '12. And at the beginning of the New Year Carl and Donald Gallup are going to make up the contents of all the other volumes. So come what may it is all planned and Yale will see it through. This obviously is as it should be and could have been sooner [but?] *ich grolle nicht* (we wont bother about the second line which is too sad — do you know it and the music Tschaikowsky wrote for it that moved me so over fifty years ago!)

And so after that was done the *élan* sent me to work on Bernard [Faÿ] — groping around to see who would help — and of all people the bawdy Princesse de Rohan — you met her didnt you — has produced the person who is supposed to pull it off or rather to introduce me to the person who will. And then a friend of Bernard's turned up who had seen him two days before and now they have asked me to recommence where I left off over two years ago. It is considered that *le climat est favorable* and the more angles the authorities are approached from the more likelihood of success. This time we have the backing of the president of the *république*. You see how one's hopes rise.

A thousand thanks for all the snaps. There is one sweet one of you. Madame Debar has come up to Paris and lunched with me. She sold the pups to a kennel reserving a brown bitch for herself. Everything is quiet at La Régie and frightfully cold. She brought me a baby hare which you should have shared — it was exquisite and for once correctly cooked. Do you know *crosnes?* They are Japanese!!! The french have eaten them for generations. They taste as good as they are pretty.

Interruption to do five thousand things in two days.

Francis' show is finally coming off next week and he is in a dither. He has settled down in the flat which he has had repainted — reupholstered — refurbished and modernised — and he has gotten to at least share the expenses the most incredibly *bien puissant* young Canadian sculptor who if deadly commonplace is at least a good manager and willing — honest and orderly (doesnt it sound like a reference for a servant). Frederica is coming over from London where she is doing heavy research for two books — for the *vernissage*.

Jane Bowles' play never came off in New York — someone told me — it may even be true — that she messed things up by falling in love with the actress who was to be the leading lady — who wasnt interested. Dear Jane — she could have used a theatrical [success?] — she left here at the height of a successful love affair and she should have concentrated on her play — which Thornton liked a bit. She is to her misfortune too true to type.

I lunched — and how — with the Knapiks a short time ago. They are handsome and more sympathetic than ever. Basket is not so well — he has had a frightful siege of rheumatism — which is alarming so early in the winter. We are both counting the days until May Day.

I went to see Libby Holman do folk and modern songs — appalling abjectly infamously perfectly. It's the quintessence of technique — what everyone says N.Y. does. But nothing else — two-dimensional — and so though astounding not interesting.

Please do not forget to let me know how your talk to the Logophilians went — what did you say and what did they say. Good for De Paul [University] if there is no intelligentsia there — they can get directly at things and at once not having to discard what others have thought they thought.

There is a new book on Proust that is upsetting the people who knew him. The mildest of the accusations — incest — is fairly proved by deduction. As for the rest no proof is offered. They gave it to me to read to see if something could be found to attack him [the author] on — but the only thing I found was scarcely [hideous?] — Jacques Bizet — the composer's son — was said to be the stepson of his mother instead of the son. His mother would have minded a bit — but certainly no one else.

The Barrys are going to Valauris for a few days in a large borrowed car and want me to go with them. To see the Picassos at the Antibes museum is a temptation but leaving Basket offers serious complications. The horrible Gabrielle is very good to him but if he was sick she would possibly — indeed very likely do great harm as she considers herself competent to diagnose and treat not only animals but persons. She couldnt be trusted to take him to the vets and leave him there in case of illness. And though he likes going to the vets he doesnt like staying there. Now I must give him his medicine — so goodbye dear Sammy for today. Much fond love from

Alice

Have you commenced to work.

Jane Bowles: Wife of Paul Bowles, novelist and composer, whom Stein and Toklas first met in 1935.

the Barrys: Jo (or Joe) Barry and his wife. Joe Barry was a writer and journalist and first met Gertrude and Alice at the end of World War II. Gertrude based the character of Jo the Loiterer in *The Mother of Us All* on him.

1 January 1951
5, rue Christine, Paris VI

Sammy dear,

Here youre being a naughty boy again and you know very well you are not incorrigible. When the adorable scarf came to warm to gladden to infuriate me — there was nothing but to take pen in hand to tell you that you were a mistaken angel on a bough and that you should see to it that your title remains as it should and as originally it was. Having said this it is now possible to give you a New Year's kiss — to wish you the realisation of all your dreams — including a black mass if you must and to thank you *de tout mon coeur.*

I am spending the day purposely alone to catch up with a great deal of neglect — cleaning and bringing out the Sam Steward basket and its treasures always invites a spell of patching mending and darning. But when the scarf just came I stopped to talk with S.S. and here we are.

Once more busy with Bernard's case which is progressing though slowly — with Basket whose rheumatism was bothersome (the poor dear doesnt walk well on the snow and in on the terrace) — with Francis and his show (very impressive well received and three pictures sold) and his two parties — Christmas day with the Barrys — a lunch party — four — but the dining room had to be heated — with the *pièce de résistance* a very fine chicken Madame Debar sent me — and with a birthday party Dil de Rohan gave at which I drank my first and most definitely my last Bloody Mary. I loathe vodka and not because it's Russian. I never did like strong drink.

That's the history of the last weeks except that I am crocheting baby blankets — four young wives pregnant — Judy Stein's wife produced a son and Jack Fisher's twins — which makes a blanket a month. And why should I talk to you or anyone about pregnant mothers. Once years ago we told Hélène if a pregnant American woman came to see us she should say we were engaged. She is — we explained — large blue eyed blonde — It is unnecessary to describe her [she] interrupted *car ces dames ne reçoivent jamais des dames enceintes.*

Have you read Lloyd Lewis' *Captain Sam Grant* — it is passionately interesting. A chapter an evening to make it last as long as possible. And I havent said a word about the drawing on the card — so very like you — your lilt and generosity and humor. How too sweet you are.

The fondest wishes for a really happy successful New Year — a million scoldings and thanks and my love

Alice

mistaken angel: Alice was playfully using the title of my novel.

Dil de Rohan: Wife of the deceased Austrian Prince de Rohan and daughter of an American woman and a British army officer. Her unusual first name, Dilkusha, comes from the name of a small village in India near which her father was stationed.

Lloyd Lewis: A Chicago writer whom Gertrude had met through Sherwood Anderson. Gertrude proposed a collaboration between them on a life of Grant, which Lewis had to decline because of the burden of his work; the war stopped all further plans, as did Gertrude's death. Lewis died in 1949; his book appeared a year later.

Hélène: The stolid Norman maid of the early days at 27 rue de Fleurus.

6 June 1951
5, rue Christine, Paris VI

Sam dear,

You were an angel of light to send me *Darkness and Day.* It has brightened the weeks and weeks of dark days we have had since it came. You were — and are and always will be I fear far far too good to me — and what an old horror I am not to have written you long ago. The days pass filled to overflowing with the most futile stupidities imaginable. The only nice things were I. Compton-Burnett and Donald Sutherland who wrote the book on Gertrude's work (both he and the book so much better than I had remembered) — and the daughter of my first friend and her husband. They were all here — have gone away briefly and will return. As I cant send you the Sutherlands and the Low-Beers it is my hope that you met the Gaunts and the Chaces who are tops (isnt that what we call them) but are topped by their servants. Was there ever portraits as rich as Bartle and Miss Fanshawe and they perhaps topped by Base and Viola. Thanks and thanks and thanks again for the lusciousness of them all.

Now your news is excellent — dont you pretend that youve lost anything from lack of practice — all you have to do is resume (didnt Greeley or Benjamin Franklin say something about that) and you'll be just as fluent as ever. Dont you try excuses — *paraît qu'ils ne prennent pas.* Why dont you do your pictures à la Chardin — *natures mortes* of people as well as objects — it's always been an alluring problem — people have a still life interest to me — their being people has been so overdone. The oldfashioned psychological problem has become part of their aesthetic. It hasnt any more value in the composition — hasnt it amalgamated with everything else so that people are people as pears are pears as gloves are gloves. It's I. C-B who makes me see this.

Max White has gone to Spain — he was suffering too much even for his fortitude from what the aquarium which is France was doing to him. He wanted the dry sun but he has a great *faiblesse* for the Spaniard so he has gone back after eighteen years to his old love. There's been no news yet from him. Before he left he cleaned the top of Gertrude's big table which was left in the most incredible mess by the workman who undertook to clean it. Clean it so he [the workman] did but after that he painted it a warm brown and then shellacked it. It was to cry. So Max devoted three days to making it beautiful again and now I know how and am getting to work on the little table tops. It has infuriated Gabrielle who thinks Americans are all the Communists say we are but she says for other reasons. Isnt that priceless. She has inspired moments a half dozen times a year. The rest of the time she is spiteful like a petty criminal. If it didnt take so much time it might be diverting.

That was an illuminating picture of Doctor Kinsey that you gave — the *auditeur-voyeur* which kept him from understanding what he learned.

Virginia has just telephoned me. She has like the sweet thing she is taken on my worries about Bernard [Faÿ] — she has her boss who she told me last evening has powerful French connections but has the common objections to poor Bernard so it might be possible to change it with the weight of Gertrude's — so Virginia is arranging a meeting for that purpose. In the meantime new plans are being made for the attack after the elections which are on the sixteenth of next month. There are here about the same percentage of abstentions as at home which is scandalous. If I were home I'd vote at least twice.

Murray Morrison as a high school boy wrote to Gertrude and then he took to writing her birthday letters which I answered. Then a few years ago he wrote to me because he was coming over which he did. He turned out to be an impossible old man of the sea at twenty five years of age. It then appeared he had gone to see or written to a number of people whom Gertrude had known. From Paris he went to London and wrote to two or three people saying he came *de ma part* and by then I'd had enough. During the winter he came over again and came to see me — the same pretentious person with the added horror of a black beard. Later he sent me an announcement of his marriage with an address here — no squeak from me — and baldly said he was returning in a few days to U.S. and wanted me to meet his wife whom he knew I'd enjoy but it was no sacrifice to refuse the opportunity by not answering — without the slightest curiosity concerning the girl who might have married him. That's the story of Mr Morrison.

I dont know what I'm going to do this summer. It was understood I was to join the Sutherlands somewhere for the month of July, but there is a loan show of post-impressionist pictures that Picasso asked me to lend four of the more important pictures here to (!) and now I must stay here for their return as the sentinel. In any case it was decided that the Knapiks and I would go somewhere together in August. Virginia is at work at finding something probably east of Grasse. I had to write to Madame Debar that I wasn't coming to La Régie — she was so kind to me but I wanted more of change in climate and the fear of who might occupy the other room. A month is a long time to be within the same walls with even a half sympathetic stranger.

Francis has been having another familiar drama (to him at least) which with perfect indiscretion he confided to anyone who would listen to him. He had been sharing his flat with a sculptor from British Columbia — the most sententious pretentious young man ever — with a cold gravy voice. What this Peter did to get himself banished from France was never confided to me in spite of the hours spent telling the story. Whether he got away incidentally with a few of Francis' all too rare pennies I dont know. In the meantime Francis achieved a blue Persian kitten whose papa and mama are world champions (which would account Francis says for his exceedingly good manners and perfect cleanliness). Francis has given me the lovely large drawing for his homage to Gertrude — it is very beautiful.

This is all for today except to ask you to keep away from electrical entanglements for the future. The idea of having electrical sparks coming out of your ears — dont you do it again. They might come out of your mouth or eyes or nostrils — you frighten me. Dont you go and belong to the *Je n'ai pas* Ménagère school.

All my thanks and love to you always

Alice

daughter of my first friend: The "first friend" was Clare Moore de Gruchy, who was the mother of Anne Low-Beer of San Francisco, who with her husband, Bela, visited Alice.

Darkness and Day: By Ivy Compton-Burnett, a favorite author of Alice's. The Gaunts, Chaces, Bartle, Miss Fanshawe et al. were characters in the novel.

your news is excellent: Having finished the work on the encyclopedia, I returned to teaching.

Murray Morrison: I had received one of his letters, and asked Alice about him.

19 November 1951
5, rue Christine, Paris VI

Dear Sam,

I've an idea about getting a passage back on the French Line. Why dont I make the reservation here. That seems sensible doesnt it. Give me the date or boat or both and over I fly to the rue Auber where I've not been since we bought our tickets *aller et retour* in '34 for the dear old *Champlain.* What a lovely boat it was and how uncertain we were about the venture of Gertrude's lecturing. Every hour I repeated — but if for any reason we dont like it we will go right back on the *Champlain* again. And how we loved it all. Here I am reminiscing like my two grand aunts — my grandmother never did not she. She considered her sisters as agreeable but weak and didnt take time to disapprove. They played concertos on two square pianos with the pedals raised as they were so short. They looked like Renoir's portrait of Malibran — that is Fanny did — Mathilde looked like nobody but herself. She weighed ninety pounds and had Manchester terriers that weighed three — and had her hair cut short seventy years ago all in ringlets black around her white face. Towards the end she was blind but could find a lost needle — she said it was magnetism. Grandma was politically minded and read the London *Times* — they'd gone to school in England — and crossed her legs and was altogether advanced and *outrée.*

And now we will go back to your coming over — which will be something to look forward to during this winter. And Emmy Curtis — almost a legendary figure is really to come to Paris and Esther [Wilcox] too — it is all so exciting and unbelievable — and Dudley Huppler too. I send messages to Wendell to tell him [Huppler] to come to see me but he doesnt. Whether Wendell doesnt want to tell him to or whether he doesnt want to the Knapiks are far too careful to tell me. Virginia is in greater beauty than ever — she is very worried about a pregnant friend who is going to have twins so it isnt easy to see her while this is going on. Virginia has a very tender feeling for this friend — at the same time that she loathes the subject of her anxiety.

There's a long and curious story about Gabrielle that must keep until you come over. She put me through two months of mental anguish and in a great flare up she consented to leave which was what I most wanted. And go she did. And it's calm and peaceful now and she's forgotten and after everything is in order again life will be possible. After all havent I found time to reminisce — more's the pity if that is the way time is to be wasted.

Max White has gone to New York to be with his aging mother. He always spoke of you warmly and wanted news of you. He's not going to like it in New York. Joe Barry is in London — the man in charge of the N.Y. *Times* there was afraid he was going to die and then was afraid he wouldnt so he Joe has to stay on until the wretched man makes up his mind what he will choose.

Basket is better. Gabrielle's shouting upset him — but he still has rheumatism and doesnt go out except on the terrace. This pen is behaving strangely — so goodnight and my love to you always.

Alice

30 January 1952
5, rue Christine, Paris VI

What can you — Sam dear — think of me except that I'm a hateful ingrate — to have kept you waiting all these weeks for an answer that was important for you to know. Later you will hear my feeble reasons for the delay — but at once to the ticket for tourist on the *Liberté* for September 5th — a note to [Jacques] Guerre after Elysée 82-38 said they knew nothing about him — remained unanswered but not returned. I write again — no answer. And only today I went over to [*La Compagnie*] *Transatlantique* to find if they had anything left and they could not tell me if anything had been reserved for you. There had not been after a thorough search in impressive ledgers. Most of their bookings are for large groups. Useless to try to explain why you could be considered a large group — so here I am returned to miserable failure. What an angelic patience you have not to have bombarded me with p.c.'s reminding me of the hideous way you were being neglected. The only excuse is that this winter has been too much for Basket's and my resistance. For two months we huddle and cling to the radiator and each other. Poor sweet thing he has been frightfully sick — more often at the vets than here — last night — but it's no use to go on. You know that he is more to me than a faithful companion and it's all wrong that he should have to go — we wont talk about it again.

It was a pleasure to have a glimpse of you in your professional role and a delightful surprise to find you more yourself than ever. Imagining you at Loyola and De Paul was seeing you in the role but no you are in the *intérieure* as you were here or at Bilignin — *inébranlable* — so agreeable to me for you rather than for the French army. Are you getting some of that into your writing — you should. Impish is altogether too easy for you — your writing should be quite new and fresh as you are. Good luck to it and bless you.

There isnt much news. Max White — who is a great admirer of yours by the way — went to Spain in early summer and was happy — it held him as it had some twenty years earlier and he would have stayed on indefinitely if he hadnt been called home by the serious illness of an aged mother. He was here briefly — he is quite irreplaceable. The Knapiks are angelic to me — Virginia more beautiful than ever and in a new way — you will be surprised — is doing bookbinding right around the corner from here and will come to see me this evening. Francis is doing some important work around Venice in late summer and at Cassis now — he rents his flat furnished and lives on it and the small sale of his pictures. It is of course a good sign that people dont like them easily but a discouraging one. His private life is quite a bit more fantastic than it was.

If Glenway Wescott could have been useful *bien* but as a judge of literature — hell. He writes pretentious unreal stilted letters to any and every body. I've seen a couple and it's my idea that he hopes that they are being kept and published — in his lifetime. He has by untiring effort over some thirty years become what he believes to be an ultimate man of the world. And still he wrote a very good oldfashioned novel (tradition of W.D.Howells!)

Esther's coming over — announced to Virginia for the first of April — is exciting me a good deal. No one in their description of her makes her like anyone else's — so we may safely say she has elusive subtle and intangible grace — which is considerable to look forward to meeting face to face — and Miss or Mrs Emily Colman [Emmy Curtis] will have — ah that it isnt possible to confide to you.

Thornton was here unchanged in spite of not being yet recovered from his long illness — he was in Princeton and Florida — is now in Arizona — it does sound as if he had a railroad pass — but he has been driving himself ahead — which doesnt leave one calm. He is polishing the Harvard lectures for a book — and ditto a play. Isabel [Wilder, his sister] was here for a week and is just gone. Their resilience when ill or depressed exhausts one.

Do you remember the Dora Maar landscape — she painted three very beautiful ones last summer and some exciting still lifes. And I've twice seen Fernande Olivier — after more than forty years — she's unchanged except physically — she's a monumental wreck. And they brought Greta Garbo to see me. And with many questions answered by me of her friends the *mystère est dévoilée* — and not so interesting. She looks without makeup not more than 36. But surely this is boring you — as it did me. Natalie Barney has privately printed a book of souvenirs of Dolly Wilde (Oscar's niece who wished she'd been his son and *Les Secrètes Amours* — poems written to her by Lucy [Delarus Madris?] — and with this your patience — this sheet and my time — are exhausted. Now I'll be looking forward eagerly to seeing you.

Love from
Alice

your professional role: I had described to her my return to teaching.
Fernande Olivier: She first met Picasso in 1904 and later became his mistress.
Glenway Wescott: American novelist, author of *The Grandmothers* and *Apartment in Athens.*
Greta Garbo: Since Garbo made no comments—only noises—while looking at the paintings, Alice considered the *mystère* to be that she was merely stupid.

5 August 1952
26 bis rue Louis-Perrisol
Cannes, Alpes Maritimes

Dear Sam,

Here we are quite comfortably settled. There is a small terrace — a wee view of the banal Mediterranean — two huge palms — a mimosa — a tree *quelquonque*(?) and a supportable heat — at least so little far. But alas the guest room is completely uninhabitable — which is a bitter disappointment to me for I had so hoped to see you quietly here in a leisurely way — not like the *tourbillon* of Paris. So if you are in the neighborhood and would care to spend a day with us let me know in advance so that Harold can prepare one of his good lunches. Are you having a good time and being good at one and the same time — you remember Gertrude's saying temptation is not tempting. At my age I was *nearly* tempted into the greatest possible *bêtise* a few weeks ago — so consider me as a happy example of human frailty saved by a Divine Providence!

Let me hear from you soon.

Love from
Alice

Postcard, 12 August 1952
26 bis rue Louis-Perrisol
Cannes, Alpes Maritimes

Awfully sorry not to see you here but will be seeing each other in Paris — where I'll be before you — so let me know as soon as you get there. J[ulian] G[reen] is an altogether delightful person. I've had an illy concealed passion for him for over a generation and his early novels are my delight. Tomorrow I'm going to try to find one of them in town. Have you met his sister — she is a strange one — and would be an intriguing heroine of a novel if her real story could be fully known — but not oh dear no a subject for her brother — do meet her. You would shed light on the murky corners. Have a good time and happily *à très bientôt*.

Love
A.

Julian Green: French writer and novelist, born of American parents.

24 October 1952
5, rue Christine, Paris VI

Sam dear,

Too many things have been happening and not enough of them pleasant — but it now would seem — except for the unexpected — the worst must be over. An unfortunate friend got us involved and there were a few anxious days. The poor sweet old Basket who is blind and deaf fell off the roof to a roof some twelve feet below and in the dark and I couldnt find him but the concierge rescued him and besides the shaking up Basket got off fortunately with a slight cut which is healing nicely. But with the misadventure he lost the little confidence he had been slowly achieving — so that he needs someone to stroke him frequently. Isnt it too sad that this is the way he is to end his days.

It is useless to say that this doesnt make the beginning of winter — autumn is winter here — more to be dreaded than usual — so that writing to you will cure me of all dismalness. You are not only sweet and good — when you are good — but gay and understanding and angelic. And the gadgets are exactly like you — all these things and some of them with sharp edges too! And I refuse to do any kitchen work that doesnt include the use of at least one. The weenie eggbeater with the long handle created a version of mayonnaise that is rapid and economical — dry mustard — salt — pepper or paprika in quantity in a bowl with one entire egg. Beat with the Sam gadget eggbeater for three minutes while you do something else with the left hand — then gradually add oil in the usual way — and when it is stiff lemon juice in small quantities — when a third of a cup of oil has been added stir in a dessert spoon of boiling water — add a few tablespoons more oil — *et voilà.* As it will be more than you need for one time it can be put in the ice chest for the next day but no longer because of the white of egg. Cannot be made without the use of a Sammy gadget eggbeater. The knife sharpener is so good that it is put away every other day far from the kitchen — Madeleine would wear it out cutting Basket's meat and I would lose too many fingers.

It seems to me that the Wendell Wilcoxes have too many things happening to their health — what one might call accidents of bad health. Last night I wrote to Wendell and I couldn't help scolding a bit. You know Adelina Patti said the habits one forms at forty are what one will live on after fifty — and she had a marvellous old age. At sixty five she married a man of thirty — and no one thought he was her grandson.

Now you must hear about Francis — he is in Portugal with Mrs. Pacevitch but before leaving was in a good deal of trouble with Luis his *valet de chambre* boy friend whom he now says is his illegitimate son. Francis is saying that he is going to recognize him so that he will inherit the title!! As yet this tale has not been confided to any English friends — who would put him straight about bastards inheriting titles — just we Americans who are indifferent about English honor — we rather like it. Of course Francis can be much less amusing than this. The tale before this had Francis involved with the Spanish ambassador — the Spanish minister of justice and a stray Spanish duke — in which a Frenchman said to Francis — Trust Miss Toklas — she has good judgment. And you may say here is where we wake up — and you would be right. We do but Francis doesnt not he.

It was quite my fault about *Mrs. Reynolds* — not Gallup's — do forgive me. Surely you have it by now. It is beautiful. The manuscript was sent from Belley during the occupation to Stockholm to someone who took it to New York. Tell me the Germans are thorough!

I am so glad you liked Glenway — I did a lot. Did George Lynes come over this summer. Perhaps he did while I was away — I'm sorry to have missed him. Joe Barry is going to lose his youth in N.Y. He wont be disillusioned — only saddened. I give him a year. He says it is so wonderful he wants me to come over to share it!!! Not that I dont think U.S. beautiful — next after Spain — and I do have my compies [compatriots] but renaissance — *ah ne pas cela* — not in any country.

Isnt the election exciting — I wade through all the speeches — pretty third-rate as they are. Shouldnt there have been a woman candidate for the vice presidency or did Mr. Truman's administration discourage them. The door bell is ringing. Much fond love from

Alice

gadgets: Knowing she always enjoyed them, I had sent her another large collection.

Madeleine: Madeleine Charrière, perhaps Alice's all-time favorite *femme de ménage.*

Luis: A casual encounter between Francis Rose and a Spanish gypsy boy in front of a bistro called La Reine Blanche in Paris resulted in Francis' hiring the young man for a summer. It was only after Luis got into some trouble with the *gendarmérie* over a stolen bicycle that Francis — called to help him out of his difficulty — examined his papers and discovered the boy was his natural son. This episode titillated both France and England for some time.

George Lynes: George Platt Lynes, American photographer of the New York City Ballet and high fashions for various magazines like *Vogue*, had discovered he was dying of an irreversible carcinoma of the blood. He made a last trip to Europe, but in his distressed condition it was just as well that he had not been able to see Alice. Lynes had very early photographed Gertrude and Alice at Bilignin.

29 December 1952
5, rue Christine, Paris VI

Sam dear,

It is hard for me to say which of your two gifts I like the best — the exquisite scarf or the joyous news that you've written fifty thousand words of a book — all written down. Thank you with all my heart for both of them. They are precious gifts that I dont deserve but no one can take them from me. What an angelic Sam you are. The scarf was worn yesterday — couldnt wait for Christmas. Nejad [Bey] asked me to be his witness at the civil marriage service and elegance was in order so the soft gentle but so elegant scarf came out of its box — was worn and greatly admired.

Ten days later. I love it and [have] been wearing it but you know you *shouldnt* have sent me another gift *ever*. Just because I hang on is no excuse or occasion for celebration. But you are just the Angel on the Bough! And so all my many thanks and I kiss you on both cheeks and wish you the happy New Year you deserve.

Back to the book — is it going well. Is it a quiet book or a turbulent one. Will you please make it long. What a beautiful way to have recommenced — with a gushing flood. If it suits you let me know how it goes.

Well my news is bad and good. Basket is no more. He died a month ago. He ate his lunch wagged his tail and collapsed. The flat is emptier than before without him. It is hard to become accustomed to his not being here. Fortunately a man had just come along to work on the voluminous notes from 1908 through '12 for the preparation of *The Making of*

Americans and the two following books. He wants me to supply names places and dates and illustrations to help fill in the foreground. As his book is not to be published for many years — discretion has been thrown to the winds and my contribution has become a *chronique scandaleuse.*

About Francis — the story has become involved as only his can. Frederica has been dragged into it for material and practical reasons — not at all certain that Francis is the father. With her permission Francis has recognized him — giving him French nationality for the moment — but when the boy becomes of age he wishes him to take Spanish nationality so that he may have the Spanish titles Francis has the right to through his grandmother! Can you beat or equal it. Bernard [Faÿ] says is one sure of the paternity — is his now legal father his father — his mother his mother! May one ask a leading question — the only one that interests me — When in the course of the story did Francis hear that the boy was his son — from the beginning — soon after — or just when. Do you know. Frederica has had an operation in London and wishes Francis to be kept on this side of the channel so that she may have a quiet convalescence. It is a very difficult task to accomplish this — but without knowing just where in the south Francis is wandering. It will be necessary to locate him and tactfully keep him where he is. If only he were here I'd menace him but you cant write that sort of thing. Fancy getting into one of Francis' stories at my age!

You knew didnt you that Dora Maar was doing a portrait of me — well she finished it and brought it to me a few weeks ago. There is some very fine painting in it and now the question is where to hang it. Of course I wont disturb any of Gertrude's hangings which means that Francis goes off the mirror — back to the door on the left of the fireplace where it had been originally and the portrait takes its place on the mirror. What will Francis say. But there doesnt seem to be any other solution.

It isnt cold but it's as moist as usual. The days are lengthening but imperceptibly — my *femme de ménage* says they lengthen in from the afternoon end! The French are so original. When once I remarked to Jeanne Roupelet that there were 13 moons a year she replied — Not in France.

Sam dear — a good happy year — good happy work — all my thanks and love.

Devotedly
Alice

Nejad Bey: A young Turkish painter, son of the Princess Zeid.
a man . . . to work on the voluminous notes: Leon Katz, who was preparing a critical edition of Gertrude's notebooks used in *The Making of Americans.*
When in the course of the story: Francis Rose discovered his paternity of the boy Luis in September 1952, approximately four months after he met him. He immediately Anglicized the boy's first name to Louis.
Francis goes off the mirror: Her statement reflects her uncertainty about Francis Rose's talent; for the next ten years there are many similar vacillations.

28 June 1953
5, rue Christine, Paris VI

Sam dear,

My shameful silence was due to a long boresome attack of pernicious jaundice and to the equally boresome writing (?) of a 75,000 word cook book in half the time — the latter to earn the pennies to pay for the former. The incompatible combination has exhausted me and tomorrow I go to the hospital for a checkup. One doesnt get over easily one's first illness in fifty-nine years! You do a little understand and so will pardon (*Tout comprendre c'est tout pardonner?*) Surely you didnt think I wasnt always thinking of you and wanting to tell you so and to thank you *de tout mon coeur* for all your attentions to me — the lovely scarf that has been a delight and a comfort and made my old suit look very fashionable and ever so elegant. It is of a color that goes with *Chinese* yellow! So many many thanks for the most beautiful of scarves. When the birthday cable came it was too much — tears not idle but tender for you and your sweet thoughts. It was angelic of you and though you have been that oh so often this was the *comble.* It bucked me up more than you can half fancy. But dont you know your friendship doesnt require any material expression for me to *wallow* in it. Couldnt you just once and for all accept the fact that a letter will say it all and *send* the *letter* and *nothing else!* (Do you see how you are driving me to early Victorian underlining. They were *not* inarticulate — there I am at it again). A million thanks for you and everything.

In return for all your news there is little to offer. Francis has changed his mind about making his son a Spanish duke — Luis is to learn English and go into the British army — first having taken British nationality. They spent the spring in Minarco (the winter on the coast near Toulon) and are now in Madrid. A visit from Luis is announced for early next month. All through this turmoil and restless moving about Francis has done a great deal of work — some very fine landscapes — especially those done in Portugal. He had a large successful show in Lisbon. Is he not incredible. Bernard [Faÿ] who was in Madrid for the winter wrote me — but *très entre nous* — is he that is Luis — the son of his father — does anyone know if he is the son of his mother. Bernard's health is no better. He has returned to the specialist in Geneva. I had hoped to go to see him but it doesnt look as if it would come off.

Summer plans are vague. For September I go with the Knapiks to the seashore south of Barcelona — a long trip and expensive for a month but it was the only thing Virginia could find. France is very expensive — what with U.S. considers no government — which of course isnt at all true — for effectively administrating essential activities — the old one is still alive — inflation around the corner and the Communists messing things up — France in spite of all this is prosperous. The president of the [Douene?] company (Yale locks and machinery) says it is astonishing the way French manufacturers can afford the latest American machinery. He is Bobsy Goodspeed's new husband. It reminds me of what an Englishman said after the other war — "Poor France is so prosperous"!

And the novel — is it by now done — did you have to do the end over again as you feared. I am so glad it is long. Long breaths are nice and healthy and sympathetic. We will make exceptions of Jouhandeau and Wendell [Wilcox] — when it is time for it to have a title and time to tell it you will let me know — wont you. The man who came over to work on Gertrude's notes is putting his work on them into shape — I wrote to you about him didnt I. There are 450 typewritten pages that Gertrude worked at for her character studies

— portraits of everyone including herself from '06 to '14 — brilliant beyond words and passionately interesting. It has been a great diversion for me this winter and now it is past time for a little light housekeeping. The flat is in a parlous state.

Je t'embrasse bien tendrement — cher ami

Alice

28 January 1954
5, rue Christine, Paris VI

Sam dear,

Isnt it hateful of me to be driven to writing after months of silence by the arrival this morning of the loveliest of lace-like woolen shawls. That is what this winter has made of me and how can you understand or forgive — you will a little bit so that I wont be too upset. So send me a p.c. to say that you do. Your beautiful — beau-tiful be-au-tiful gift is not really for the likes of me but it is so adorable and so like you it isnt hard to forget *that* in its actual possession. It will be worn for grand occasions — for example when Frederica Rose comes to see me. She will cast first an appraising and then an appreciative eye upon it and the ensuing silence will be full of meaning that only women can interpret. And all this time you have not had one word of thanks — *Je t'embrasse de tout mon coeur et je t'embrasse — Sammy chéri.*

News! There really isnt any. Winter is winter and there is no use going into that — most particularly not the kind we've been indulging in these last few days — minus fifteen centigrade outdoors — plus twelve here in the salon — but it is supposed to break today and the first airplane has flown over the house this very minute — which is more encouraging than any meteorological (too many syllables?) report. We indulge in so much foolishness — P.T.T. strikes and a proposed plan of having lanes around the Arc de Triomphe to relieve the traffic congestion — and a mauve and green and red curly decorative cabbage — non-edible of course which is the latest and still rare novelty. None of this is front page news like Hemingway's accident has been in *Le Figaro* — but when we were in Chicago and they shot a young gangster (Baby something) he was first page news because he was bad — the good boys were definitely not — they were second page news. Appalling this exaltation of crime in U.S.

Enough of this — where are we with the long novel — is it not by now all revised and ready to show to an editor — *toutes félicitations monsieur* — make haste for I am longing to read.

And the jaundice cured by dark Karo syrup in ten days! It took over twenty times as many days to cure me. Dont you believe that it was the sun — it's liver and I'm delighted to know that the last memory of your early indiscretion is completely out of your system. A.A. should put everyone on a diet — no fats of any kind — no spices — *enfin* lean meat and fish (no eggs) raw and cooked vegetables and fruit — and it's really a very pleasant *régime* — above all no fats — neither butter or oil or their substitutes. But go on to it gradually because jaundice likes to return! That's why the cook book was so drab. But I've gotten finally some advance pennies — due in June! — and am blowing them into heating. And Francis has done some really beautiful line drawings for it [the cookbook] and a dust cover. And Francis — well he and Frederica are reconciled. She has bought the small top story of an old house in Ajaccio overlooking the bay and is building a small studio on the roof for Francis who in return seems to have offered the sacrifice (?) of renouncing his son Luis. Every one who met him said that he was just a bad boy from Marseilles. Francis still says Luis is a very gifted painter. While the work on the flat is going on Francis is in Frederica's rooms in Nice where he seems to be working madly and well. His flat here is still rented to an American couple.

Yes the Katherine Anne Porter had a story back of her venom. She was quite an admirer of Gertrude's work previously to a visit of a well mannered good looking young G.I. whom I found talking to Gertrude on the sofa here. Do I read Katherine Anne Porter said Gertrude to me. Oh God no — said I and left the room. Whereupon the youth said — But you know my aunt. To which Gertrude answered — So very many people came to the rue de Fleurus. When the article appeared in *Harper's* (you probably saw it amongst a book of criticism of K.A.P.) Joe Barry answered it and very well indeed but *Harper's* didnt print Joe's protest but gave it to K.A.P. who wrote him an enormously long incredible letter in which "as an artist I" occurred several times ending with — In case on re-reading my article you find other things to object to please let me know before it is reprinted in a book of essays. Of course Joe didnt answer her but sent her letter to Yale Library. Dont repeat this please — only you and Jo and Sutherland know the *bas fond* of K.A.P.'s point of departure.

Don't be too lonesome because of your sister having left Chicago. Without any unfaithfulness to her or to legendary Emmy [Curtis] isnt it time you found an Egeria — what Thornton might call a serpent of the Wabash. But that is another story.

No more room — time for a bowl of soup. Endless thanks and love from an appreciative and loving

Alice

Hemingway's accident: On January 25, 1954, Hemingway was on a sightseeing trip by chartered plane in Uganda, leaving from Nairobi. The plane came down in an inaccessible spot near Kampala, and the party was rescued by a launch.

the jaundice cured: My own mild case of jaundice was cured by the old-fashioned method of "sugar-drip"; no hospitalization was required. I had told Alice that I had not known I had it because my tan hid the yellowness; she thought I meant the sun had caused the jaundice.

Katherine Anne Porter: American writer and essayist, and an early admirer of Gertrude's work, especially *The Making of Americans.* After the incident with her nephew, Porter attacked Gertrude in an article entitled "Gertrude Stein: A Self-Portrait" (*Harper's,* December 1947). The attack, together with an exchange of letters pertaining to it by Donald Sutherland, is in *The Collected Essays and Occasional Writings of Katherine Anne Porter* (New York: Delacorte, 1970).

2 August 1954
5, rue Christine, Paris VI

Sammy dear,

Your letter came in spring and now it is not — most markedly not summer — where is summer — where is leisure — alas not to be found hereabouts. Words — idle words — not so when *you* write them — surely your novel is interesting — it just naturally must be and dont be impatient or depressed — just the end of the school year when you wrote —

makes everything go drab. You are please to write me *at once* that you have just read the novel once again (perhaps in S. Francisco) and are surprised to find it really most awfully good. Then we'll both be feeling a lot better.

Yes I would like to see Eleanor Rohr if she is here before or after September when I'm vacationing with the Knapiks somewhere in the south — near Cannes — near Grasse — not on the French Mediterranean — which is infested. The house we go to is not yet definite — it should [be] — having waited so long it will be easier because it is too long.

Well Professor Philip Sparrow I didnt give or show or mention your card to Francis — not I — *entre nous* I have engaged to keep him fairly respectable — he has cost his wife too much — probably in both tears and dinero. He doesnt drink or whatever else it may have been and if he did come to see me with a very pretty American sailor — in uniform of course — the relation was uncomfortably correct. Tattooing at any time — anything — anywhere indeed — no siree (good Californian) he's going to behave until he leaves for Corsica on the 12th where he joins his wife and will work there. I told you that their flat was sold and they were out-bid and only salvaged the two servants rooms on the fifth story — which Francis has put into not only living quarters for himself but a quite suitable place to paint in — and whom do you think helped work on it with him — the Windsors — if we are to believe Francis. Lately there's been another case of his telling the truth.

There's been no news except the scandals re the Picasso paintings brought for a big show from Moscow and Leningrad — but you'll have seen that in the newspapers. Now there is a new one on — so we've had two stupendous exhibitions — one following the other — the new one of late work '50–'54 is much the more interesting.

Heaps of love to you, Sammy dear — always

Alice

Eleanor Rohr: Alfred C. Kinsey's secretary had expressed a desire to meet Alice, and I had asked Alice's permission.

Philip Sparrow: The name I took when my disgust with university teaching turned me to tattooing; it was the same name I used for the dental journal articles. It came from a poem by John Skelton.

American sailor: Robert Vinal of San Francisco.

20 November 1954
5, rue Christine, Paris VI

Dear Sam,

Oh dear — it is very sad that S. Francisco no longer seduces you. Not for me to say whose fault it is — not for me to choose between you and it. Sometime you must try it again and discover if it doesnt fascinate you anew without blame to either of you.

Dont take on [Senator Joseph] McCarthy — it is months since he worried me — he no longer exists — trial headings I just skip. Besides there are French politicians quite as fanatic and a lot more corrupt.

Eleanor Rohr made not the slightest sign in my direction.

Has *Finer than Melanctha* arrived — Yale said it had been sent — Wendell got his sent at the same time. Let me know at once because they will be reminded if not.

Here there is not very much news. The most cheerful is the possession of a catalyste [catalytic] portable radiator. It is fed gasoline C (whatever that may be) and heats at least better than the old inadequate electric radiator and will be far less ruinous. It hasnt to be sure yet gone below 41° Fahrenheit — *nous verrons ce que nous verrons.*

The month with Virginia and Harold near Grasse was deliciously calm and restful. The little house was on a hillside amongst olive trees and near fields of jasmine (essential oil for Paris perfume). A ten minute ride on the bus took us to Grasse and its southern market — including Italian specialties. Harold built a spit outside the kitchen and cooked incredible food — which brings me to the recipe book — a copy of which just this morning has been posted to you. The story of the Haschisch Fudge is a scream. It was contributed by a friend who lives in Africa — and who met Gertrude twice at dinner parties before [he knew who] she was and didnt talk to her at all. It is my ignorance not to have suspected what the few leaves were — of course I didn't know their Latin name. So when *Time* did that vulgar malicious paragraph I was furious. Harper's got frightened and put the question up to the Attorney General who said it was illegal only to sell buy or use the drug — but it is not in the American edition — would you like a copy of the recipe. But you will love

Francis' lovely illustrations. He has returned from Ajaccio where he has been for several months with Frederica. There has been a re-re-re reconciliation and it has done him a world of good. He is really sage and industrious and economical and has become a good boy for the moment at least. I am going to try to climb the six flights of stairs to his two weenie rooms to see his new pictures.

What has happened to your novel — dont you send it to publishers. You should. And why dont you write an article on tattooing that would be publishable — witty and exotic. You could do it ever so well and it would be priceless — in both senses of the word. Go to it.

And now I must go to the kitchen and cook lunch. All good things to you Sam dear and fond love

Alice

a friend . . . in Africa: Brion Gysin, a writer and painter, had met Gertrude and Alice briefly in the 1930s. He was a close friend of Paul and Jane Bowles'. Alice included the recipe without being actually aware of what it was; even the introductory comments were Gysin's.

7 March 1955
5, rue Christine, Paris VI

Sam dear,

Why are you so good to me — why oh why did you send me the fantastically intriguing book. You see what it has done — prevented me from thanking you for it for the week since it arrived. It is seducing — first there was the exciting table of contents — then the seductive illustrations — finally the absorbing text — then I wasnt lost for anything else. Only now have I found enough resolution to put it aside long enough to tell you this and to thank you trillions of times. (It is leaning up against my chair — wailing Lift me up and open me — you'll love what you havent read even more than what you have). So thanks and thanks again.

My news is briefly told — indeed there is none — just the usual winter weather report — which you will be spared. *En passant* the room is quite comfortable with the new catalytic heater. It was my fond hope that you would be over this summer until your letter came and even now after so many weeks it is not an accepted fact. It might still be a mistake — or more assuringly just an unexpected change of plans. Dont use the old excuse that the French do not like us or U.S. We've been more disliked and the U.S. less appreciated. The new ministry has made it unpalatably clear that there are more serious problems — Africa and the budget are nearer their pockets. Why the *Figaro* has had to fall upon "The Question Black and White in U.S." so dont fear you will be held responsible for McCarthy or the McCarran act. By June they'll probably have forgotten our existence. They have no races really.

Francis as I must have written you went through a complete reconciliation with his beautiful intelligent sensitive sympathetic wife during last summer — returned here in late autumn a reformed character — earned his living during the winter and is now very sure of himself — working hard at his painting and commercial work (designs for textiles — wallpaper and so on) and is — it must be confessed — quite dull — mixes his phantasy and the more or less orderly life. He flies about seeing everybody — going to all the *vernissages*. I am still and always shall be very fond of him but unquestionably he is not vastly diverting.

I am having Gallup send you Gertrude's book. Kahnweiler has just written a charming preface to the next volume (publication in October).

About tattooing as a profession. It worries me — the insecurity of its being a reliable livelihood and a safe amusement — but one must run some risks to keep lively. Does this seem hopelessly sententious and aged — forgive me — both of which have been in my way for years. You were sweet about the cookbook — but just wouldnt you be that in all conditions.

Write to me soon — that is when you have time and inclination — and all my grateful thanks for the precious book.

Love and devotion from

Alice

Kahnweiler: Daniel-Henry Kahnweiler, whom Gertrude and Alice had known since 1907. Besides having one of the leading art galleries (Galerie Kahnweiler) on the rue Vignon, he published Gertrude's *A*

Book Concluding With As A Wife Has A Cow. A Love Story in 1926, with illustrations by Juan Gris; and two years later *A Village. Are You Ready Yet Not Yet*, with lithographs by Élie Lascaux.

the fantastically intriguing book: I had sent her a large illustrated book, *Gunfighters and Outlaws*, with an intelligent text about the personalities of the Old West.

Whitsunday, 1955 (May 30)
5, rue Christine, Paris VI

Dear Sam Dear,

The better the day the better the deed. It has taken a lot of waiting to find the time to tell you how grateful I am to you for your friendship — that you should be ashamed to prove its existence by showering me with gifts — that it cant be denied that receiving them is not an exciting pleasure but that these are not the only way to keep me excited and pleased — why dont you write me an extra letter. Does this sound like a complainful [pen?]? That's not the intention — as you well know. What should have been said is — I have the cooling gadget — it works wonders — saves my life and hours and hours of precious time. And a trillion prillion thanks for sending it to me out of the blue — delivered by the postman — into the kitchen it went into immediate action. For guests an American meringue pie was being prepared as the *pièce de résistance*. Do you know it — the meringue is baked — covered with whipped cream — covered with *crème pâtisserie* — covered with soaked in rum berries or candied fruit covered with whipped cream. The trouble has always been to get the *crème pâtisserie* cool without spending the time to cool it by stirring. Oh but doesnt the little steady cooler work the miracle — cant use it without smiling at it. Thank you and thank you again.

As for the book [on outlaws] — even young Frenchmen are breathless — horrified shocked and surprised that such things were — that the book has been written about them — that it was sent to me — that I enjoy reading it — that I am proud to have it — rising crescendos ending with a crash in three voices — which only shows how foreign one is after forty eight years residence. Then I showed it to a Mrs. Sprigge — essence of middle-class British pretentiousness — who is doing a biography of Gertrude. She was horrified but tried to cover it — when I dropped that Gertrude would have loved it — that she had a particular weakness for Billy the Kid. It's a peach of a book and ever so well presented.

I've just returned from a few days jaunt to Reims to visit the cellars — drink champagne and scent the aromas of the vineyards — taken there by *H*[*ouse*] *Beautiful* who accepted some cooked with champagne recipes. It was an amusing — a delightful jaunt — we averaged about a bottle and a half apiece a day — and with two superlative meals a day. Our last host asked for the menus and lists of guests of our previous ones. As a matter of fact two of the founders of the biggest houses were men whose widows established them permanently and on a much larger scale than the men had conceived and two are now being run by widows. Oh France is certainly of and for women. And now we're off to Bordeaux to taste cognac! I use an awful lot in cooking but cant swallow it raw.

News about Francis continues to be surprising — he is earning his living painting and doing commercial work — he has paid his debts and made no new ones and likes it. There is a young man who hovers about but he is not a boy friend nor does he seem to want to be nor will Francis let him be. He would like to sleep with — but if I'm not careful the post wont deliver the letters.

The Knapiks are in fine form — Harold had one of his compositions played by full symphonic orchestra at Nantes. Virginia has a new boss at the embassy and likes him and the new work.

What do you think of the enclosed as an idea — can it be useful to you.

All thanks and love to you — Sam dear — always from

Alice

the cooling gadget: A small chrome-plated tube of a heavy metal alloy, to be kept in the coldest part of the refrigerator and then inserted into the substance to be cooled.

the enclosed: A clipping from *Le Figaro* (28–29 Mai 1955) suggesting that the blood type be tattooed on the body between the eighth and ninth ribs, since that location was most protected from wounds and accidents.

19 January 1956
5, rue Christine, Paris VI

Dear Sam,

Is it too late to wish you so very many happy New Years — not too late at least to thank you for yours — nor to tell you how much I enjoyed the [lad?] being tattooed — though he didnt seem to look like you — his chief beauty was a vacant innocence more suitable to him than resembling you. How do you and he like the new flat and will you be working — that is tattooing there and how does that accommodate itself to teaching — and does the tax collector visit you. Am I asking too many questions — dont answer any that seem — or are indiscreet to you.

Winter has come and as soon as it did the catalytic stove went out of order and was being sent back and forth between here and the repair shop during which I froze — 50° Fahrenheit here. Now it is marching with a pervasive odor of? — Friends complain but it is really quite bearable. Not but a few days more and two months before spring is officially here. The forsythia were out and the sap was running in the trees a month ago.

I have translated a rather beautiful book by a young Belgian girl — short stories about insects and birds — mice cats and dogs and poets — the latter of whom she does not respect — her father is one and her mother is a *bas bleu* — and I'm going to Brussels to give a *causérie.* What do you suppose I'll say to them — I refuse to think about it — if one could only gossip.

Francis is down in Corsica with his latest boy friend — Bostonian. Francis likes them to be American — they are less brutal — even the gangsters. His wife is in England — so that her flat in Ajaccio is free as Francis will be for her when she comes here presently. Do you remember Max White — he has become a Catholic — three of my friends have. Did you know Daniel Rops was elected to the Academy. We did what we could to prevent it and he failed the first time but five months later he got in.

By the way of tattooing — did you know who the *Tattooed Countess* was — she was the type writer for the president of the great wheat (?) manufacturing company and he married her and left her his vast fortune. When we knew her she was living on an enormous estate outside of Minneapolis with hothouses orchids grapes oysters in the dead of winter. Tell your lady patients how far a tattoo can take them. Are you coming over to do the few remaining crowned heads — why not — you could see Europe and I could see you.

From Tangier there's been a letter from Brion Gysin saying Morocco is fairly unpleasantly lively but Tangier is quite quiet.

Have you seen a very vulgar article on *Teaching Gertrude Stein* by an Elizabeth Sprigge who is writing a biography of Gertrude. The worst of it is that I got *Harper's* to take it God help me!

Write to me when you have time.

Much love dear Sam from
Alice

a young Belgian girl: Anne Bodart's *The Blue Dog, and Other Fables for the French* (Boston: Houghton Mifflin, 1956).

the Tattooed Countess was: Both Alice and Gertrude believed that the original model for Carl Van Vechten's novel was Mahala Dutton Benedict Douglas, who inherited the Quaker Oats fortune from her husband, Walter, who had gone down with the *Titanic.*

28 January 1956
5, rue Christine, Paris VI

Naughty — very naughty — unpardonably naughty Sammy,

What do you mean by such madness — to send me the book which has just come. Half moved by your thought of me — half furious with your wild extravagance — half of a twitter to get to reading all the wonder the book holds (already one and a half "me's" and that's not yet all). There's someone in it I knew — and when you come over you'll hear the rest of her story here in Paris during the other war! So I am trying to say thank you thank you thank you in gratitude and forget what a bad boy you are to bestow such a precious gift upon me. Why should you — tell me.

All of a sudden it grew so warm that I shut down the catalyste for four hours so no matter what happens later — and less than two months to spring — today has been humanly bearable — so that it is a Red Letter Capital Day [last four words in red ink].

Do you know any old local herb recipes. I'm a-collecting them. And do you know the difference between marjoram and oregano — none of the dictionaries — French or American seem to — nor the French cookbooks differentiate but the American cookbooks do. What is Professor Philip Sparrow's opinion on this? hein?

Always — dear Sam — so many thanks and very much love from

Alice

21 September 1956
Nice — Alpes Maritimes — until
the end of the month

Sam dear,

Your letter gave me so much pleasure — months ago! And this is the first free moment — stolen at that from — but more of that later. The long cold winter — the dark rainy spring followed by a sunless summer combined with overexertion indoors laid me low — Once on the train coming down here at the beginning of the month for the annual all too short vacation the boresome pains and aches commenced to disappear. But *tais tu* — or you'll rightly believe I've become a complainful pussy!

Here it is restful and quite sunny and I spend my days trying to achieve fifty thousand words from the box of recipes — to be delivered to Harper's at the end of November! Not likely. Half that has become my goal. And your packets of oregano and marjoram put me on the road to a [deal?] of discovery and wild invention. Did you know that oregano was wild and more strongly flavored marjoram. I certainly didnt. It was angelic of you to send me them — they helped to shake me out of a torpor which had become my normal state. Many many thanks and *please please* send a list of the spices for a spice necklace. It would be precious and help enormously my culinary curiosities. Why not a string of mixed spices to dip into a saucepan of boiling water or wine before anything else is added — so that after a few minutes the string could be removed — dried and used again and again — a saving of time and effort over the usual measuring after opening tins and bottles. Tell me more!

It is nice here but dreadfully dull and for the Mediterranean coast incredibly ugly. I like to turn my back on a landscape of great distinction — but this one one can face without flinching. And the little house is hopelessly *petit bourgeois*. But the sun and air are delicious and in Paris I'll miss them.

Have you received the new volume from the Yale Press — you should by now. Mine will be waiting in Paris for me. You can fancy what each new volume means to me. There are two more to follow. Some way or other I must hang on to see them — they are my *raison d'être*.

About your having stopped teaching — it was high time and still the right moment — bravo — bravo — bravo. Isnt there any newspaper that pays little but more than nothing for the things you can do so very well — so naturally like the Sparrow of the dental review — less local with subjects of a wider field. You can carry conviction without interference to wit — humor and diversion. It is something the French do — and well — and we dont do at all. Maybe you have thought of something of your own by now.

Have I written you about Francis and his international scandal — if not — in my next. His wonderful wife straightened it out and he has emerged — in a much better situation than before. That's the way he is — and he is painting very well.

So much love to you Sammy dear

Devotedly
Alice

2 November 1956
5, rue Christine, Paris VI

Sam dear,

De-lighted that you'll be over and soon — *mirifique* to see you. Of course I'll be here — if I can get away it will be later. Some recipes for Harper's may help — it was due for the end of this month but — there seems to be nothing up in the empty head. But I'll get it off in time.

Thanks for the clipping re Francis — his son (look where he has landed!) and the Frog Man. It not only got to Chicago but *Pravda* took it up too! He has been in England where he has made a lot of money.

Thanks again — and always — for the story of the herb scented beads. With your permission your description will go into *Aromas and Flavors* (it quite frightens me) and with that it is quite unnecessary for me to see a necklace.

Do you know a French book on tattoo? I saw one in the window of a *recherché* — and perhaps a little *louche* bookshop (they surely sell more or less than books — but what — you tell me). I couldnt see the name of the author and the shop was closed. It *looked* serious — I intended to get it for you — so let me know more. I fear it is — if not old old still possibly out of print — but no time should be wasted in my securing it.

So looking forward to seeing you and so much love

Alice

Oh, the telephone — I was next to it all Monday morning when at 9 o'clock they said they were putting it through. Did they? They did not. A weekend wire is quicker cheaper and more reliable. And that's alright about Julien Green's leaving the manuscript here — of course. If I'm not in the concierge is perfectly reliable.

the clipping re Francis: What Alice called "Francis' international scandal" made headlines over the world. A retired Royal Navy commander, Lionel Kenneth Philip Crabb, a good friend of Francis and a frogman, had disappeared in Portsmouth harbor after diving near the Soviet warship that brought Premier Bulganin and Secretary Khrushchev to Britain for an official visit. Francis claimed to have received the last word from Crabb, a note saying, "I'll be in clover the first of the month. I've sold my invention." Subsequently, Francis said, the note "disappeared." Newsmen and intelligence agents searched for Francis, who went into hiding, and could not be located either at his apartment in Paris nor in Lady Rose's house in Corsica. Deepening the mystery, according to the London *Times* (June 17, 1956, et seq.) was the disappearance of four sheets from a hotel register in Portsmouth, where Crabb had been seen entering with another man, said either to have been Francis or his son, Louis Rose. Apologies from the Admiralty did little to soften the Soviet anger; it was thought to be an attempt on the lives of Bulganin and Khrushchev. Crabb was never seen again.

the herb scented beads: It was popular in the American midwest, especially Ohio, to make necklaces of allspice and flour, tightly rolled into balls and strung with glass beads separating the spice balls. The warmth of the wearer's skin created a small intense perfume.

the manuscript: A translation of Jean Genet's *Querelle de Brest,* which I had made.

2 January 1957
5, rue Christine, Paris VI

Dearest Sam,

The better the day the better the deed but it is a month minus a day that the bad news was written and if it was bad then it has been worse since. At once I took to resting up — as much as my life admits — to be as fresh as a daisy when you arrived. And I havent gotten around to the bookshop — not precisely in this quarter — to see if the tattoo book [is the one you already have]. It is not likely to be the one you mention — there would be no point in their trying to make a point of selling a book published today in Paris. But I shall get to the little shop where I saw it and I hope still find it there.

And the new quarters on the respectable side of the street — are they flourishing so that when the weather is better here and still unfavorable for business in Chicago — you can take a flying leap over. That is what you must look forward to.

Emmy [Curtis] sent me a pretty card and her good wishes.

Francis is still in London making money designing for textile fabrics. He didnt return after his convalescence with the Guards officer at the smart nursing home.

Dont believe your newspaper accounts of the situation here. There is no rationing except gasoline oil and *mazout* and I have priority rights at my age — so that unless the winter is going to be extremely disagreeable I'll not be too uncomfortable. There was a moment when the French took to their old happy habit of hoarding — sugar this time — *cela n'a pas pris* — the government flooded the market and the legal price was maintained. *Tableaux!*

I dont think it is going to be a catastrophic winter — in any case only three more months to go. And the days are perceptibly longer — on the evening end. Is that universal or just a choice French thought. Arent they *impayable*.

So very many fond good wishes to you — Sam dear

Love from

Alice

when you arrived: My 1957 Christmas visit had to be postponed a month.

tattoo book: Alice was not referring to the one I had in my collection, *Le Tatouage du "Milieu"* by Jacques Delarue.

the new quarters: A new shop had been opened on the east side of State Street in Chicago.

25 January 1957

5, rue Christine, Paris VI

Sam dear,

You were really too sweet to send me the burlesque pictures — the only thing that would or could completely and entirely take me out of the distressing *tristesse* of this winter weather. And would you believe that there are two of my favorite heroines of my early youth — Lillian Russell and Fay Templeton — and that my memory of them is not at all as they are pictured in the book. Lillian Russell gave no suggestion of knowing a Diamond Jim Brady and Fay Templeton was less than half the weight — who wore a pair of tights a high belt a bunch of violets and a smile — so proper that my mother took me to a matinee! And one afternoon before the other war on the rue de Rivoli on the way to Gagliani's Gertrude and I stopped breathless at the sight of Lillian Russell — yellow hair turquoise eyes pale rose complexion in a black tailored suit buttoned down the front like a riding habit from neck to waist into which she had evidently been poured. How otherwise had she gotten into it. Oh yes she had an enormous black velvet picture hat with long black feathers. Of course none of any of this was of the mode of the moment. She progressed very slowly. Dumbfounded the traffic stopped — staring at her — made room for her to pass. It was probably one of her last triumphs.

There are probably dozens of more treasures for me to

discover — the book came this morning and so I havent dug into it yet.

Angelic Sammy — all my grateful thanks and love

Alice

the burlesque book: A large illustrated book, companion to *Gunfighters and Outlaws,* on the history and personae of the burlesque theater.

14 September 1957
La Brebeche — Magagnosc par Grasse

Dearest Sam,

Try to forgive me a little without knowing too much of the reasons for the long silence. There were many weeks of too much work with the natural exhaustion that followed broken by the shock of the unexpected death of a friend — by Francis getting himself into a scandalous scrape and being taken to hospital — all this without the comfort of having seen you. Your not coming [this summer] was a terrible disappointment to me.

La Sprigge's book was wiped off the slate by Gilbert Harrison's review of it in the *New Republic* and Donald Sutherland's in the *Nation.* Excellent both of them — did you see them. She put it over her British critics but not ours.

James Purdy bores me. He asked me to write something about his latest effort — that I would be amongst friends — Carl [Van Vechten] and Edith Sitwell but I ignored his request and his book. He — his subject matter and his treatment of it lack taste.

Strictly *entre nous* Thornton [Wilder] was not pleased with Ruth Gordon's changing more lines at every performance. Then she wanted to play in French in Paris. How Thornton got out of that is beyond my imagining — for she is a formidable lady — an *arriviste* and a money maker — pretentious and insensitive. What more?

Two weeks ago tomorrow Virginia — Harold and I were driven down here by a friend of theirs. It was a lovely trip — sunny by way of Grenoble — the *route Napolienne.* The friend went on to Mallorca and we are here in a convenient if not too comfortable house in a little garden with huge olive and willow trees with the fragrance of not too distant fields of jasmine blossoms. I sit all day in the garden and havent yet ventured to go to Grasse — to say nothing of Cannes where I want to go to see Picasso — who never comes to Paris any more. If I can manage it I shall take the treatment of the mud baths (not alluring in themselves) at Acqui in Piemonte. Anita Loos was lately miraculously cured of long standing arthritis. It would be pleasant if it did as much for me. I am writing today for terms. The cure is short — three weeks — so that the return to Paris would be before the end of next month.

About Francis — he suddenly appeared in Paris about a month ago complaining of Frederica — she had sold the two wee rooms in the Quai d'Anjou — she could no longer afford to pay the taxes. He hasnt been painting but was earning a lot for textile designs — he apparently has great aptitude for them. The next thing one night quite late there was a telephone message from a strange rough voice — announcing that Francis was at the military hospital at Levallois — then the visit of one of the resident doctors who was very upset by the *voyou* whom Francis brought with him from London and who had beaten him up in a drunken brawl — and who had brought him to the hospital and who called it a serious heart attack. The doctors say there is nothing the matter with him except his character. It is too sad.

There was a nice visit from Mrs Rozeck — an unusually sympathetic sensitive person — she spoke so warmly — appreciatively of you. What a charming courageous thing to have come over with her three little girls.

The equinoctial mistral is blowing and I must go indoors. When you have time write to me — Sam dear — to say you do forgive me.

All my fondest love
Alice

James Purdy: American novelist and short story writer. Alice later changed her mind about his work and came to admire him a great deal. Her first opinion, however, resulted from an irritation that he had sent her his book without her requesting it — a mistake in judgment on the part of Carl Van Vechten, who had asked Purdy to send it, assuring him that Alice would react favorably. Had Van

Vechten himself sent the book, her reaction in all probability would have been much different.

La Sprigge: As she did in most instances, Alice hated the end result of Elizabeth Sprigge's book, *Gertrude Stein: Her Life and Work* (New York: Harper, 1957).

Mrs Rozeck: A student of mine who had become infatuated with Gertrude's work.

6 October 1957
Acqui — Piemonte — Italia

Sam dear,

Your nice long letter was forwarded from Paris to Grasse whence I came here. The hot baths have been famous since the days of the Romans — but it was the enchanting Anita Loos who recommended them to me and they have indeed been beneficial. I am walking much better and without a cane. On Friday I go to Milan and then fly back to Paris — hoping that I shall be fortified against the wet winter and the work. So much for me — except for the pleasure of looking forward to seeing you. Where will you be staying? And dont you dare bring me the weeniest gift. I'd hate you and it if you did. Beware my new old anger.

Now about Francis — go easy — he was in a wretched state when he was taken to the British military hospital having been battered up by a young boy friend he brought with him from London. He was an ignorant ruffian who telephoned me late one evening but I'd have nothing of him. A nice resident doctoress had gotten him into a Jesuit retreat somewhere in the suburbs of Paris and I shall see him upon my return. A word of advice — Francis has been in difficulties with the police and in a political mixup — as a foreigner you should be careful. Poor poor Francis — he has few friends left either in London or Paris.

It's a heavenly day — really *dominical* — autumnal — to be indulged in with a ladle not a spoon. By the way do you eat garlic. The regime here is liberally construed but garlic is considered indelicate so they chop four cloves of it for me for my evening meal. It is a soporific you know. The Knapiks enjoy it as much as I do so I've formed a habit. As for *aillo n'en parlons pas.*

Do you know James Purdy and his two books — he is or

was a friend of Wendell [Wilcox]. His books bore me exceedingly. I was shocked to learn he wasnt an ignorant young man. He wrote to me as if he were — that is part of a game. His second book has just been published and *Punch* scored it severely.

Now I must take my daily promenade — isnt it wonderful to be able to do so.

So much love Sam dear — and *à bientôt hein*?

Alice

A word of advice: This is the word of warning that one never ignored from Alice. Although after this Francis and I corresponded for a number of years, I never again mentioned him to Alice. The same thing had happened with the Daniel-Rops, and others. It was a choice of pleasures: you knew either Alice (and Gertrude) or the others — not both.

aillo: Possibly Alice means *ailloli,* or a mayonnaise-type sauce made with mashed garlic.

15 January 1958
5, rue Christine, Paris VI

Sam dear,

It is hard to think that it isnt possible to telephone you at half after nine but good to know you have escaped the great cold up on the top story of 3 bis Place St. Sulpice. And the little heat the old heater ('28) was giving has no more to give and there has been no time nor energy to get across town to investigate two small ones. I am still on a hunt to find many things besides heaters — a *femme de ménage* — a plumber — a new tarif for stamps — *basta.* The list could drag on endlessly.

My news is just chill — fatigue — good health and happiness — why? Impossible to explain or understand. Often because of one or a combination of these I fall asleep or doze in my chair. I sleep under three layers and in two of wool and like it.

I have nine recipes to send to Poppy Cannon tomorrow morning — no wonder Bessie of Harper's was enraged with my carelessness — but I wrote to him sharply before he had a chance to do so.

Have you seen Thurber's last book — he is witty wise and writes like an angel. His drawings please me less.

I am economising paper because goodness knows when the weather will permit me to get over to my stationers (or anywhere else). You may yet see what la rue de l'Ancienne Comédie can produce.

The Knapiks are delighted with the kitchen alarm clock you gave them but nothing to the pleasure the spoons gave me. They are used for Sunday sauce.

The pen has gone on the blink. I have changed the *cartouche.* Is it any better. Good enough to [send] my absent Sammy my love.

Alice

It is hard to think. During all my visits to Paris, Alice always telephoned me at 9:30 A.M. In the winter of 1957–1958, the heating system at the Hôtel Récamier gave way.

31 January 1958
5, rue Christine, Paris VI

The spoons are darling
Sam dear,

Glenway Wescott wrote to me to ask me to tell you to see him on your way home. But you had flown centuries before. He is quite delightful — he and J[ulian] Green — quite unlike as they are — are equally charming — oldfashioned. Glenway has given *causéries* on Gertrude to clubs — in spite of her harsh phrase in the *Autobiography* on his work.

Here it has been very cold — no heat — at moments no light or water — no Madeleine. Now it is warm — yesterday three little electric radiators — a *femme de ménage* (slightly smelly) since Monday — no plumber yet. Bernard Buffet is going to have a profile in the *N[ew] Yorker.* Francis is teaching painting in London — is painting for a show in the autumn — seems sober and well to do!

Did you get back to the tattoo book on the rue Jacob? I shall get there again soon.

Fond love from
Alice

her harsh phrase: In *The Autobiography of Alice B. Toklas,* Gertrude had written that at no time had Glenway Wescott interested her and that he had a certain syrup but it did not pour.

3 April 1958
5, rue Christine, Paris VI

Sweet Sam,

What a miserable time of Asiatic grippe and poisoning. Are you taking good care to recover your strength. Be sure you are and let me know that you are. I am praying for you. I came back into the Church having been baptized as a child — easily and happily. My parish is Saint Séverin but it is too far for the arthritis. There is however a small chapel just around two corners and that is a comfort — and an English priest from Chaillot who comes here.

The rest of my news is good too — all except Madeleine's successor who cant see or hear or remember and who prefers the light work to leave the heavy to me! I have done an article for the *Atlantic Monthly* on the Haute Couture and I am about to do a book of reminiscences in collaboration with Max White who has come up from Rome for the purpose — which will be fun for I've passed the burden to him. And Harpers is doing the recipes with an introduction by Poppy Cannon (in which Cézanne Hemingway Picasso and Matisse were all contemporaries) and the tone to be over laudatory became embarrassingly untrue. But all these will bring in enough pennies to pay for the plumbing repairs and a trip this summer for the cure at Acqui. 5 rue Christine has been sold to speculators who will sell the flats — but the French law protects me and they cant put me out.

Isnt this enough news for one letter.

All my prayers for a joyous Easter — too late — and for all good things to you Sammy dear

Love from
Alice

I came back into the Church: Several persons have speculated about her early baptism into the Catholic Church, all records presumably having been destroyed in the 1906 San Francisco earthquake and fire. In an earlier letter (September 8, 1949) she says that as a child she fell off a log into the water and was promptly taught Our Father — a curious punishment for one of the Jewish faith. Janet Flanner reports (*The New Yorker*, December 15, 1975) that Alice told her that as a little girl in San Francisco she had been created a Christian in the most casual way by a Catholic girlfriend who had sprinkled her with holy water and pronounced the proper formula; in Catholic belief this would have constituted a valid baptism.

30 April 1958
5, rue Christine, Paris VI

Sam dear,

Your letter left me "flabber and gasted" as you say — it was much nearer to what I hoped you would be feeling — that was greatly encouraging and you are definitely on the road to joining your sister in her faith — her and my prayers for you will be answered — and I shallnt get in your way of your finding yourself with the grace peace faith that will overwhelm *you any day.* Yes dear that is the way it is and shall be world without end. A mass for you will help.

Max White is here working on the book with me. You know he was converted three years ago by Father de Chardin. He came up from Rome where his health suffered from the cold. He has the happiest memories of you — speaks warmly of your gifts and thoroughness. He sends you tender thoughts.

It was good of you to send Gertrude's letters to Yale. They are safe there and belong with all the others. When I first went back into the Church I lost her and then suddenly it was clear — she had been with God all her life and that brought her back with a radiance I had never known.

Francis' son has married and will make him a grandfather one of these days!

Sam dear — dont think that wont get you anywhere — say the prayers you remember.

I pray for you and will have a mass said for you.

Love
Alice

On the back of the envelope in which this letter was contained, she wrote "The most gorgeous flowers have come from you just now—rose colored purest tulips — blue iris — yellow Shasta daisies. Naughty boy — you could come over instead! Thanks thanks and again thanks."

7 August 1958
5, rue Christine, Paris VI

Sam dear,

Yes Max [White] was a surprise — he just disappeared into thin air. Harold [Knapik] came down at once after having first gone to Max's hotel — they only knew he had left. He had dined at the Knapiks — stayed until midnight and not mentioned his imminent departure. Harold and I went over the situation pretty thoroughly and concluded that I was well out of a mess — for Max was exhausting me (four hour seances six times a week) — that he was not satisfied with me — that he didnt think as a novelist he should be biographising — and quit. By the time we came to this there was nothing but relief. The publishers were pleased — they had found him difficult and are now hunting for a successor. I tell you all this because it is a very real Max story.

The rest of my news is not brilliant. An infected foot has left me immobilised. The doctor doesnt permit me to stand — but ablutions and simple cooking are achieved. It is getting better and the pain is decreasing. I hope to get off at the end of the month to spend September in the Midi with Harold and Virginia and then go to the baths at Acqui which were wonderfully beneficial last year.

No Sam dear — the past is not gone — nor is Gertrude (life everlasting — Father Taylor — my confessor — has made that clear). It left me in a dither when suddenly it came to me — where was Gertrude. She *is* there waiting for us. Father T. and Bernard — a Madame Azam and an Edward Waterman made me what Holy Church intended we should be — what a disparate group we would otherwise be. I pray for you — my dear — you will return — your sister's prayers cant be unavailing.

You know Gertrude told Hemingway — in the early days — he couldnt earn his living doing newspaper work and write — he should like Sherwood [Anderson] earn his living running a laundry. Keep tattoo and writing apart. Your detachment article is alright for the man in Switzerland or another.

Now I must close the shutters and get a glass of orange juice and finally creep into bed.

God's blessing — Sam dear

Love from your devoted
Alice

29 November 1958
5, rue Christine, Paris VI

Sam dear,

To tell you once more how much I am looking forward to seeing you on the twentieth and to tell you that it is not my fault if you have gotten now a cookbook of which I can not be proud. The Knapiks made a mistake in copying the address I gave them.

There is a manuscript an ex-soldier sent me and which is blasphemous — which I have told him — and which I am keeping for you to see because there is a great deal of tattooing (?) in it.

I am having to get the repairs in the flat finished and to myself (we are both falling to pieces gradually) before you arrive. I am praying so hard for you to come back — perhaps for Christmas. My father confessor says masses for you.

Blessings — Sam dear

Love from
Alice

a cookbook: Alice deplored the popularization of her *Aromas and Flavors of Past and Present* (New York: Harper and Brothers, 1958) by Poppy Cannon and the substitution of "American ingredients," finally dissassociating herself from the introduction and the book in general.
an ex-soldier: John Breon, who had written admiringly to Gertrude in 1945 and wrote *The Sorrows of Travel* (New York: Putnam, 1955).

8 January 1959
5, rue Christine, Paris VI

Sam dear,

After you left the other evening I read the book you gave me — intensely interesting — I didnt go to bed until I had read the modern half where the history I know came in. To think I should have known Kipling — who at that time was my great favorite. Well! Well. Then I went to bed and got up to do the housework. And now Mad[eleine] has returned and the flat is clean again — and the plumber is finished and the electrician this morning and the catalyste is to be returned Tuesday at the latest. That is my news.

And yours? Did you get to Rome?

And I am ever so sorry you took so much time to write at

such length about John Breon's novel but pleased that we agreed though I didnt have Matthew Arnold or Plato to support me. It is indeed an able but fearful book and the litany drove me quite mad. Miss Mary Storer [?] is coming to see me Sunday evening and I shall have to hear her on the book. She was on the faculty at Beloit when he was a student there. And so was Chad Walsh a fair poet and very High Church — what can he think of it? Miss Storer will tell me though I would prefer not.

One more bit of news. I have an appointment with my oculist for Monday afternoon so within a week I may be seeing again. I hope so.

It was lovely seeing you again — yes come next year — I may hang on until then. The book must get done. And the cheque was found — put away with some receipts and some old *Punches* kept for Harold Knapik that Virginia found. So that divining string was mistaken. It (the cheque) wasnt in the *meuble* or in the scrapbasket. With a pair of gloves I went through the *boîte d'ordure!* and the glasses that were missing were in the bag of the bag of the vacuum cleaner! And now there is nothing missing.

Dont forget you said you would say the Creed frequently and read the missal and when Father Taylor returns he will bless the beautiful rosary you gave me and I shall say my penance with it. Be a good boy so that my prayers be effective.

Bless you dear Sam — God and all the saints.

Love from
Alice

the cheque was found: The full story of the "divining string" is related on pages 105–7.

5 August 1959
Postmarked St. Maxime — Var

[Written above the printed rue Christine address:] No I am not here nor have not been for some time for any length of time

Sammy dearest,

It's a long too too long a time since you've heard from [me]. After a bad winter a bad spring commenced and in April I went down to Acqui again — was benefited and went over to meet Frederica Rose at Marseilles where there [were] fifty Picasso masterpieces at an incredible show — and Picasso the adorable Jacqueline the son Paulot his wife and her daughter and a host of friends at his beautiful home at the Chateau de Vauvernargue. It was wonderfully exciting and after flying home I collapsed! It was a short but dreadful illness. *Schwamm darüber* (did you learn that in Switzerland). Finally — indeed quickly my good doctor cured me and sent me to a romantic spot near Paris to recuperate which I did in six weeks — got back to Paris for three days and was brought down here (Saint Maxime) in the Riviera to stay until the Assumption with a friend of Virginia Knapik. All for 82 mildly exciting.

So many many thanks you sweet Sammy for the lovely roses. Why are you so good so devoted to the old lady — to buck her up? It does — bless you. What makes you so faithful?

Now I must answer a long ago letter. Do not be discouraged with hell — remember there is forgiveness of sins — doesnt that compensate? And the communion of saints and all the rest of the creed? Tell me — are you beginning again to believe? I want you to be happy and blessed.

All my thoughts and love to you

Alice

28 December 1959

5, rue Christine, Paris VI

Sam dearest,

What wonderfully good news you gave me for Christmas — the best I've had since Gertrude died. My good Father Taylor came that morning to give me Holy Communion and I told him (for he has been saying masses for some of my friends. "Good," said he, "you see what prayer will do. And now Picasso!") You are my sweet Sam, you have made your sister and me all happy and my prayers now for you will be different ones but just as faithfully, night and morning. I am sorry you will never have met Father Taylor he goes back to the Soudan as a White Friar in June. He has been attached to the Gros Cailloux for several times. It was through a friend that he received me into the Church. She the friend Madame Azam in Rome for Christmas expected to meet me there but I couldnt make it (too cold to travel and too expensive this year.) She wrote and said the only two persons I knew in Rome are the Pope who was the legate here and my neighbor and friend for eight years and the Ambassador and one cant expect to see much of either of them especially at Christmas tide can one?

Bernard Faÿ came to Paris on his way to spend Christmas at Solesmes (you must go there some time) — Edward Waterman took me there — a monk a friend of Bernard's prayed for me. And that was the beginning. Edward is a bad boy and a good Catholic!

Please send me Emmy's [Curtis] address. I'll write to her. She sent me a Xmas card but her address was on the envelope which got lost.

I like your stationery. The rose reminds me of a very unpleasant book by Brinnin. He sent me a copy which I spent a month correcting to send to Yale for reference, not for circulation.

Harold Knapik has been very ill — he is at the American hospital. Osborn Andreas has offered them a house in Colorado where they will go in spring. They go to Chicago as soon as he is well enough to travel. I shall miss Virginia greatly.

My loving thoughts for a blessed New Year — Sam dear.

Devotedly

Alice

With this letter was enclosed a color postcard of The Holy Lamb, a detail from Van Eyck's *The Adoration of the Lamb*.

What wonderfully good news: After a long and involved struggle with my conscience, and in the end feeling like a hypocrite, I decided to tell Alice that her prayers had been answered and that I had returned to the Church. There were many considerations: my love for her, some increase in happiness for her in the declining years, a strengthening of her own belief and faith. It was difficult to justify such a deception, but her joyful reaction was a partial reward, and no harm was done.

unpleasant book by Brinnin: In customary fashion, Alice disapproved of *The Third Rose: Gertrude Stein and Her World* by John Malcolm Brinnin (Boston: Little, Brown, 1959), referring to him in conversation as "that upstart crow."

11 February 1960
5, rue Christine, Paris VI

Sam dearest,

There are too many reasons why I should have written but now there is an added one — your wondrous book has arrived and there is a most surprising reason. Do you perhaps [know it]? Before I commenced to read when I was just looking through the beauteous pictures I found the early Man Ray photograph of Gertrude with an Ezra Pound on the same page and a lovely very young one of Anita Loos and one of poor dear Scott Fitzgerald. Would anyone [have] suspected it? And so many thanks for many reasons for your generous gift. You are always being too good to me. But as you well know I thank God night and morning for the best gift. You know what my good Father confessor said — If in answer to prayer you have His ear and you should ask Him to bring one of [your] friends to Holy Church — would you not want Picasso? You must have a priest — go to see him — which of course I dont — though when I told Picasso that my early worry was Gertrude he gave me the same answer Bernard did — "She is in Heaven waiting." That was surprising. Probably I'm no less clear to you — Sam dearest.

I have been considerably upset by the Knapik news — Harold as you know has been very seriously ill at the American hospital — he is getting better but will leave there walking on crutches and on a diet — for three years. It has been a great strain on wonderful Virginia. I see her frequently — Harold not in months. Andreas has offered him a house he owns in Colorado which they have accepted for spring — but they fly to N. York in a week where he will see de Cuevas about his ballet and then go to Chicago where he will arrange more musical matters. I shall miss Virginia more than I can say.

The rest of my news is the household — which I spare you.

Write to me soon. Pray for me — which I do for you night and morning.

Loving thoughts from
Alice

wondrous book: A large pictorial book entitled *The Jazz Age.*

6 May 1960
5, rue Christine, Paris VI

Sam dear,

Your letter too long unanswered was a contentment and an encouragement. I rejoiced at the good news it brought — night and morning prayers are not unavailing. (There is nothing that is as peace-[making?]) How can one resist the creed?

Your illness and operation frightened me — do take care of yourself — dont be neglectful. You are wonderful at helping the cure — but Sammy better avoid the crisis. Get your answer always as you did for tattooing "King of Kings — Lord of Lords" — a direct answer — inspired you are.

Today is the first warm day — the sun without wind — the window open next to me — the air balmy — and it is making the winter fatigue less troublesome. Arthritis made walking almost impossible even with a cane. Then something called *Verve* sent a man to interview me for records and gave me perhaps a more needed than deserved advance. He took me to a recording station where I read from the *Autobiography* and answered questions. As taxis are difficult to find we walked thirteen blocks — Fine! Except the next day I was a rag. However the advance will pay for the trip to the baths at Acqui and a visit with the John Browns (he is the U.S. cultural attaché) at Rome where he will I hope have me presented to His Holiness. If I can manage to get the flat in order I'll fly down to Milan (taxi to Acqui) a week from Monday.

So many people write or telephone to know more about

Gertrude — serious students (good) — not so serious — and not students at all. It keeps me busy. A dreadful young woman wanted a catalogue (!) of the pictures.

All the *inédits* are published now.

I hope you havent seen Malcolm Brinnin's book — vulgar and mistaken. La Sprigge brought me some flowers and sent her greetings!!

Now I have gotten to the gorgeous flowers you sent me (you know my feelings against such extravagance). Never have I seen such wildly beautiful tulips and lilacs (surely hothouse) on stems a yard high — brilliant yellow — a new tulip as big as your head — dark purple to mingle with the double lilaç lilacs. They have made the room very fragrant and of an elegance and I dont mean to be cross but they would keep you a week in Paris. But *de tout mon coeur je t'en remercie — Je t'en embrasse — Mille tendresses de ton plus vieille amie.*

Alice

Your illness: An operation on a kneecap.

something called Verve: On April 29, 1960, Alice recorded for Verve records some readings from *The Alice B. Toklas Cook Book* (her experiences with Gertrude in France, the American tour, experiments with food during the occupation of France, the gardens at Bilignin, the famous recipe for hashish fudge with her own comments) and two versions of her first meeting with Gertrude Stein — the first from *The Autobiography of Alice B. Toklas*, the second her own recollection of that meeting.

23 August 1960
Via Anton Giulio Barrili, 44, Roma

Sam dear,

Here I am — as much to your surprise as mine. I am a paying guest since two weeks with the nuns of the Adoration of the Sacred Blood — a Canadian cloistered order — all but three working sisters immured. I am very comfortable except for the heat and very happy — mass mornings at half after six — benediction Sundays and holidays.

How did I get here? John Brown had wanted me to come down and stay with him — he is cultural officer at our embassy — after my cure at Acqui in spring but it seemed better to rest — but he came to Paris in June and I flew back with him and spent three delightful weeks with them. His wife is a great person and when I decided to spend the winter in Rome she found this convent. You should see her make the arrangements with cigarette in her mouth with the good Sister Saint Paul. So here I am. And where are you and how are you. And are you coming down here instead of Paris at Christmastime. If not why not?

I havent been in Rome for nearly fifty years when Gertrude and I were here and stayed up above the Piazza d'Espagne — and I've only been in town now three times. I hope to go to Saint John Lateran and to Santa Maria Maggiore — but it is very hot. When it is cooler I shall.

It is dark in the room now — sunrise is so slow and sunset so fast.

You are in my prayers twice a day (sometimes I say them three times) and I always love you — dear Sam.

Ever your devoted
Alice

Here I am: This was the fateful winter in Rome during which the Stein family seized Gertrude's collection as a "national treasure left unprotected."

Roubina Stein, Allan's widow (Gertrude's nephew had died in 1951), secured entry somehow to Alice's apartment, although Alice was always extremely careful to make sure that the concierge never revealed her out-of-town absences. What ruse was used to enter the apartment is not known. Once there, Roubina Stein inventoried the pictures from the list made at the time of Gertrude's death and found some items missing — which Alice had sold, as Gertrude's will permitted. Mrs. Stein did not communicate with Alice, but secured a court order declaring the pictures endangered by Alice's absence. The paintings were removed the day before Alice returned from Rome.

Ruined by this move of Roubina Stein's was a small plan that Alice had cherished and devised after the death of Allan Stein. By negotiating with Roubina Stein, the eldest son Daniel, and the lawyer who was guardian of the two minor children (Michael and Gertrude), Alice hoped to be able to offer them enough money for their lifelong comfort — to be furnished by a sale of the paintings en bloc, so that the collection would not be dispersed. The removal of the paintings made this impossible. A major selection of the paintings was sold immediately for six and a half million dollars to a syndicate of four trustees and one patron from the Museum of Modern Art — an institution that both Gertrude and Alice hated. The paintings were thus "dispersed without sentiment."

19 October 1960
Via Anton Giulio Barrili, 44, Rome

Sam dear,

It was lovely getting your letter with the news that you will be here at Christmas time with your Swiss friend and a Monsignor — that you are happily in the arms of Mother Church now — which is the good Lord's gift to us all.

When you get to Monteverde the convent that is — the working sister who sees the world — Sister Saint Paul (Canadian) will let you wait for me in the parlor and then you and Rudolf [and I] will go to a nice little restaurant in the lovely Piazza Navona which (the restaurant) has the adorable name of *Tre Scalini*. The food is Italian but not necessarily mucilaginous macaroni!

It has grown frightfully cold — the heater goes on at the beginning of the month — every few days it rains. Never do I have colds — but I got the epizootics(?) and sneezed my head off — twenty three times yesterday. But I woke up cured this morning! And you know I wouldnt pray for myself.

Rome needs rain — it has been dry for three months. There will otherwise [be] no vegetables — no truffles — no mushrooms — nor any of the common ones — the delicate bell peppers — egg plants — *courgettes* and fruity tomatoes. There are still miniature artichokes. It takes all of the state of California to equal little Italy.

Now about the wrong address — the fault was not my little red address book — it [was] my poor tired old eyes which are completely on the blink. My pen is a Sheaffer Skrip cartridge — which slips in one's hand then doesnt register. And there are interruptions — the good Sister Saint Paul comes with a letter — with the cleaner's package — the laundry (twice). Gertrude said nuns were like birds — they are happy in their faith — and to a certain degree we share it with them. If I were sixty years younger I would want to enter their order — The Adoration of the Sacred Blood. The big beautiful Crucifixion opposite my door has taught me that and so much more.

To you — Sam dear — my tender thoughts — prayers and love.

Devotedly
Alice

10 December 1960
Via Anton Giulio Barrili, 44, Rome

Dearest Sam,

You are really coming! Too good — so good it is true. No dont come out — it is a good distance and you would have to come and go back — I would only have to go. So telephone — the number is 580 890.

I'll find out if the restaurants close on Christmas as they do in Paris.

Eyes somewhat better but not yet good enough.

The midnight mass in the Sistine Chapel is for you my dear — it holds several hundreds. People I know were there the other day for a requiem for defunct cardinals and a Paris friend who knew H[is] H[oliness] when he was nuncio there was received with ten others. H.H. is like you. He has time for everything including explaining Huysmans' Oblates. Fortunately life has always been simple. Heaven is less so.

Soon now — very soon, Sam dear — you'll be here.

Blessings — love
Devotedly
Alice

4 January 1961
Rome

Sam dear,

Your pretty p.c. from Pompei came this morning — by the time you were in Chicago — such is the Italian past. Nor do I complain of your having been in Rome without letting me know. By accident you were on the terrace at Doney's — the opposite of looking [for] you at Culoz. Never mind — next time I'll find you sooner. Did your Monsignor show you the sybils' cave at Naples. The scandal of the hour of my return here [at the convent] from the dinner party is now forgotten. The Sweets are on their cruise. Do you know the story of Freda? She spends half the year here with Peter and the other half year with a friend of Bob's in Los Angeles. She would like Peter to be appointed as consul in L.A. but he says if he leaves Rome he wants to go to Paris. So much for that.

I am so glad you saw the Pope. It is a permanent event —

isnt it — it doesnt fade. There are some people who live two blocks from the Piazza San Pietro. I spent New Year's day with them and they took me to the Piazza Navona to see the lighted booths — gay — and to see the electric wreaths decor at many of the palaces. Rome is festive. Now we have twelfth night and then calm down.

There was neither time nor occasion to tell you of the very nice father confessor Madame Azam found for me in the neighborhood. He is at the head of the school of the canons regular of the Immaculate Conception. In the meantime poor Father Taylor has been ordered from Paris back to England and is not certain of returning to Paris.

Sam dear — you are in my thoughts and my prayers are always two or three times a day for the Lord's blessing and protection — addressed to the beautiful crucified Christ you brought me. (My prayers to Him are a new comfort).

Devotedly
Alice

you were on the terrace: See page 108.

13 October 1961
5, rue Christine, Paris VI

Dearest Sam,

So very many strange things have happened to me — but Our Saviour through your Crucifix has given me a blissful peace. My heartfelt thanks again to you — Sam dear.

A long happy winter in Rome — the baths at Acqui — return to Paris where I found the walls bare. The heirs found them [the pictures] insufficiently insured and unprotected. Then I slipped and broke my knee — which [is] still in a cast. I was moved to a nursing home at Ville d'Avray — a ghastly month there but able to hobble with a crutch — then fell again and broke my wrist — fortunately the left. At my age falls are natural — arent they?

Madeleine comes to take care of me — she has been very good to me. I have a useless Spanish *soubrette* as a servant but Madeleine is hunting a successor — thinks she has found one.

You do know — dont you Sam dear — of all *ces événements* — how peaceful my life is.

Do you remember our Belgian host and his Austrian lady love of Christmas Evening where we stayed too late? She was converted and they were married — to everyone's delight. He is no longer [consul?] at the Belgian embassy at Rome but ambassador to His Holiness.

My handwriting will have told you of the state of my eyes — *n'en parlons plus.*

My kind editor came over from N. York to work over the manuscript of my book. He is very satisfied with it and is providing a secretary to enable me to finish it this year and a young woman to read aloud to me several evenings a week.

You are — Sam dear — in my thoughts always and in my prayers twice a day.

Much love
Devotedly from
Alice

my handwriting: With her advancing age and near-blindness, Alice's handwriting had grown much larger and more sprawling; her letters were now filled with omitted words, repetitions of the words and phrases, interlineations, occasional misspellings, and uncustomary gaps in thought and expression. It was amazing that she could write at all.

22 February 1962
5, rue Christine, Paris VI

Sam dear,

Who but you would have written me such a letter and thought of writing it in such a manner that I could easily read it — Angel child that you are. May the Good Lord bless and protect you always.

I have just had a series of adventures. Gertrude and I always went to Pierre Balmain's "collections" — so this year having with the aid of an excellent masseur who had already got me to walk down the stairs to the front door and back twice — and with [the] aid of Raymond — a young Pekinois whom he brought back with him a few months ago we went off to Pierre's to the collection. I was led to the seat of honor between Princess Isabelle of France and our ambassador — ex-general Gavin and his wife — but there I sat on a little chair without moving for three hours. The collection was fabulous — [beige?] and white and rose — no blue — a few greens — but nothing to compare with the brocaded Chi [at this point an amanuensis takes over the handwriting] nese jacket they brought back from Pekin for me and a Chinese coat with fur strips. I felt very appropriately dressed but came back exhausted and a few nights later went to the Ritz hotel where Pierre was decorated with the Legion of Honor. He made a speech which I didnt hear — and saw there his friend the daughter of the widow of the Prefet at Grenoble who has a home there — Chindrieux and one in Paris and I had a pleasant conversation of Paris' early days and also with Madame Jouhandreau and her husband and a number of people I didnt know. So much for my fashionable life.

I'll write to you again when I have more news to tell. My book is going to be sent off or to show to Robert Lescher when he comes over. Joe Barry says that Lescher wrote him that he's very pleased with the book which is very encouraging.

Do you remember Robert Sweet that night at Christmas? He has been very unhappy. His wife fell in love and ran away with an actor and he doesnt know what to do about it. She wanted him to see her and talk to her about [things] but he quite rightly refused and he now threatens to come over to see me. Gertrude was very fond of him and it was he who took us to Germany in a bomber immediately after the war.

My plans are somewhat vague but I go to Acqui in spring after having seen John Brown in Rome and my convent for a few days.

Let me hear from you my dear and all my thanks for your letter.

Prayers and God's blessing,
Devotedly
Alice

Who but you: In large printed capital letters I had written her at length.
Pierre Balmain: Well-known designer. He had met Gertrude and Alice at Bilignin while delivering clothes from his mother's shop in Aix-les-Bains. Gertrude and Alice helped him to begin his career in Paris.
Robert Lescher: Editor, Holt Rinehart and Winston. The book was *What Is Remembered.*

12 June 1962
5, rue Christine, Paris VI

Dearest Sam,

Only your handwriting is legible to my feeble sight. I re-read it often and pray for you three times a day.

My book is finished and the editor took it off with him almost two weeks ago. It doesn't end as well as it should but I could do nothing with him or it. They wont print it until January or February when you will have your copy. It should have ended more gaily.

Do you remember Robert Sweet at the Christmas dinner in Rome? His wife sat on the other side of the host. Well — poor Robert has had a sad story. She went to see her son act and there fell in love with [the] leading actor and brought him out to California where Bob S he didnt want to see him. And very soon after the actor died. Bob wired me the whole story and said he wanted to come to see me but I said he shouldnt. Now the book is done and the editor has gone back to U.S. Poor Bob.

And poor Emmy — I fear to have her news — but write it. It is too sad.

Dearest Sam — I think of you all the time and pray Our Good Lord will bless and protect you.

My dearest love to you always — and when will you be here?

Devotedly yours,
Alice

23 March 1963
5, rue Christine, Paris VI

Sam dear,

Your letter would have been sheer delight if it hadnt had the news of your Emmy's death. You had fortunately the satisfaction of seeing her through the best and hardest of her days. You are doing that for us all. The Good Lord bless and protect you.

And your seventy hours journey to Dallas — how can it be so long? And your sister must be overjoyed to see you — as we all are when it comes to that.

Do you remember the place we stayed at in the Cher near

Bourges. Marie Geneviève is Mayor now and all the mayors of France came to Paris and she came to see me and wanted news of you. She has bleached her hair but is otherwise as she was —

This letter abruptly breaks off, with closing and signature missing.
seventy hours: Alice had misread my printed *seventeen.*
Marie Geneviève: Madame Debar at La Régie, Soye-en-Septaine, Cher.

6 May 1963
5, rue Christine, Paris VI

Sam dear,

If I havent thanked you long ago for your sweet wire for a birthday that should rather [have been] forgotten than remembered it is because there have been too many reminders of my age.

But I thank you with all my heart. It was a cheering moment when with aid of a magnifying glass I read it — so like dear Sam I said.

Now will you please tell me how your affairs progress. Is there any hope of your coming over here. I am not going to Acqui this year. It would be too fatiguing and expensive.

Do you remember the place where you came down to see [me] in the Cher? Madame Debar who no longer grows tobacco but has been made the mayor of her village and came to Paris for a congress of all the mayors of France! Well I may go down there about the 15th of October when Donald Sutherland will be here with a car and drive me down. Why dont you come over and join me there?

Did I write you that the Barrys are divorcing? Well they are not. I hate divorces. Instead they went down to Morocco on a second wedding trip. She has written a successful book — a collection of her newspaper articles.

Francis Rose is living in Brighton in an ancient house — with a boy friend and is writing a book on Gertrude and painting for which he has asked me to do a foreword. I

A young Englishman comes to read aloud to me and he will read Francis' manuscript to me which has come this morning. I fear there will be corrections to make which Francis did not ask for.

I pray for you night and morning — asking our Lord to bless and protect you. Now I ask a special prayer for you Sam dear.

Always devotedly
Your fond
Alice

20 July 1963
Chez Madame Debar — Soye-en-Septaine

Dearest Sam,

Isnt it a coincidence that your letter should reach me here and that I dont like it as I did when you were here. Mme Debar is bigger and handsomer than she [ever was] — her maid (le Gouvernement) is *un numéro*. The Donald Sutherlands drove me down and will probably call for me on their way back from Spain.

Your letter upset me — to have to give up your work shocked me. Wouldnt Paris with trips to the South be pleasant and profitable living — as good over [here] as Chicago? You will understand my prejudiced point of view.

I have no news except that I am old tired and dont see [or know?] much [Letter continues on back of a postcard with picture of the church at Soye-en-Septaine] I have prayed for you every night and morning since I went back to the Church. I would like to think Our [Lord] answered them. May He bless and protect you.

Love to you
Fondest love to you Sam dear from
Alice

give up your work: The law regarding age limits for tattooing had been changed in Illinois.

27 October 1963
Saturday morning
5, rue Christine, Paris VI

Sam dear,

It is so good to know that I am to see you upon your return. You will have word from me upon your return from your journey [at your address on] rue Erlanger.

Your television — which I have never seen — is frighteners.

Love and prayers
Alice

9 November 1963 (Pneumatique)
Saturday
5, rue Christine, Paris VI

Dearest Sam,

Your address disappeared. Jacinta couldnt remember having seen it! But Madeleine found it stuffed in the side of the arm chair!

When will you lunch with me? I must see you!

Isnt the weather too lovely?

Love and prayers
Devotedly
Alice

Appendices
Index

APPENDIX I

Although circumstances prevented Gertrude Stein and Samuel Steward from meeting during Gertrude and Alice's tour of the United States, Gertrude read his novel, and in her *Everybody's Autobiography* (New York: Random House, 1937) she twice referred to him and his novel, the first on pages 227–28

> We did like Columbus Ohio. It would seem that a great many years ago a professor of English of the University of Ohio in Columbus came to see me and it had been a pleasure to him and to me. We exchanged a few letters and that was long ago.
>
> He had taught all his classes to read me and now he was dead, I had not known about this and he was seconded not in his professorship but in his feeling about my work by Sam Steward who had been in Columbus but was now in Helena Montana and would we go there, we never did get there and later he was in the University of the State of Washington and they threw him out because he wrote a book called Angels On The Bough which is a very interesting book. It has something in it that makes literature. I do not know quite what but there it is. That is one of the things that is so perplexing, why do books that are books that do everything why do they not make literature, I do often worry about that, anyway the Bulletin of the American Association of University Professors realize this and now he is teaching in the Loyola University of Chicago who also know this thing.
>
> Well anyway we have never met but he is interesting.

and the second time on page 269.

> Then there is Sam Steward. Sam Steward I have never seen, he had sent me a little book it was not what I liked it had more fancy than imagination and so I told him and now he has written another one Angels On The Bough and that is a good one, that too is clear and has in it more than clarity, he and Max White both suc-

ceed in saying something more than they say, their clear line creates something, it gave me pleasure, they took away his job from him at the University of the State of Washington on account of his book but now he has another one in the Loyola University of Chicago. We are expecting him this summer I think that he is interesting.

APPENDIX II

Gertrude Stein, like Tennyson's Ulysses, was "a part of all that she had met," and everything that happened to her usually found its way into her writing. When she discovered that Samuel Steward was allergic to many foodstuffs she amused herself by writing about him in *Alphabets and Birthdays* (New Haven: Yale University Press, 1957), pages 50–51.

And now for S.

Sammy and Sally and Save and Susy.

Sammy had his aunt and his aunt had Sammy and his aunt's name was Fanny and Fanny had Sammy.

Sammy was his name and he was funny and he had an aunt Fanny and she was funny.

Sammy could not eat bread or potatoes or chocolate or cake or eggs or butter or even a date, if he did he fainted away, that was his way, a very funny way but it was Sammy's way. His aunt Fanny was not funny that way, but she was funny in another way, whenever she saw a cat or dog a turtle or a bird or a third, a third of anything she had to turn away. She was funny that way.

But Sammy had his aunt Fanny and Aunt Fanny had her Sammy.

Poor dear Sammy.

Now what could he eat, what could be a treat, poor dear Sammy.

A lemonade perhaps or a beefsteak, or a plate or a but dear me no not ice cream, he could not eat cream, nor a birthday cake, he could eat the candles but not the cake, poor dear Sammy. Sample and example.

His Aunt Fanny did not care that Sammy could not share what she ate, she just went on cooking and eating and Sammy just went on looking and fainting. They were very funny Sammy and his Aunt Fanny. Poor dear Sammy.

And in spite of all Sammy grew tall tall enough to go to school.

In school they were taught

Sample and Example.

There was a pretty girl and she had a curl and her name was Sally. They called her pretty Sally and she was a sample. And then there was Sammy there just was Sammy poor dear Sammy and he was an example.

And then one day pretty Sally in play asked Sammy to come to her house on her birthday.

Sammy did.

There was a great big cake with frosting and a date and Sammy feeling faint said he could not eat icing or the date or cake but he could eat candles if they were to be given. But no said Sally oh no don't you know, we burn them, there are no candles when we come to eating we burn them and if we did not burn them I would not have my next one not my next birthday, oh naughty Sammy wants to take my next birthday away.

And poor Sammy had nothing to say, to see all that icing and cake made him feel faint so he just did have to go away.

Now you may think this is a funny story but no it is true, anybody even you could know Sammy poor dear Sammy and his Aunt Fanny, he lives there too and it is true all the story of Sammy all the story of his Aunt Fanny all the story of Aunt Fanny all the story of Sammy is true. Poor dear Sammy.

INDEX

The names of Gertrude Stein, Alice B. Toklas, and Samuel Steward do not appear in this Index as separate entries since the entire book is devoted to them. Each literary work of Stein and Toklas is listed under its own heading, as are their ideas and opinions on various topics, such as "Superstitions," "Writing and writing habits," "Drinking and drunks," and so on.